Defining a Nation

"Reacting to the Past" Series

Defining a Nation: India on the Eve of Independence, 1791

Ainslie T. Embree
Columbia University

Mark C. Carnes
Barnard College
Columbia University

PEARSON

Longman

New York Boston San Francisco
London Toronto Sydney Tokyo Singapore Madrid
Mexico City Munich Paris Cape Town Hong Kong Montreal

Senior Acquisitions Editor: Janet Lanphier
Editorial Assistant: Stephanie Ricotta
Executive Marketing Manager: Sue Westmoreland
Production Coordinator: Virginia Riker
Senior Cover Design Manager/Designer: Nancy Danahy
Cover Photo: India, Varanasi, Dasaswamedh Road, people and rickshaws on street.
   © Getty Images, Inc.
Senior Manufacturing Buyer: Alfred C. Dorsey
Printer and Binder: Command Web Offset Company
Cover Printer: Coral Graphic Services Inc.

Library of Congress Cataloging-in-Publication Data

Carnes, Mark C. (Mark Christopher), 1950-
Defining a Nation: India on the eve of independence, 1945 / Mark C. Carnes ; Ainslie T. Embree.
    p. cm. – ("Reacting to the Past" series)
  Includes the rev. ed. of India's Search for National Identity.
  Includes bibliographical references and index.
  ISBN 0-321-35585-7 (alk. paper)
  1. India—Politics and Government—1765-1947—Problems, exercises, etc. 2.
Nationalism—India—Problems, exercises, etc. 3. India—History—20th century—Sources. I. Embree,
Ainslie Thomas. II. Embree, Ainslie Thomas. India's Search for national identity. Rev. ed. III. Title.
IV. Series.
DS480.45.C34 2005
954.035'9—dc22
                                        2005008747

Please visit our website at http://www.ablongman.com

ISBN 0-321-35585-7

1 2 3 4 5 6 7 8 9 10—BJP—07 06 05 04

Table of Contents

The Train to Simla

Through the train's window, smeared with grit and soot, you can barely make out the faces of the torrent of people surging along the station platform. But that swirling chaos **is** India: A red-turbaned Sikh, with a long dark beard; three dark barefooted children begging for food; a Muslim woman swathed in black; a nawab in a London-tailored linen suit; a young man dressed in the white homespun cotton—*khadi*—that Gandhi equates with Indian independence from British domination. And sprinkled throughout are British soldiers in khaki, walking with that brisk, purposeful swagger that won an empire—and may now have lost it.

So many people! The numbers spin in your head: 400 million in all. 300 million Hindus. 100 million Muslims. Millions more Sikhs, Pashtuns, Parsees, Christians, Jews. And many are so needy, so poor: 60 million Untouchables, among them the children begging on the platform.

Yet somehow you have the train compartment all to yourself. You look at your watch. The train should have left the Delhi station two hours ago, before the summer sun begins baking the Ganges plain. The war has taken a toll on train schedules; the British army diverts locomotives and rolling stock whenever they wish. But then they always have. Railways have long been the rope that bound British India. To be sure, Britain had acquired India in the age of sail, back in the 1700s, when the British navy blasted the French and Dutch trading outposts from the harbors of India and established a monopoly for the British East India Company. Company officials had then used revenues from its trade monopolies to recruit and hire an army—most of it Indian—that over the course of a century subdued most of the native princes, Hindu as well as Muslim.

But effective control of the vast subcontinent came only with the construction of the railways in 1853. The telegraph system and a postal service followed in the next year. Then came tea from Assam, cotton from Bengal, coal from Orissa and Bihar, opium from the basin of the Ganges and Brahmaputra Rivers. Great mountains of products and resources moved along iron rails to Calcutta, Bombay, Madras—formerly sleepy ports that now became teeming centers of commerce and industry. And as Indian raw materials flowed out, British manufactures—especially cotton textiles—flowed in, with disastrous consequences for the artisan weavers and spinners of rural India. A few years ago, when Gandhi initiated his campaign for Indians to boycott imported manufactured textiles, he was fighting a battle first waged, and surely lost, over a century ago.

You recall Gandhi's Salt March fifteen years ago—in 1930—surely one of the most extraordinary protests in history. Ten years earlier, Gandhi had persuaded the Indian National Congress (INC, the Congress) to cease collaborating with British rulers, and he then launched his *satyagraha* movement, the word derived from *satya* (truth) and *ahimsa* (nonviolence, or love), a concept of civil disobedience that Gandhi claimed was rooted in ancient Hindu texts. At the time all India, it seemed, rose up in opposition to Great

Britain. Many boycotted British-made goods, ceased attending British schools and colleges, and quit their jobs in the British civil service. Even many Muslims, though unsettled by the Hindu overtones of Gandhi's campaign, took part in the campaign to achieve *swaraj*—independence. Gandhi sought to draw Muslims more closely into the campaign. You recall his 1919 meeting with Muslim leaders, just a few blocks from this train station, when he spoke in support of the Muslim caliph of Turkey.

Gandhi called off the first civil disobedience campaign when members of Congress attacked and burned a police station, murdering the constables. The people of India were not sufficiently schooled in doctrines of nonviolence, or so he had said. But in 1930 he announced resumption of the civil disobedience campaign through the Salt March to the sea, there to gather salt and dispense it freely, in open defiance of the British monopoly on salt distribution. Slowly he walked toward the sea, leaning on a bamboo cane, stopping at every village along the way. Huge crowds followed, and the eyes of the world watched. Weeks stretched into months. When he finally crossed the beach to the sea, he declared: "Watch, I am about to give a signal to the nation." Then he leaned over, scooped up a handful of salt, and lifted it up—an offering for the multitude. The crowd, now numbering in the tens of thousands, surged across the beach and dipped pans and pails into the salt deposits. The British, who had ignored Gandhi's walk to the sea, arrested hundreds and then thousands of his followers. Massive civil disobedience flared up throughout India. Perhaps 100,000 in all were imprisoned. A pinch of salt, sprinkled into the winds, and so falls an empire!

But not yet. Gandhi will not be walking to Simla. Like you, and like everyone else at the conference, he will take a train. A thought occurs to you: Might he be on this one? No. The train station would have been swamped with hundreds of thousands seeking merely a glimpse of the man who had become the conscience of India. Even rumors of his appearance would delay the train for hours. Again, you look at your watch.

You find it ironic that most of the nationalist leaders of India, when they are not in jail, spend their time on trains. They organize an independence movement by means of a technology that had ensured their nation's subjugation. It was just a mile out of the station, too, where a Hindu terrorist had detonated a bomb that had destroyed the train of Viceroy Irwin; you recall the train cars, blackened by the explosion, and you thought it a miracle that the Viceroy had not been hurt.

You notice a commotion on the platform. Some British soldiers are running toward an Indian conductor, pointing to your compartment and speaking animatedly. The conductor frowns and shakes his head. Yours is a first-class compartment, more than is allowed for regular soldiers. But the conductor shrugs his shoulders—evidently the other cars are filled—and the soldiers clamber up the steps. You move to the window seat and arrange your papers. A few seconds later, several of the British come into your compartment, shirts drenched with sweat.

"Mind if we join you?" asks a sandy-haired soldier.

You gesture to the seats, and they sit down. A few minutes later you hear a thunk below your feet as the gears of the train engage. Soon it glides silently forward: one of the newer locomotives, sent from England just before the war.

"I saw the bunker where they found Hitler. Him and Eva," a corporal says. "Said to myself, 'War's over.' Thought I'd be havin' a pint at the Black Ox in Devonshire in a few weeks. Now I end up in bloody hell." The others laugh.

"Wait 'til we're fighting Japs in the streets of Tokyo. You'll wish you were in hell."

"The Japs shoot back," another adds. "Over here, with Gandhi's crowd, you hit 'em on the head, and they say, 'Why, thankee very much, governor. Why not punch me stomach?'" More laughter.

"India—a nation! What a joke," Devonshire adds. "It'll last about as long as the whiskey in this flask." He passes it around. One of the soldiers hesitates, glances at the others, shrugs his soldiers, and then offers it to you. You wave it away and again look out the window.

Now their voices are lower, but you can still hear. "They won't fight even to defend themselves," another soldier says. "They tell us to 'get out'—to 'Quit India'—but if we 'ad, they'd all be bowing down to Hirohito and learning Japanese."

"But **we're** not going to Japan. Not unless the admiralty figures how to get the Royal Navy up the Himalayas to Simla." More laughter.

"Once you get all the Indian leaders together, you'll need an army to keep them from killing each other."

"What a nation! They hate each other as much as us."

"And to be led by a man who gives speeches in his underwear."

The laughter, initially raucous, stops.

Sensing that they are looking in your direction, you open your briefcase, bulging with papers: treaties, population studies, reports on geographical and economic resources, newspapers in many different languages: Bengali, Urdu, Hindi, Marathi. You have much on your mind: the fate of all India. You cannot get the numbers out of your head: 300 million Hindus, 100 million Muslims, all ruled, at present, by several thousand Englishmen. You glance out the window and are blinded by the morning sun. You consider moving to another seat, or pulling down the shade, but you have been cooped up too long. And you know that as the train winds through the foothills of the Himalayas, the view will be spectacular.

Conversation subsides. You hear mention of "Iwo Jima," and the soldiers shake their heads. Most seem to be glad that they have been detailed to Simla—on a diplomatic mission—rather than being sent to fight the Japanese. You learn that a task force was gathering at the British base in Bombay, preparing to transfer to the Far East. Where, exactly, no one could say. The Japanese positions in East Asia are crumbling—their attempted invasion of India had collapsed the previous year—and now they are everywhere on the retreat.

The train crawls through the congested old city of Delhi. Children play along the track.

"There's the Red Fort!" exclaims a soldier with a trim, black mustache. You catch a glimpse of the great stone building. "I learned about it when I read history," he adds.

"Oh, Lordy. Him and his Cambridge days," Devonshire replies.

"If you had eyes, you'd see that it's a treasure, one of the marvels of the world. It's made of red sandstone and was built by Shah Jahan, a Muslim emperor in the mid-1600s. About the same time that Christopher Wren built St. Paul's Cathedral. Shah Jahan also built the Taj Mahal. It was a tomb for his wife."

"Hope she died first"—and some more chuckles.

The train passes the crumbling walls of old Delhi, some of them built by Muslim warlords in the twelfth or thirteenth centuries. Many of the stones have been scavenged for huts and hovels for the Untouchables, who, prohibited from living in the main residential center, inhabit the outskirts of the city. You see that some of the walls have been blown apart. Were they destroyed by artillery during the great Sepoy Mutiny a century ago?

Back then, the British East India Company, which had ruled most of India as a commercial venture, had hired Indians, called *sepoys*, to fight in its armed forces. For decades, sepoys had chafed at racist British officers and harsh discipline. Then, early in 1857, they were issued new Enfield rifles, which required soldiers to bite the tip off the gunpowder cartridges before loading. Rumors circulated—apparently true—that the cartridges were lubricated with grease from pigs and cows. This simultaneously infuriated Hindus and Muslims alike: Hindus revere cows as expressions of a cosmic life force; and Muslims are forbidden to eat pork, which they regard as defiling.

You stare out the window. It was at Meerut—just 40 miles to the east—where on May 10, 1857, a contingent of sepoys—Hindu as well as Muslim—refused the new cartridges. The British threw the soldiers into prisons and bound them in irons. This enraged other soldiers at Meerut, who turned on the British officers and shot them. The sepoys went on a rampage, butchering British men, women and children. Then the sepoys marched to Delhi, persuaded the Indian troops there to join the mutiny, seized the Red Ford, declared the aged Mughal emperor to be the new ruler of India, and set about the work of strengthening the walls. They also slaughtered more British men and women.

The revolt spread to Lucknow, Cawnpore, and other cities in northern India. Within days much of northern India was in rebellion against its British masters.

The officers of the British East India Company immediately mobilized. A combined British-Sikh force was put onto trains and sent to Delhi. They deployed on the ridge of hills just ahead, beyond the walls you had just passed. You feel the train slow as it begins its ascent.

The sepoys, firing cannon from the fort, attempted to drive the British from the hills. But the British and Sikhs held their positions. The sepoys attacked and were driven off. Refraining from further attacks, they resolved to make their stand behind the walls at Delhi.

Several months later a much larger British-Sikh army arrived, this time on trains carrying heavy siege guns. Those guns blasted the fortifications, and the British-Sikh soldiers poured through the gaps. Within days the sepoys had been rounded up and killed; the British reprisals were as gruesome as the earlier massacres of British in Delhi. But the Sepoy Mutiny had one lasting effect: No longer would India be ruled by the British East India Company. Henceforth the British government would govern India directly as a colony of the crown.

You smile at the irony: That decision in 1857 is the reason why you are moving north to Simla. Because word is out that, 88 years later, the British are thinking of abandoning India, the "jewel" in the crown of British colonialism. The British governor—the Viceroy—has summoned all the Indian leaders to a conference at Simla to see if India is now capable of self-government. That begs the larger question: Is India a nation? For that matter, what does it mean to be a nation?

In ancient Greece, people felt their allegiance to their city: They thought of themselves as Athenians or Spartans. But India consists mostly of tens of thousands of villages. In China, people shared a deeply ingrained set of beliefs and practices called Confucianism, but India has no common beliefs or practices. The people of Puritan New England regulated their lives according to the Bible, which, though interpreted in many ways, constituted a common source of beliefs; so, too, the people of revolutionary France regarded the writings of Rousseau and the *philosophes* as beacons for a new set of beliefs, a new form of worship similar to the affection the Americans had for the Constitution of the United States. But the various peoples of India consult a bewildering variety of texts: the ancient works of Hinduism and Buddhism, as taught by a multitude of gurus; the Quran, as interpreted by different Muslim holy men; the more recent writings on resurgent Hinduism and Islam. What **idea** can serve as the foundation for a new Indian nation?

A knock on your cabin door. The Indian steward brings in tea and biscuits, bows slightly to you but ignores the soldiers. Then he departs. You pass the biscuits to Mustache, who thanks you, and then you stare out the window. To the east, the Jumna River gleams as the sun burns off the morning mist. The Jumna originates high in the Himilayas, its waters nourished by the tears of Shiva, a Hindu deity. Or so the story goes. Several hundred miles farther east, the Jumna flows into the Ganges. According to another Hindu legend, the Ganges always renews itself and brings renewal to those who bathe in its waters.

You smell cow dung, which is used for fuel and fertilizer, and soon you see a herd of cattle grazing by the river. To Hindus, the cow is life: a giver of essential nutrients, a universal expression of mother-force and thus of life itself. Some Hindus insist that Indian independence will bring an end to the slaughter of cows by Muslims, who eat beef. Your briefcase contains a fat folder on the Cow Protection Movement.

But you have many similarly thick folders, each documenting obstacles to Indian nationhood. You reach into your briefcase and pull out the one on language. English, like the railroads, helped to unify the subcontinent. But if India breaks away from the British empire, will it declare its independence from the English language? And what language would replace it? Most Indians speak Hindi, but there are other major related languages: Bengali in the east, Marathi around Bombay. zin the south they speak Telugu, Kannada, and Tamil, languages from an entirely different language family—Dravidian. In the Muslim provinces to the west, one hears Pushto and Urdu and even a smattering of Persian. And then there are the local languages—Kashmiri in Kashmir, Khasi in Assam, Sinhala in Ceylon.

"If these people are mostly Hindu"—you are startled by the voice of one of the soldiers—"why do all of the palaces have Muslim names?"

"Same reason we're now going to call Berlin Churchillville," Devonshire answers.

"And this"—Mustache speaks again, waving a hand as if to take in all India—"this plain is where the great battles were fought. It is the fulcrum of the entire subcontinent, high rich farmland just to the west, beyond those hills. All of the rivers on that side of the train"—he waves his hand toward the far window—"flow to the west, through the arid high country of the Punjab. Then they merge with the Indus River and pour into the Arabian Sea. All of the rivers on this side of the train"—he reaches past your face and taps the window—"flow into the Ganges and then into the Bay of Bengal. Two different rivers, two different peoples. Muslims in the west, Hindus in the east. Except far to the east, toward Bengal, where there is a province filled with Muslims. Don't know why. Panipat—the village up ahead—has for centuries been the site of crucial battles. The most important ones occurred hundreds of years ago."

"What did they fight with," Devonshire smirks, "bow and arrows?"

"Elephants, too," Mustache continues. "In 1526 Babur, invading India from his base in Afghanistan, charged across the plain and won a decisive battle at Panipat, allowing him to establish the Mughal empire. Thirty years later, his grandson—Akbar—perhaps the greatest Mughal ruler—won another key battle at Panipat. More challenges to the

Mughals came—and nearly always the armies converged at Panipat. Another Afghan invader attacked in the 1760s, and then the Sikhs, who were gaining power in the Punjab, attacked the Mughal armies at Panipat a decade later. Always the Mughals won."

"Until we came." Another soldier, with a red face—hopelessly sunburned—called out.

"Right. The British East India Company ruled the most important provinces, especially those with trading potential. But it left hundreds of native princes in power—Hindu or Muslim. The Company didn't much care, so long as the native rulers behaved themselves. It even built up some native institutions. The Company struck deals in most villages with the *zamindas*, well-to-do locals who were rather like the lords of the manor in feudal England. The zamindas loaned money and collected taxes, taking their share and sending the rest to the British. For a time the zamindas even dispensed justice. System worked like a charm. Still does, in many places. Even Gandhi regards them as part of the fabric of rural India, with its spinning wheels and all."

"If British India worked so well, why are we leaving?"

"Who says we are?" Mustache continues. "Churchill says the Indians can't govern themselves. That's why they're dragging all of these Indian leaders to Simla. They'll put 'em all in the same room and lock the door. By teatime they'll all be dead, having murdered each other. We'll be given the job of burying them all."

The others laugh heartily.

And then the conversation stops. You know they are looking at you. You stare hard at the reports on your lap and jot some notes. The report consists of columns of numbers. In India, it is always about numbers, big numbers. Some you cannot get out of your head: 400 million. 300 Hindus. 100 Muslims. The numbers matter, especially now. World War II will soon be over. The democratic powers will defeat the German dictator and the Japanese emperor. Everywhere democracy is in the air, and it will doubtless come to India, too.

The train slows to a stop. No one seems to depart or get on, and then the train resumes its journey. Within a few hours it will begin its torturous, twisting climb through the foothills of the Himalayas; by the end of the day it will be winding around steep mountains toward Simla.

India's climb to nationhood, too, will be a difficult one. The ultimate destination—at Simla—is nationhood. But the grade is steep, and the obstacles many. And if the train lurches off the track, many will die.

Introduction

What is a nation?

Is it a people who share common values, such as the Chinese of the Ming Dynasty, steeped in Confucianism, or the Israelites, who followed laws put forth by their God? Is a nation a geographical entity, such as the city-states of ancient Greece or the peoples encompassed by the Roman Empire? Is a nation a form of contract, whose people agree to come together to achieve something greater than what they could accomplish individually, as in Rousseau's concept of the general will and the republic embodied by the Constitution of the United States? Is a nation an expression of racial identity, such as seventeenth-century Sweden or the tribes of east Africa?

This game seeks to answer these questions as they apply to the Indian subcontinent after World War II. More, the game raises the question of how various notions of nationhood are applied in the creation of new states. Few issues are more salient to our own times. During the six decades since World War II much of the world has undergone upheaval. Old governmental systems have collapsed and new ones have emerged—and are still emerging.

This game begins in India in June 1945, at the British summer capital at Simla in the foothills of the Himalayas. The game's sessions cover approximately one to two years.

BASIC MATERIALS

The game consists of this booklet as well as each student's role (see "Roles" below). The Instructor will distribute the roles, probably during the second class session.

An indispensable component of the game is *Sources of Indian Tradition,* Volume 2 (published by Columbia University Press). This volume, especially second or later editions, contains essential selections of the writings of the principal figures of this historical moment.

The historical context is described in Ainslie Embree, *India's Search for National Identity* (Appendix B, this booklet). Students researching particular roles can find more information in the Recommended Readings (Appendix C).

HISTORICAL MAPS

The following maps provide useful information on the physical composition of the Indian subcontinent in 1945.

Map A. India 1945: Major Cities, Rivers, and Princely States

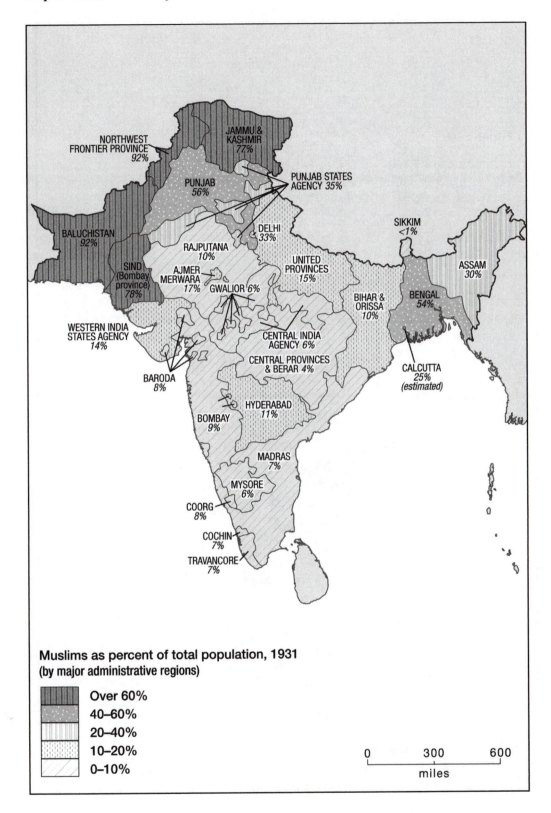

NORTHWEST
FRONTIER PROVINCE
92%

JAMMU &
KASHMIR
77%

PUNJAB
56%

PUNJAB STATES
AGENCY 35%

SIKKIM
<1%

BALUCHISTAN
92%

DELHI
33%

SIND
(Bombay
province)
78%

RAJPUTANA
10%

AJMER
MERWARA
17%

GWALIOR 6%

UNITED
PROVINCES
15%

ASSAM
30%

WESTERN INDIA
STATES AGENCY
14%

BIHAR &
ORISSA
10%

BENGAL
54%

CENTRAL INDIA
AGENCY 6%

CENTRAL PROVINCES
& BERAR 4%

BARODA
8%

CALCUTTA
25%
(estimated)

HYDERABAD
11%

BOMBAY
9%

MADRAS
7%

MYSORE
6%

COORG
8%

COCHIN
7%

TRAVANCORE
7%

Muslims as percent of total population, 1931
(by major administrative regions)

Over 60%
40–60%
20–40%
10–20%
0–10%

0   300   600
miles

Map B. Muslims as a Percentage of the Total Population Of India, 1931

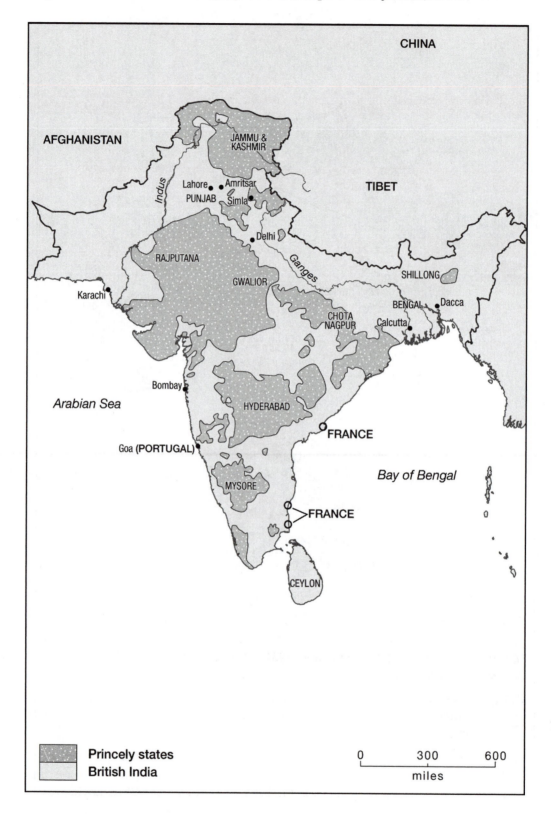

CHINA

AFGHANISTAN

JAMMU & KASHMIR

TIBET

Indus

Lahore • • Amritsar
PUNJAB
Simla •

Delhi •

RAJPUTANA

GWALIOR

Ganges

SHILLONG

Karachi •

BENGAL • Dacca

CHOTA NAGPUR

Calcutta

Bombay •

Arabian Sea

HYDERABAD

○ FRANCE

Goa (PORTUGAL) •

Bay of Bengal

MYSORE

○
○➤ FRANCE

CEYLON

Princely states
British India

0   300   600
miles

The Historical Moment: June 1945

World War II is drawing to a close. Last month Nazi Germany surrendered. Japan's empire in the Pacific has collapsed, and Americans are making plans to invade Okinawa in preparation for the eventual conquest of Japan. The Soviet Union, governed by a communist hierarchy led by the formidable Josef Stalin, has filled the vacuum in Eastern Europe caused by the collapse of Nazi Germany. Many expect that communism will spread through war-ravaged Western Europe. Many, too, expect that in the wake of the inevitable withdrawal of the Japanese army, China will descend into chaos with the resumption of the civil war between the communist forces of Mao Zedong and those of nationalist leader Chiang Kai-shek.

There is talk of a new League of Nations, a "United Nations," but few think that any such international organization will be capable of ensuring peace and stability.

Nowhere is the situation more confused than in India. Great Britain is emerging from the war victorious, but its economy has been crippled. Whether it can retain India, the "jewel in the crown" of British imperialism, is doubtful. Now Prime Minister Winston Churchill, who has spoken against granting Indian independence, is seeing his support evaporate in Parliament. Within India, protests against colonial rule have intensified throughout the twentieth century, and the advent of Mohandas Gandhi has energized Indian politics as never before. Gandhi has combined a vision of Indian independence with a new means of attaining it: nonviolent civil disobedience.

In 1942 this point was hammered home to British officials with tremendous force. At the time, the Japanese army had swarmed over Southeast Asia and was advancing through Burma into India. The British proposed to coordinate and control all India for the purposes of defeating the Axis powers. In return for India's wholehearted support for the war, Britain would invite India to join the British Dominion as an equal member afterward. The Congress party, which had spearheaded Indian nationalism since the late nineteenth century, rejected this proposal outright. Gandhi likened it to "a blank cheque on a failing bank." Congress reasoned that Britain could renege on its promise once the war was won; and Congress bitterly resented the provision that a province could choose to separate from India and become an independent nation. Congress thought this clause favored the Muslim League, which proposed to cobble together a separate Muslim nation—"Pakistan"—from those Muslim-majority provinces within British India.

Despite Congress's refusal to contribute to the war effort in 1942, Britain made plans to defend India from the impending Japanese invasion. Gandhi called on Indians to insist on immediate independence from Britain, even if it weakened the British war effort. "I have made up my mind that it would be a good thing if a million people were shot in a brave and nonviolent rebellion against the British rule," he declared. Congress endorsed his call for nonviolent protests against British rule through the "Quit India" movement. Gandhi encouraged his people: "Take a pledge with God and your own conscience as witness, that you will no longer rest till freedom is achieved and will be prepared to lay down your lives in the attempt to achieve it."

Gandhi attempted to enforce nonviolent discipline, but in so vast and populous a nation, some of the protests turned violent. The British Viceroy outlawed the "Quit India" movement and arrested most of the leaders of the nationalist movement, including Gandhi. This ignited more riots and even a spate of attacks on railroad bridges and telegraph depots. (The Muslim League, which feared that the violence might easily shift focus from the British to the Muslim minority, refrained from taking a visible stand on the matter.) Field Marshal Viscount Wavell arrived the next year to spearhead the defense of India from the Japanese. In 1944, Gandhi and Muslim secularist Ali Jinnah met to discuss the future of India: Gandhi insisted that India be a single nation, encompassing all faiths and peoples; Jinnah declared that India contained two separate states, one Hindu, the other Muslim. The talks went nowhere.

Three months ago [March 1945], as the Japanese threat receded, Wavell went to London to confer with the Foreign Ministry and Prime Minister Churchill. He returned several weeks ago. On June 14, he announced in a radio broadcast his plans to convene at Simla an executive council of Indian political leaders to discuss the fate of the subcontinent. The next day, he ordered that imprisoned Congress officials be released.

Churchill, an ardent imperialist, has made noises about retaining some form of British rule or influence over India, but this appears unlikely. During the war, the United States pressured Great Britain to allow colonial peoples the right to self-determination after the war, a principle that was encompassed in the Atlantic Charter. Britain signed the document, as did all the Allies. Whether they would fulfill the provisions of the Charter now that Germany had surrendered remained unclear. Apart from Britain's legal obligation to retreat from colonial domination, there is the painful economic fact that Britain has been nearly bankrupted by the war. It now lacks the resources and perhaps the will to impose its rule on 400 million Indians.

Special Rules: Departures from the Historical Context

The game seeks to replicate the situation at Simla in June 1945, but it offers several counterfactual premises.

OMISSION OF LORD WAVELL

The game hypothesizes that Lord Wavell died, suddenly and of natural causes, just days after making his radio address of June 14, 1945. He has been replaced by one (or perhaps more) British Interim Governor(s) General. They will not only direct the proceedings of the conference, they will also supervise whatever functions are still held by the British government in India. They can make decisions as they see fit, subject to review by their superiors in the Foreign Office in London, and by the Prime Minister (i.e., the Gamemaster). The Prime Minister may promote the Governors General to Viceroy(s) if he is pleased with their performance.

INCLUSION OF THE NIZAM OF HYDERABAD AND THE MAHARAJA OF KASHMIR

Since 1857, Great Britain ruled much of India directly. But when Britain consolidated its hold on the subcontinent in the nineteenth century, it sometimes eschewed direct rule and instead entered into treaty relationships with hundreds of native Indian princes, who held titles such as "nawab" and "Nizam." These treaties generally allowed princes to retain sovereignty over their lands and subjects, and placed the princes under the protection of the British military, but ceded to the British government vast powers pertaining to foreign affairs and military matters. Thus the fate of the subcontinent is now complicated by the existence of these "dependent" native princes.

If, for example, Britain withdraws from India and gives the keys to its governmental buildings and operations to Gandhi and the Indian National Congress, the largest of the Indian nationalist organizations, the effect on the hundreds of "dependent" principalities would be unclear. Thus the withdrawal of Britain from the Indian subcontinent would oblige each of the princes to work out his own arrangements with whatever authority replaced Britain elsewhere on the subcontinent. There remains, too, the question of whether Britain can legally withdraw from these treaties unilaterally.

In fact, the British did **not** invite the Indian princes to the Simla conference, and instead called them to a separate meeting of the "Princely States," proceedings that were scrutinized by Indian nationalists. However, the game assumes that the two sets of meetings—that with the most prominent leaders of Indian nationalism and that with the independent princes—were joined into a single meeting at Simla.

The most important of these princes, and the one who will serve as a surrogate representing, loosely, most of the other Muslim princes, is the Nizam of Hyderabad (Nee-ZAAHM of HIGH-der-ih-bad); very large classes might also include the Hindu Maharaja who ruled Kashmir.

INCLUSION OF THE HINDU MAHASABHA

The British Governors General also did not invite adherents of the Hindu Mahasabha (mah-hah-sabba). The Hindu Mahasabha was a Hindu cultural organization, not a political group. However, its ardent championing of the Hindu cause (protection of cows and Hindu shrines, advancement of Hindi as the language of the government, instruction in the classic texts of Hinduism) had political implications. Some members of the Hindu Mahasabha have created a paramilitary political arm known as the RSS. By mobilizing Hindu sentiment and channeling it at times into militant opposition, these Hindu radicals perhaps possess the power to wreck any decisions brokered at Simla. Thus, while the leaders of the Hindu Mahasabha did not attend the conference, their views—potentially shared by 300 million Hindus—loomed over its proceedings. The game mirrors that **virtual** presence by including an **actual** leader of the Mahasabha at the conference.

INCLUSION OF THE COMMUNIST PARTY LEADERSHIP

Some games also include a leader of the Communist Party of India, although the British did not invite the Communist leadership to Simla or to any other organizational meeting. Prime Minister Churchill is profoundly suspicious of Soviet Premier Stalin, and he has insisted that British officials closely monitor the Communist Party in India. In 1928 a series of labor disturbances swept through the major industrial cities, especially Bombay. The next year, the British arrested some thirty Communist leaders for conspiracy to overthrow British rule, and they were convicted and sent to prison. In the 1930s the Congress included in its list of complaints against the British the conviction of these Communists. The actions of the Communists at Simla will doubtless be watched closely.

INCLUSION OF INDETERMINATES

Nearly all versions of this game will include indeterminates. Some roles, moreover, contain substantial latitude in many matters. Thus, while it may seem that everyone at Simla has his own preset positions this is wrong. The Governors General are new to India, and thus they will likely be responsive to what they hear and learn at Simla. Even the major parties—such as Congress and the Muslim League—contain a range of viewpoints. In larger classes, one member within each of these groups is undecided about many issues concerning the goals and strategies of the organizations to which he or she belongs. This person's decision will define those goals and strategies. Some roles will be defined as indeterminate: a "representative" or "spokesperson" for "rural India," or a "representative" or "spokesperson" for "urban India." Although no such person was convened at Simla, these players in some way represent undecided public opinion. They will thus have considerable influence in the event of referenda or elections.

DURATION OF THE SIMLA CONFERENCE

Historically, the Wavell-Simla conference lasted only a month: June 1945. It immediately became mired in a series of sharp disputes between leaders of Congress and the Muslim League. A particularly acrimonious issue was that of Muslim representation in a post-independence legislature. Congress included among its delegation Maulana Azad [sometimes identified as Maulana Abdul Kalam Azad], a prominent Muslim politician. Mohammed Ali Jinnah, leader of the Muslim League, insisted that it alone represented the Muslims of India and demanded that Congress drop Azad from its delegation. Congress, led by Jawaharlal Nehru and others, refused. This impasse wrecked the conference.

The failure at Simla led to another British-initiated diplomatic effort in 1946, known as the Cabinet Mission. It proposed British withdrawal and called for a Union of India in its place, to be achieved through the work of an interim coalition government of all major Indian parties. The Cabinet Mission negotiations rekindled tensions between Congress and the Muslim League but ultimately resulted in a framework for independence and the partition of India.

For the purposes of the game, the Simla conference *assumes* that the first Simla conference did not collapse—and will not collapse. Instead, the "Simla conference" of the game will last about a year, with each public session occurring after a lapse of about two months. During this period, the British Governors General (or Viceroy), in consultation with whomever they wish, will address as best they can whatever developments transpire during the game. They may or may not choose to set up an interim government composed wholly or in part of Indian leaders.

Roles

The following is a list of the players and a summary of their public motives. (You must understand, of course, that—as in life—individual players may have secret motivations.) You can—and must—gain a further understanding of everyone's objectives by reading the corresponding sections in Stephen Hay, ed., *Sources of the Indian Tradition,* Volume 2. The information also provides some sense of the powers (political, historical, military, cultural) each may possess. Diligent players will also undertake research on their own to uncover information about the other parties to the conference.

SUGGESTED ROLE DISTRIBUTION

Faculty may alter this distribution as suits their pedagogical purposes. Concerning Congress party and the Muslim League: **Congress** (INC) includes multiple roles. Every version of the game includes Maulana Azad, a Muslim, who is included on a separate line in the assignment table below. The Hindu leaders of the INC are divided into as many as five different roles: (A) represents a secularist (Nehru); (B) a Hindu partisan; (C) an indeterminate within INC; (D) a leader from Bengal; and (E) another indeterminate within INC—an historian of Indian nationalism. The **Muslim League,** similarly, contains different roles: (A) represents a secularist, Ali Jinnah; (B) a Muslim partisan; (C) an indeterminate within the League.

ROLES	CLASS SIZE (NUMBER OF STUDENTS)										
	13	14	15	16	17	18	19	20	21	25	30
British Governor General	1	1	1	2	2	2	2	2	2	2	2
INC (Hindu)	2	3	3	3	4	4	4	4	5	6	8
INC (Muslim: Maulana Azad)	1	1	1	1	1	1	1	1	1	1	1
Gandhi (A & B)	2	2	2	2	2	2	2	2	2	2	2
Muslim League	2	2	3	3	3	3	3	3	3	4	6
Sikh Leader	1	1	1	1	1	1	1	1	1	2	1
Nizam of Hyderabad	1	1	1	1	1	1	1	1	1	1	1
Dr. Ambedkar, Untouchable	1	1	1	1	1	1	1	1	1	1	1
Indeterminate Representative of "Rural India"	1	1	1	1	1	1	1	1	1	2	3
Leader of the Hindu Mahasabha	1	1	1	1	1	1	1	1	1	1	1
Maharaja Singh of Kashmir	0	0	0	0	0	0	1	1	1	1	1
Communist Party	0	0	0	0	0	1	1	1	1	1	1
Follower of Bashdar Khan (Pashtun)	0	0	0	0	0	0	0	1	1	1	1

BRITISH GOVERNOR(S) GENERAL

The British Governors General, having been summoned to succeed Lord Wavell somewhat hastily, cannot be assumed to possess perfect knowledge of the situation in India. As recent arrivals, they need to be appraised of each group's requests and objectives. To that end, the Governors General will devote the initial public sessions of the conference to hearing and discussing everyone's views.

(**Advisory**: All Simla participants should listen to these statements attentively and read the position papers carefully. When someone proposes something with which you disagree, you should ask to rebut it then, when it is still in everyone's minds.)

The invitations to the conference indicate that the British seek to propose and implement a plan for Indian independence. The conference may adopt a plan for British withdrawal and for an Indian government, including a Constitution.

The British have publicly proclaimed that their mission is to accomplish Indian independence and broker an equitable settlement that will allow an honorable withdrawal of Great Britain. Prime Minister Winston Churchill, who has ultimate power over the Foreign Ministry and its officials (such as the Governors General of India) has made no secret of his wish to retain some vestige of India as the remaining "jewel" in the tarnished crown of British imperialism. At the very least, he doubtless has requested that a post-independence India remain within the British commonwealth, the trade and cultural alliance composed of former colonies.

In addition to hosting the Simla conference, the Governors General control the civil and military bureaucracies that run India. Simla, though a favored summer resort in the Himalayas, has since the late 1860s been the seat of the British government during the summer months. That is, the British Governors General can issue orders to the Indian civil service, to the British military and police authorities, and to provincial officials.

At the level of the central government, the top positions are staffed by British officials who were recruited through civil service examinations and training directed from London; the majority of the middle-level administrators as well as nearly all of the service personnel are native Indians. (At the provincial level, prior to World War II, native Indian civil servants controlled education, welfare, and agriculture, with British officials responsible for security and the court system; when Congress announced the 1942 "Quit India" campaign, many Indian civil servants and local elected officials resigned from the government and Britain reverted to direct rule of the provinces. That system remains in place at present.) The Governors General also control the British armed forces and can issue orders to the Royal Indian Army and the Royal Indian Navy (forces whose officers are British but most of whose soldiers and sailors are Indian).

This means, for example, that for the duration of the war the Governors General can order the arrest and imprisonment of nearly anyone in the country on virtually any pretext. They can also outlaw organizations, direct the movement of military forces and police units, and otherwise issue orders to all agencies within the civil service. They can do so publicly, by making announcements (and posting them on the website); or they can proceed in private, through communiqués to the Gamemaster (who will also function like the colonial bureaucracy—slowly, perhaps even inefficiently, but in accordance with the directions of the Governors General).

The powers of the Governors General are circumscribed chiefly by Great Britain's fast-dwindling economic resources, and by increasing resistance to British rule on the part of Indian members of the civil service and the military. Many Indians suspect that British influence is waning, and some regard various Indian politicians, of one faction or another, as their likely future bosses.

MEMBERS OF THE INC: THE CONGRESS PARTY

Since its founding in 1885, the Indian National Congress (INC, or Congress) has spearheaded the campaign for Indian independence from Great Britain. It is safe to assume that all members of Congress lose if, at the end of the game, India has not been granted independence and the British remain as an intrusive administrative, political, or military force on the subcontinent.

Although three-fourths of the population of India is Hindu, and an equivalent proportion of the Congress leadership is Hindu, Congress claims to represent all the peoples of India. Indeed, the president of Congress is Maulana Azad, a prominent Muslim. Congress leaders, moreover, have cultivated relationships among Sikh leaders and Dr. Ambedkar, the most visible spokesman for the Untouchables.

Congress proposes that Great Britain depart from the subcontinent, allowing Congress to inherit administrative control of what has been the British raj. The Congress leaders conceive of the transition as a turnkey operation: the British administrators will depart from their posts, and Congress leaders will replace them. Congress would thus inherit a strong centralized governmental structure. Congress leaders further suggest that with the collapse of Japan, and with China embroiled in civil war between Communist and nationalist factions, a united India holds the promise of becoming one of the strongest nations in the world. Congress also dismisses claims by the independent princes; when the British depart from India, the British treaties protecting such princes and upholding their sovereign powers will become null and void, in fact if not in law. Some princes have already announced their likely affiliation with Congress; others, such as the Nizam of Hyderabad, a Muslim, have insisted that their principality will retain their own independence even if the British depart. (Map A shows the major princely states.)

Congress is not fully united. Among the Hindus within Congress, there are disputes over whether India should become a modern industrial power, as the Hindu Mahasabha proposes, or whether India should cling to its rural village traditions, as Gandhi advocates. Some advocate that India's government be modeled after the parliamentary democracy of Great Britain, while others, especially Jawaharlal Nehru, are drawn to socialistic and even communistic systems. Still others repudiate Western models and insist that any Indian government uphold traditional Indian (and especially Hindu) traditions. Some go so far as to demand the establishment of a new Hindu nation: Hindustan. The Hindus' confidence is a function of their numerical supremacy: there are well over 300 million Hindus and 90 million Muslims. Many Hindus reason that once the British leave, the Hindus will inevitably dominate whatever government is left behind. Yet everyone recognizes that holding India together will be no easy matter. Muslims and other groups may seek to weaken Hindu confidence by underscoring the elements of division: the exclusion of the Untouchables from Hindu society; the vulnerability of the Sikhs; the independence of various principalities, and so on.

Congress is also divided between Hindus and "nationalist" Muslims, such as Maulana Azad. Azad, like Gandhi, wants Congress to become the umbrella organization representing all Indians. To that end, he does not want the party to endorse explicitly Hindu causes, such as cow protection and Hindi as the national language.

Inseparable from the legacy of Congress is Mohandas Gandhi, the central figure in India's independence movement. Gandhi, though influential among Hindus and the

Congress leadership, does not seek to create a secular, modernizing state along the lines of the Western nations (see Gandhi, below). This may cause some friction within Congress, as well as with the "westernizers" and "secularists" in Congress, of whom Jawaharlal Nehru (NAY-ROO) is most prominent.

REPRESENTATIVES OF THE MUSLIM LEAGUE

The claims that Congress speaks for all Indians have been sharply challenged by the rise of Ali Jinnah and the Muslim League, which has fared well in some local elections. Jinnah and the Muslim League complain that a unified India will be dominated by Hindus who will inevitably deprive Muslims of their rights. Yet cooperation between Congress and the League is not unimaginable; indeed, Muslims and Hindus worked together, as did Gandhi, Nehru, and Jinnah, in the Indian independence movement. The Muslim member of the INC, Maulana Abdul Azad, seeks to restore this sense of common, Indian purpose. Azad especially speaks for the 30 million or so Muslims who live in provinces where Hindus are in a large majority. (See Map B, Muslims as a Percentage of the Total Population, 1931.) If India breaks into two separate nations, one predominantly Hindu and the other Muslim, the Muslims who remain in "Hindustan" will constitute a small minority, fearfully exposed to the huge Hindu majority. Jinnah is not, some would say, a separatist; he also bases his claim for Pakistan, and his "hostage theory," on these very demographics. The hostage theory holds that the Muslim majority could gain negotiating leverage by the fact that Hindus would remain as a vulnerable minority in the Muslim majority provinces; likewise, Muslim minorities in Hindu majority provinces would occupy a similar situation. Better for a single nation, with Muslims as a substantial minority, than to divide the subcontinent into two religiously orientated nations with vulnerable minorities.

Formed in 1905-1906, the Muslim League grew out of an intensification of Muslim nationalist sentiment during the preceding decades, but particularly in response to Hindu (and INC) opposition to the partition of Bengal into two sections, one chiefly Hindu, the other chiefly Muslim. Hindu nationalists bitterly protested partition of Bengal (see below) and instigated and other acts of violence against Muslims. Alarmed by this Hindu partisanship within Congress, many Muslims left the Congress party and formed an elitist lobbying group, the Muslim League. The Muslim League claimed that Muslims, on grounds of cultural and historical importance, should be given separate representation in the civil service, in the legislature, and in any upcoming constitutional arrangement. The creation of the Muslim League, in opposition to the independence-seeking Congress, foreshadowed Muslim concern over what would happen to Muslims, given their much smaller numbers, if the British left.

The position of the Muslims in India was changed by World War I. Turkey, the only state with an Islamic ruler—the Sultan of Turkey and caliph of the entire Muslim world—was allied with the Central Powers and opposed by the Allies, including Britain. The British attack on Turkish forces at Gallipoli and elsewhere inflamed Islamic opposition to Great Britain throughout the world and forced the Muslims in India to reassess their support for British rule. In 1916 Congress and the Muslim League worked out an agreement (Lucknow Pact) to actively and collectively oppose British rule and to seek Indian independence.

The defeat of Turkey and its dismemberment by the (Christian) Allies in 1920 ignited protests among Muslims throughout the world. This movement in defense of the caliph was known as the Khilafat (kih-LAH-fut) Movement. The Muslims in India joined in protesting the British actions, and Gandhi exploited this to bring the Muslim League into an alliance with Congress to expel the British from India. This is known as the "non-cooperation" movement. The civil disobedience campaign broke down in the mid-1920s, and it was revived in the early 1930s.

By then, however, the Muslim League had been reinvigorated by Muhammad Iqbal (1877-1938), a brilliant Muslim writer. Iqbal initially denounced nationalism as a Western evil; he favored instead a sense of worldwide Islamic affiliation unconstrained by national boundaries. But when the Khilafat Movement collapsed in the mid-1920s, Iqbal increasingly favored creation of an Islamic state within India. This notion became central to Jinnah's proposal of Pakistan as a separate Muslim state. During the 1930s, however, the Muslim League saw its influence diminish; moreover, Jinnah was uncertain of the merits of an explicitly Islamic state.

By 1940, Jinnah, in his presidential address to the Muslim League at Lahore, sought to use the militant clout of the League to force independence on India: "Islam and Hinduism are not religions in the strict sense of the word, but in fact are different and distinct social orders, and it is only a dream that the Hindus and Muslims can ever evolve a common nationality . . . . To yoke together two such nations under a single state . . . must lead to a growing discontent and final destruction of any fabric that may be so built up for the government of such a state."

As an alternative to a Hindu-dominated single Indian state, Jinnah and the Muslim League will likely propose the partition of India into a predominantly Hindu state and a predominantly Muslim state consisting of mostly Muslim areas in western India, east and south of the Indus River, and in eastern India, especially Bengal. The League proposes to call this Muslim state Pakistan.

Unclear at present is whether the League proposes that "Pakistan" be constituted as a secular state or as one based on Islamic principles, perhaps even on the strict precepts of Islamic law, or the *shariat*. The members of the League may differ on such matters, perhaps heatedly. But in all likelihood, the Muslims will seek to persuade the British of the need for a separate Muslim state, carved out of India. A less happy outcome, though not entirely unpalatable to the Muslims, would be the creation of an Indian state in which the federal government possesses very limited powers. If Muslims can largely control what transpires in the Muslim provinces of a loosely federated Indian state, then affiliation with the Hindus would not be so terrible, or so some members of the Muslim League may assert. The Muslim League rejects entirely the leadership of some Muslims who have professed their support of the Congress and Congress's goal of a strong, united, and centralized India.

ADHERENTS OF MOHANDAS GANDHI

Mohandas Gandhi is a major moral force in the Indian subcontinent. During the early 1900s Gandhi had worked tirelessly and courageously to support rights for Indians and other minorities living in South Africa. His system of nonviolent action, *satyagraha* (saht-iy-a-GRAH-ha), against repression achieved some tangible results and made Gandhi a major international figure. In 1919 Gandhi came "home" to India to tumultuous acclaim and to great turmoil. The British had imposed strict censorship rules during the war. When they enacted the Rowlatt Acts to continue such political control afterward, Gandhi called for a nationwide work stoppage *(hartal)* in protest. Although the protests were to be nonviolent, sometimes the mobs grew unruly and outbreaks of violence were common. When one large group assembled in a walled garden called the Jallianwala Bagh in Amritsar, a British general ordered the army to fire on them. Nearly 400 perished, and over a thousand were wounded. Appalled, Gandhi retreated from his nonviolence campaign, arguing that the people of India had been insufficiently tutored in nonviolent precepts. Then came the Khilafat Movement and eventually the resumption of nonviolent anti-British protests, which flared up intermittently for the next two decades.

Gandhi's purposes are difficult to reconcile. On the one hand, he enshrines the rural villages of traditional India, characterized by the economic self-sufficiency of local craftsmen and farmers, by adherence to religious teachings (both Hindu and Muslim), and by social stability. He disapproves of Western concepts. Thus Gandhi refuses to wear manufactured textiles and instead can be seen in simple handwoven and handspun cotton clothes. (The flag of Congress includes a spinning wheel, a symbol of India's artisanal economy.) "Real freedom for me will only come when we free ourselves of the dominance of Western education, Western culture, the Western way of living . . . . Emancipation from this culture would mean real freedom for us," Gandhi declares. He also opposes modern medicine and foods. His vision of an ideal society in many ways corresponds with the Brahman conception of India.

On the other hand, some Indians denounce Gandhi for failing to advance Hindu political power. Moreover, his ideal society appears to be at odds with traditional Hinduism, especially his pronouncements on behalf of the Untouchables (whom he identifies by the term *harijan*, "children of God") and his calls for accommodation with the Muslims. He champions nonviolence and seeks to defuse the tensions among ethnic groups, especially Muslims, Hindus, and Sikhs.

But Gandhi's views are at times difficult to pin down. Moreover, although Gandhi has agreed to come to Simla, he has announced his intention of not attending the sessions because he is not at present an officer in the Congress party. However, leaders who espouse his principles—and sometimes his contradictory principles—will attend and present his views. And it is possible that Gandhi will himself decide to appear at the conference, or otherwise give speeches that will be heard throughout India. Gandhi himself retains great influence among Indians, especially those in Congress.

THE NIZAM OF HYDERABAD, A MUSLIM PRINCE

Formerly a feudal potentate, the Nizam—perhaps the richest man in the world—rules all of the state of Hyderabad in south central India. (See Map A, India 1945: Major Cities, Rivers, and Princely States.) Five-sixths of his subjects are Hindu. The Nizam is the most powerful and indisputably the richest of hundreds of Indian princes whose ancestors brokered treaties with the British to preserve their rule in return for special concessions to the British (revenue, police powers, foreign relations, etc.). Like many other princes, the Nizam now wants to preserve at least some semblance of his rule. During World War II he contributed to the British war effort several score warplanes. He doubtless worries that Indian independence will allow Hindus in the national capital to rule Hyderabad. He prefers that Hyderabad become a separate, and largely autonomous state within a loose Muslim (or perhaps Hindu) federation.

THE MAHARAJA OF KASHMIR

The Hindu counterpart of the Nizam of Hyderabad—a Muslim prince among a predominantly Hindu population—is Maharaja Hari Singh, the Hindu prince of Kashmir and Jammu, where three-fourths of the subjects are Muslim. Singh is the great-grandson of Maharaja Gulab Singh, founder of the state of Jammu and Kashmir. Like most other leaders of the hundreds of Princely States, Maharaja Hari Singh seeks to maintain some autonomy; yet he worries that if Kashmir is autonomous, the Muslim majority may seek to do away with him.

REPRESENTATIVE OF THE SIKHS

The Sikhs (pronounced "sihks" or, in the West, "seeks") constitute less than 2 percent of the population of India, though they possess considerable economic influence in the Punjab. Sikhs, an unusually enterprising and energetic people, transformed the Punjab into one of the most prosperous agricultural regions of India. The Punjab is a dry region, though five major rivers flow through it; Sikh ingenuity in devising irrigation, along with the skill of Sikh farmers, known as Jats, have made the Punjab the breadbasket of India.

Sikh means "disciple," a reference to the disciples of the Sikh guru Nanak (1469-1539). Nanak sought to "purify" Hinduism by purging it of polytheism and inegalitarianism (the caste system). The teachings of Nanak and his nine successors (together, the ten gurus) are recounted in the *Granth Sahib*, the sacred book of the Sikhs.

Defining a Nation: India on the Eve of Independence, 1945

The popularity of Sikhism, as propounded by Nanak's fifth successor, the guru Arjan (1581-1606), threatened Mughal rule in northern India. He was captured and tortured by the Mughal emperor, but he refused to recant. Before he died, he got word to his son, Hargobind (1606-1645): "Sit fully armed on the throne and maintain the army to the best of your ability." Hargobind's tenure as sixth guru was characterized by his militarizing the Sikh religion and its society. Govind Singh (1675-1708), the tenth and final Sikh guru, declared that "the Sword is God and God is the sword!" Singh also founded the Khalsa, a religious brotherhood of Sikh males. (*Singh* means "lion," and all Sikh males are given this name.) Govind Singh also wrote a prayer, recited daily by Sikhs, to promote the cause: "The Khalsa shall rule; none who object to it shall exist. In humiliation the refractory shall submit and those who seek refuge shall be protected." By the eighteenth century, as the Mughal empire declined, the Khalsa acquired influence over larger sections of the Punjab. But in the nineteenth century the British East India Company fought two bitter wars against the Sikhs, defeating them in 1849. The Punjab was then added to British India.

Because the Sikhs had proven to be formidable soldiers, the British East India Company sought them out to serve in the Company army, even allowing them to take their military oaths on Sikh scriptures and to wear the Sikh turban. Appreciative of British patronage, the Sikhs sided with the British during the Sepoy Mutiny of 1857. Though less than 2 percent of the population of India, the Sikhs accounted for one-fifth of Britain's armed forces. The Sikhs regarded themselves not as subject peoples to the British raj but as "favorite sons of the Empress Mother," Queen Victoria.

Of the 1.2 million Indians who served in the British military during World War I, over 350,000 were from the Punjab—the center of Sikh power and influence. During the unrest following World War I, the Sikhs joined with Hindus and Muslims to seek Indian independence or autonomy. In 1922 Bhagat Singh, a young Sikh revolutionary, was convicted by a British court of political murder. When Singh and his accomplices were hanged, riots broke out in the Punjab, leaving hundreds dead. Gandhi expressed sadness at the violence but praised Bhagat Singh's bravery. "I would not flinch," he said, "from sacrificing even a million lives for India's liberty."

The Sikh representative(s) will doubtless propose an independent Sikh state in the Punjab. The Sikhs worry that their religion and culture will be extirpated if they are forced to live in a nation dominated by either Hindus or Muslims. The Sikhs, though long regarded as the finest soldiers in India, could hardly be expected to prevail in armed confrontation with either the Hindus or the Muslims of India.

Perhaps the Sikhs can persuade the British to grant them their own nation in the Punjab. Throughout the raj, the Sikhs have been the staunchest supporters of Britain. Or perhaps the Sikhs will join Congress, hoping that their support for the majority party will persuade it to grant some autonomy to the Sikhs in the Punjab. Or perhaps the Sikhs will work with other minorities, perhaps even the Muslim League, to counterbalance the electoral power of the Hindus.

DR. B. R. AMBEDKAR, UNTOUCHABLE LEADER

Dr. B.R. Ambedkar, an Untouchable educated at Columbia University, seeks to ensure that the departure of the British will result in political power for the Untouchables (identified as "Selected Castes" or, more precisely, "Out-Castes," in the bureaucratic euphemism of the day). He wants not only that Untouchables be treated decently, or accorded constitutional "rights," but that they acquire political power to ensure and preserve such rights.

A pivotal moment in Ambedkar's consideration of the problems of the Untouchables came in 1932. That year, in response to his requests, the British government agreed to "reserve" 71 seats in provincial executive councils for Untouchables. These "reserved" seats could only be held by Untouchables. Gandhi, however, was outraged at this fragmentation of the people of India into separate political entities. He thought this move was characteristic of a British policy of "dividing" India so as to ensure its subjugation. In protest, he went on a hunger strike. The British government, fearing that Gandhi might die and thereby plunge India into chaos, withdrew the proposal. Ambedkar assented to this decision, but bitterly he resented Gandhi's actions.

Ambedkar will likely propose that the British affirm the rights of Untouchables and ensure that, in all future legislative bodies and governmental administrations, Untouchables are accorded representation in proportion to their numbers in Indian society. The Untouchables, though constituting about one-sixth of the population of India—more than 70 million people—will likely lose nearly all elections because everywhere they constitute a minority, indeed, a despised minority. His goal is a type of political affirmative action, in which one-sixth of all legislative seats, administrative offices, and governmental positions are "reserved" explicitly for Untouchables.

Ambedkar may approach Congress to support such measures. Yet there is the chance that in so large a group the needs of the Untouchables may be ignored. Moreover, many Hindus, especially Brahmans, believe that affirmative action on behalf of the Untouchables subverts the natural social order, undermines the social stability inherent in Hindu religious precepts, and threatens to plunge India into chaos. Some Hindu politicians may also insist that political strength depends on resisting the efforts of minorities to fracture the Hindu-dominated polity.

Thus Ambedkar may instead seek to join forces with the other important minorities in India. Insofar as the Untouchables are nearly as numerous as the Muslims, they would be an influential minority. But can any minority that opposes Congress expect to receive favorable or even fair treatment at the hands of Congress?

REPRESENTATIVE OF THE HINDU MAHASABHA

The Hindu Mahasabha, though founded in 1906 to protect Hindu cultural traditions and promote a Hindu state called Hindustan, did not attain prominence until the 1920s. By then, tensions between Hindus and Muslims had sparked frequent riots. Hindus would be offended by the Muslims' public slaughter of cows; and Muslims would become enraged when Hindu processions, drums pounding and trumpets blaring, marched past mosques during scheduled prayers. Fights ensued, often with heavy casualties. The Mahasabha's guiding force was—and is—V. D. Savarkar, who spent years in a British penal colony in the Andaman Islands on charges of terrorism. Savarkar was released in 1935, and since then he has become the leader of the movement. The Hindu Mahasabha has had an increasingly powerful effect on the leaders of Congress, who recognize that Mahasabites are capable of mobilizing, often in an instant, legions of militant followers. The Hindu Mahasabha functions as a cultural movement capable of inspiring radical Hindu politicians and also of influencing politicians in the Congress party. It opposes those who heap praise on Western institutions and it seeks to persuade Congress to veer away from socialist schemes.

The Hindu Mahasabha proposes to push foreigners out of India and to prevent the tearing of "Mother India" into two separate regions. Some of its adherents endorse the nonviolent strategies of Gandhi; others, having been reared on the nostrums of extremists such as Tilak and Savarkar, are willing to endorse radical, even violent, solutions. Unlike Gandhi, who endorses the values of the rural villages, the Hindu Mahasabha seeks to build a strong, modern (and thus industrial) nation. The Hindu Mahasabha, though intent on creating Hindustan, breaks with some high-caste Hindus in its desire to break down caste barriers. A strong Hindu nation, the Mahasabha insists, requires that Hindus be united.

LEADER OF THE COMMUNIST PARTY OF INDIA

Communists view the ethnic tensions within India as part of the effort among British and American capitalists to disguise the class tensions that are at the heart of relations in India. The British divide the Indian people by keeping alive religious and ethnic tensions (the partition of Bengal in the early 1900s is an obvious example), thereby obscuring the British colonial (and capitalistic) subjugation of the workers and peasants of India. The communist leader seeks to build a party within India to lead it toward real power.

VARIOUS INDETERMINATES

The indeterminate persons represent unexpressed (and perhaps unformed) public opinion. In India, the "public" consists mostly of the hundreds of millions who live in rural villages. The indeterminates—and, through them, the peoples of rural India—

influence the game in complicated ways, especially in the concluding sessions. Most partisans need to appeal to one or more of the indeterminates.

FOLLOWER OF BADSHAH KHAN (PASHTUN, NORTH-WEST FRONTIER PROVINCE)

The Pashtuns are a small minority with considerable influence in the remote highlands below the Hindu Kush mountain range, stretching from Kandahar to Kabul (now Afghanistan). Badshah Khan is a devout follower of Gandhi. Like Gandhi, he believes in nonviolence; unlike Gandhi, he controls a formidable army that patrols the wild wastelands south of the Khyber Pass. What he wants for the Pashtuns in a "new" India is by no means evident at the outset.

Basic Game Rules

VICTORY OBJECTIVES

Each group has different victory objectives; even within groups, objectives differ. The rules of the game are flexible and evolving. Players will likely be pressured to compromise "their" views (as outlined in the "roles") but players who compromise too far will cease to be faithful to their core identity and constituency. If this happens, they will lose. Determining exactly when this point has occurred is the prerogative of the Gamemaster, whose judgment will be made after the game is over. This unseemly potency and subjectivity may offend. But life, too, unfolds in ways that defy our notions of fairness and objectivity.

TACTICS AND WEAPONS

Technical: Access to the Podium

All players will have the right to stand at the podium and be heard. The GM may interrupt the Governors General to ensure that this right is respected. If the Governors General persist in ignoring such requests, the GM may report their autocratic behavior to the Prime Minister in London, who may order their recall or dismissal. On the other hand, the British Governors General may choose to employ the GM as a police force to ensure decorum during the game. In certain circumstances, those in power may circumscribe players' access to the podium.

Parties will try to win their objectives by persuading the Governors General to accede to their wishes, and then by persuading the others to go along with them. Persuasion may require additional inducements. Some possibilities (there are others) are indicated below.

Nonviolent Protests and "Direct Action"

The Muslim League, INC, Mahasabha, Sikhs, Communists, and/or Untouchables may at any time call upon their followers to respond to some decision, action, or policy. Any such proclamation must be made in class, in public, at the podium. A public call for "direct action" will likely trigger adherents in impoverished sections of various villages and cities to rise up violently against specified religious or class rivals. The effectiveness of such protest/action is determined by how many leaders support such action and the numbers of their followers. If, for example, one member of the Muslim League calls for a "direct action" day against Congress, it will be less effective than an episode in which all three members of the ML call for such action. Similarly, a "direct action" initiated by the INC would be more effective than one initiated by the Muslim League, if only because the INC had far more adherents. The magnitude of the violence can be affected by the other parties as well. If, say, the entire Muslim League calls for a "direct action" day and the entire INC calls for protest on the same day, the likely result would be tens of thousands of casualties. On the other hand, some groups, especially the Gandhians, can help defuse violent tensions by deploring a "direct action" or a "nonviolent protest" before it gets underway. But no one knows, in advance, the outcome of any protest or direct action.

Civil War

The Muslim League, INC, Sikhs, and Nizam of Hyderabad may declare war on whomever they wish. A war declaration will be a signal to violently inclined adherents to go all out against their foes. This represents an escalation of violence, but it will not produce a war in the usual sense of the term. None of the parties possesses large, well-trained armies with heavy weapons. Even rifles are in short supply throughout the subcontinent. All of the above factions have military units or drill teams with guns or security forces, but no one has the basic materials to raise and equip a large army. A sensible precursor to a war declaration is the building up of military forces, partly by acquiring arms. This may not be simple.

All parties may issue calls for nonviolent protests, such as non-cooperation. Remember: One can never anticipate all the ramifications of violence; the GM will input all the evidence pertaining to any situation in his master laptop computer (named Die-roll) and announce the outcome.

In the event of a continent-wide election, or referendum, the following percentages constitute the "core unshaped demographic profile" of the electorate of India, assuming a franchise of all adults:

Muslims	21%	Christians, Jews	1%
Caste Hindus	52%	Hyderabad	6%
Untouchables	15%	Kashmir	2%
Sikhs	2%	Communists	1%

In some instances, the nationwide vote can be precisely controlled by a particular figure at Simla. For example, the Sikh leader "controls" the Sikh vote or 2 percent, the Nizam of Hyderabad controls 5 percent (the vote of Hyderabad, unless the army of the Nizam has been neutralized), and the Maharaja of Kashmir controls 2 percent (the vote of Kashmir, unless his army has been neutralized). (Neutralization of either army at the outset of the game is unlikely because only the British at present have armed forces.) The leader of the Communist Party of India controls 1 percent.

The voting allegiance of all other groups depends on more complicated factors. For example, the **Muslim** vote (21 percent) is apportioned by the following "controls": Maulana Azad controls 4 percent, and the Muslim League, if unanimous, controls 15 percent. The other 2 percent can be apportioned by chance, or according to factors (quality of speeches, etc.) as the Gamemaster sees fit.

Of the 16 percent vote of the Untouchables, Ambedkar controls 9 percent and Gandhi 4 percent. The remaining 2 percent is controlled by the Indeterminate representative of "rural India."

Of the 52 percent vote of the Caste Hindus, 9 percent is apportioned to the indeterminate representative of rural India, and 28 percent to the Hindu leaders of the Congress party, if the position is unanimous among the Hindu leaders of the INC. Gandhi (if Gandhi A and B concur) controls 12 percent. The other 3 percent is allocated by the Gamemaster based on criteria he may or may not make public.

Special Note: these allocations are illustrative. They will be changed depending on the size of the class and the particular configuration of roles the instructor chooses to include. Moreover, the Gamemaster may alter this distribution for various reasons (an especially powerful speech or argument, an unexpected action that might have far-reaching implications on public opinion, etc.).

"Reserved Seats" Versus "Restricted Electorate"

In the 1930s, the British introduced the concept of reserved seats in provincial legislatures for specific minorities, such as Untouchables, Muslims, and Sikhs. That is, if Untouchables constituted 15 percent of the population of a province, then 15 percent of the seats would be "reserved" for Untouchables. But Dr. Ambedkar insisted that only Untouchables be allowed to vote for the reserved Untouchable seats; the Muslim League, that only Muslims could vote for the reserved Muslim seats. Gandhi and the Congress party vehemently objected to these provisions.

The issue can be more readily understood by considering how it would apply to the United States. "Reserved seats" could mean that 15 percent of the Senate and the House of Representatives would be "reserved" for African Americans. But if the electorate were unrestricted, then everyone—whites, blacks, Asians, members of the Ku Klux Klan, and so on—could vote to see which African Americans would hold those seats. The "elected" African Americans might not reflect the will of African Americans.

A restricted electorate provision, when coupled to "reserved seats," can be understood as follows: The electorate would be said to be "restricted" if only African Americans could vote in the election to choose the African American representatives. That is, as applied to the United States, only African Americans could vote for the seats in Congress that were "reserved for African Americans."

Electoral Simplicity

Literacy in India is very low. If there is to be a referendum of all adults (male and female), the issues must be simplified and converted to visual symbols. No one can expect all voters to read a paragraph or even a sentence. A referendum vote on cow protection, for example, could show two symbols: one, a cow; another, a cow with an X over it. A vote on partition, similarly, could show a symbol of one nation; another of two nations.

The British Governors General would control and administer any election or national referendum, unless India has gained independence. Afterward, an election or referendum would require sufficiently broad support (as determined by the GM) to cope with the enormous administrative problems of conducting an election during a time of confusion and transition.

FUNDAMENTAL CONSIDERATIONS

Players will inevitably be occupied with technical issues of constitution-making and government creation. But those who are most successful will take on the biggest issue—the meaning of nationality—and devise a coherent conception, consistent with their victory objectives, and relate it persuasively to the rest of the class. The technical issues will likely fall in place if the overall argument is persuasive.

Schedule of Assignments and Class Activities

The schedule that follows assumes a class of about twenty students. Larger classes may require more time to allow all roles to be voiced and debated. If more than twelve class sessions are scheduled, the extra time can be used to develop more thoroughly the history of India and the ideas outlined in the *Sources* readings. Students should begin readings in advance of class.

SCHEDULE OF ASSIGNMENTS AND CLASS ACTIVITIES		
Class	Instructor Activity	Student Activity **Before** Class
1	Introduction / Q & A: Hinduism and Islam; historical context outlined in *India's Search* (Sepoy Mutiny to 1945)	Read game packet, including following sections of *India's Search for National Identity* (Appendix B): Read entire selection up to "Negotiations for Independence" (in Chapter 6) (DO NOT READ LAST SECTIONS UNTIL GAME IS OVER)
2	Discussion of ideas in *Sources*; End of Class: Distribute Roles	Begin reading *Sources*, especially Chapters 2-4 (See "Reading Assignments" in next section)
3	Continue discussion of ideas in *Sources*; 15 minutes for factions; meet with Governors General	Complete *Sources* reading and read Appendix A of this booklet
4	First ½: Quiz on Readings; Meet with Factions	Reread materials pertaining to your role; prepare for Quiz on Readings
5	Game begins	British Gov. Generals make initial statement; Faction meetings
6	Game: Full session 1	Sikhs, Nizam, Maharaja, Communist: presentations to full session (prepare and submit paper #1)
7	Game: Full session 2	Untouchables and Gandhi adherents make presentations (paper #1)
8	Game: Full session 3	INC, Muslim League: presentations to full session (paper #1)
9	Game: Full session 4	Governors General issue draft recommendations to Prime Minister, followed by open discussion
10	Game: Full session 5	Reply by various parties (second papers)
11	Game: Full session 6	Reply, continued / Implementation of Revised Plan (Governors General option) (second papers)
12	Post Mortem Discussion: Game issues, Historical Outcome; Hand out game evaluations	Read remainder of *India's Search* for post-mortem discussion.

Defining a Nation: India on the Eve of Independence, 1945

The game requires that students master the ideas of the figure on which their role is based, and that they also become familiar with the ideas of nearly everyone else. Moreover, students must learn considerable historical context.

FIRST CLASS: HISTORICAL BACKGROUND

Before the first session, students should have read all of the game booklet and plunged into the first half of *India's Search for National Identity*, the historical narrative that appears as Appendix B. The following paragraphs provide a general introduction.

Ancient Origins of Indian Civilization

For thousands of years, the history of the Indian subcontinent resembled those of agricultural peoples elsewhere. Most lived along the Indus River or its tributaries; by 1000 B.C. the Ganges River had become another center of settlement. As was true of other ancient civilizations along the Nile, Yangtze, and Tigris-Euphrates Rivers, most people were farmers. As agricultural yields expanded, population increased. Cities gradually emerged.

Very early the belief developed that groups are defined by graduated degrees of purity and impurity that differentiated them from other groups. These groups were further based on ties of kinship and occupation.

Political systems evolved as well, as tribal assemblies tended to give way to hereditary dynasties. Kings and princes constructed irrigation systems, granaries, and walled fortifications; they also raised armies to provide protection from envious hill-country warlords or desert marauders.

Over time, hereditary elites consolidated power in various ways: by interceding with deities that otherwise would destroy crops and unloose plagues and famines; by accumulating knowledge of the stars and calendars, so as to know when rivers would flood and the first frost would destroy crops; by developing the art of writing to record and preserve information; and by championing deference and obedience.

Indian history during the first millennium was characterized by a succession of dynasties: each gaining power, expanding its geographical dominion, and subsequently crumbling into hundreds of little principalities or small republics.

Introduction to Hinduism

Hinduism is the name that Westerners and most Indians have given to the very complex systems of beliefs and practices that evolved on the Indian subcontinent over hundreds of years. It is impossible to date its origin or its founders, because it has grown and changed through the centuries, and, like all religious systems, it continues to change and adjust to different historical conditions.

Having emerged in India approximately 3500 years ago, Hinduism is one of the oldest religions. Its structures of authority are related to great sages and saints, and to teachers known as "gurus," many of whom have widespread reputation, although many are local. Countless Hindu sects have arisen, each based on its own set of scriptures. Yet most Hindus nevertheless accept the sacredness of one set of ancient texts, probably dating from 1400 B.C. to 500 B.C., called the *Vedas*. The Vedas consist of hymns and descriptions of rituals, chiefly sacrifices, used by the Brahmans, a priestly class, to win favor of the gods. These texts outline a mythology that divided society into four classes, or *castes*, in descending grades of purity and knowledge. The Brahmans, the priestly caste, are the highest caste, followed by warriors, farmers and traders, and laborers. This is the basis of what Westerners, but not Hindus, refer to as the "caste system." Hindus regard it as a way of life or of societal order.

Although not all modern Hindus accept the caste system or its theological underpinnings, nearly all variants of Hinduism adhere to several other concepts. *Samsara* (transmigration of the individual soul) posits that after death a person's soul is reborn into another person's body; when that person dies, the soul migrates to another person in a cycle of life, death, and rebirth. Those who behave virtuously in one life will advance, by the law of *karma*, to a higher spiritual state in the next. Eventually, after many such cycles, a fully spiritualized soul attains *moksha*, liberation from the life-death cycle and union with the cosmic truth.

Hinduism embraces many deities, although two are especially prominent: **Siva**, the creator, preserver, and destroyer of the universe, appeared in the *Svetasvatara Upanishad*, a Vedic text dating from about 400 B.C.; and **Vishnu**, a god who is incarnated in many forms. The most widely known of these incarnations are **Rama**, of great importance in modern India, and **Lord Krishna**, the central deity in the *Bhagavad gita* ("Song of the Lord"), a text that appeared around 200 B.C. Lord Krishna is the focus of an immense variety of artistic and literary representations.

The English term "deities" fails to fully convey how Hinduism is perceived as layers of related metaphors. For example, it is incorrect to say that Hindus "worship" cows: rather, cows evoke a constellation of life-affirming concepts: milk, infancy, mother, and life. Hindu "deities" similarly evoke the sights and sounds and peoples of a particular place. Hindus perceive the metaphorical meanings of its sacred traditions in different ways.

English translations of the Vedas and the Bhagavad gita are available online at: http://www.hinduwebsite.com.

The Rise of Islam

Islam, founded by the Prophet Muhammad (570?-632), took root in much of central Asia. The fundamental principles of Islam are outlined in the *Quran* (sometimes spelled Koran), which Muslims regard as the word of God as revealed to the Prophet Muhammad. The Quran is comprised of some 114 chapters, called *surahs*. The Quran often refers to both books of the Bible, and accepts much of Judeo-Christian narrative.

But according to believers, the Quran supersedes these earlier renderings of the word of God. It holds that though Abraham, Noah, Moses, and Jesus were important prophets, Muhammad was the greatest and last of the prophets; that God forgave Adam for disobeying God's commands; and that God is indivisible (not, as in Christianity, Trinitarian). Because man's ultimate duty is submission to the divine will, Islamic law, *Shari'ah* ("the path leading to the watering place"), states the principles to guide Muslims.

The greatest influx of Muslim peoples into the Punjab occurred in the 1100s. Muslim warlords gained ascendancy in parts of northern India and increasingly penetrated south India. Yet many Hindu princes held out against the Muslim advance and some forced it into retreat. Often Muslim rulers fought each other.

The most important of these confrontations occurred in the early 1500s. Babur, a Turkish warlord, moved eastward, conquered the Punjab, and in 1526 defeated most important Muslim sultan of India at Panipat. This marked the founding of the Mughal Empire. One of Babur's descendants, Akbar the Great (1556-1605), won yet another major battle at Panipat (1556), ensuring his control over much of the subcontinent.

Although the Mughal rulers were intermittently challenged by Muslim and Hindu princes, their most serious challenger was Shivaji (1627-80), a general who led the Hindu Marathas and seized much of the region around Bombay. The Mughal Empire was in trouble.

About this time, too, European merchants were exploiting the new route to India by sailing around Africa and through the Indian Ocean. The Portuguese, French, Dutch, and English all established trading ports in India. And then the European powers came to blows, with the British prevailing during the worldwide war between England and France fought from 1756 through 1763.

Imposition of British authority over much of India was chiefly the work of the British East India Company. One prince after another yielded to the demands of the British. With the defeat of the Sikhs in 1846, British control of India was almost uncontested. Then came the Sepoy Rebellion of 1857. This is where Embree's *India's Search for National Identity* begins (Appendix B).

SECOND AND THIRD CLASSES: PRIMARY SOURCES

Before the second class, students must also read much of *Sources of the Indian Tradition,* Volume 2, listed as follows. These writings are important because they will inform the views of nearly **every** person who is attending the Simla conference. Students will understand the objectives and motives of other players by understanding the texts on which their ideas are based, as outlined below (a specific faction, or factional subdivision, is indicated in **bold**). By 1945, Gandhi had become by far the most famous and influential figure in India. Everyone should study his writings.

Sources of Indian Tradition[DJ1]*, Volume 2*

CHAPTER 2
Read the Introduction: "Leaders of Hindu Reform and Revival"
(INC, Hindu Mahasabha)

CHAPTER 3
"Nationalism Takes Root: The Moderates" (Introduction only) **(INC)**

CHAPTER 4
"The Marriage of Politics and Religion: The Extremists"
(INC, Hindu Mahasabha)
Bankim Chandra Chatterjee: Nationalist Author
Bal Gangadhar Tilak: "Father of Indian Unrest"
Lajpat Rai: "Lion of the Punjab"

CHAPTER 5
Leaders of Islamic Revival, Reform, and Nationalism
(Muslim League, Jinnah, INC, Azad)
Mohamed Ali: Patriot and Defender of the Faith **(Islamicist ML)**
Muhammad Iqbal: Poet and Philosopher of the Islamic Revival **(Islamicist, ML)**
Muhammad Ali Jinnah: Founder of Pakistan **(Jinnah)**
Maulana (Abdul Kalam) Azad, Muslim INC **(Azad, INC)**

CHAPTER 6
Mahatma Gandhi: Nationalist India's "Great Soul" **(Gandhi, INC, Ambedkar)**

CHAPTER 7
Other Leaders (INC, Ambedkar, Gandhi, Nehru)
Vinayak Damodar Savarkar: Hindu Nationalist
(Hindu Mahasabha, Gandhi, INC)
Jawaharlal Nehru: Democratic Socialist **(Secular INC)**
Bhim Rao Ambedkar: Spokesman for the Untouchables **(Untouchables)**
Manabendra Nath Roy: From International Communist to Radical Humanist
(Communist)

CHAPTER 9

Pakistan: Defining an Islamic State **(Secular ML)**
Jinnah (more)

Major Documents

In addition to *Sources of the Indian Tradition,* many important writings—chosen specifically for this game—appear in Appendix A.

FOURTH CLASS: QUIZ

To ensure that students have read the materials on which the game depends, there will be a short-answer quiz for half of the fourth class session. Half of the questions will be from *India's Search,* half from the readings in *Sources.* The exam will likely be taken from the sample questions below.

Sample Questions: India's Search for National Identity

CHAPTER 1: ONE GREAT NATION

1. Indian intellectuals began thinking in terms of an "Indian nation"
    a) with the rise of Hinduism 3000 years ago
    b) after the subjugation of the Hindus by the Mughals in the 1500s
    c) with the introduction of European ideas about nationalism in the 1800s
    d) after Gandhi initiated the independence movement in the early 1900s

2. Great Britain promoted the concept of an Indian nation in all of the following ways except
    a) building railroad, telegraph, and postal systems
    b) requiring the use of a single language—English—in government
    c) administering India as a single administrative region
    d) bringing Indians together in the British civil and military bureaucracies

3. By the late 1800s British law was applied to Indian affairs in all of the following ways except
    a) the rules of evidence in court proceedings
    b) applicability to all Indians, regardless of religious status or political rank
    c) matters of personal law, such as marriage and divorce
    d) the creation of a court system

4. Which of the following is true of British-sponsored education in nineteenth-century India?
    a) It eliminated illiteracy
    b) It reduced the power of hereditary Hindu upper castes
    c) It taught Hindus and Muslims to appreciate their own cultures
    d) It introduced upper-class Hindus and Muslims to Western ideas

5. Ram Mohan Roy, an important Indian thinker of the mid-1800s, regarded Hindu practices such as the marriage of children and *sati*, the burning of widows on their husbands' funeral pyres, as

   a) symptomatic of the British domination of India
   b) venerated Hindu traditions that should be upheld as a shield against the modernizing ideas of the West
   c) superstitious corruptions of the pure Hinduism of antiquity
   d) crimes that should be stamped out by the government

6. The following quote is from what famous writing?

   > Mother, to thee I bow.
   > Who hath said thou art weak
   > When the swords flash out in twice
   > Seventy million hands,
   > And seventy million voices roar
   > Thy dreadful name from share to share

   a) Bankim Chandra Chatterjee, from the novel *Anandamath*
   b) Charles Dickens, *A Tale of Two Cities*
   c) B. G. Tilak, Commentary on the Bhagavad Gita
   d) Lajpat Rai, The Coming Political Struggle

7. In Hinduism, a cow is

   a) worshiped as sacred
   b) consumed during a sacrificial rite
   c) cherished as a symbol of fertility and motherhood
   d) the chastener of Muslims

8. Sivaji (Shivaji) was

   a) a cow that was worshiped as divine
   b) a Hindu prince who became a cow-god
   c) a Maratha (Hindu) warrior who dislodged the Muslims of the Mughal dynasty in the 1600s
   d) a Muslim warrior who defeated the Hindus and ensured the establishment of the Mughal dynasty

9. What pivotal event occurred in 1885?

   a) the Sepoy Mutiny
   b) the founding of the Indian National Congress (INC)
   c) the founding of the British raj
   d) the founding of the Muslim League (ML)

CHAPTER 3: SEARCH FOR A CENTER

10. In 1905, Lord Curzon, Viceroy of India, decided to partition the province of Bengal, with 78 million people, into two provinces. All of the following were consequences of this decision except

   a) East Bengal, one of the provinces, would have a Muslim majority
   b) the Indian National Congress denounced the partition as illustrative of the British policy of "divide and rule" and called for a boycott of British manufactures
   c) Muslims became increasingly wary of the Congress
   d) Hindu radicals in Bengal commenced a campaign of terrorism against the British
   e) Curzon was assassinated

11. What pivotal event occurred in 1906?

   a) the Sepoy Mutiny
   b) the founding of the Indian National Congress (INC)
   c) the onset of the Great War
   d) the founding of the Muslim League (ML)

12. World War I stimulated Indian independence by

   a) increasing the role of Indian leaders and bureaucrats in military and civil administration
   b) increasing the power of the British government
   c) weakening the power of the British government
   d) defeating the Japanese

13. The British-proposed constitution of 1919 contained a provision for dyarchy at the provincial level. Dyarchy meant that

   a) on certain matters, British administrators would make decisions jointly with Indian administrators, as directed by elected Indian provincial legislatures
   b) decisions would be made by random die roll
   c) British administrators would make all decisions
   d) Indian administrators would decide matters of war and peace, and British administrators decide matters of finance and trade

CHAPTER 4: THE EMERGENCE OF GANDHI

14. Gandhi's concept of *satyagraha* stands for

   a) violent opposition to *sati*, whereby Hindu widows immolate themselves on the funeral pyres of their husbands
   b) nonviolent action against oppression
   c) violent resistance to oppression
   d) opposition to British imposition of a salt tax

15. Gandhi's 1919 call for a *hartal*, or strike, culminated in which of the following?
    a) the "Black Hole" of Calcutta
    b) the firing on civilians at the Jallianwala Bagh, an enclosed square in Amritsar
    c) the arrest of key Congress leaders
    d) the arrest of key Muslim leaders

16. Gandhi's 1921 non-cooperation movement included all but which strategy?
    a) the withdrawal of children from British schools and colleges
    b) the boycott of foreign goods
    c) the boycott of the law courts
    d) the campaign for Indians to be elected to local and provincial positions

17. Khadi is
    a) a ritual anointing oil used in Hinduism
    b) a Hindu god
    c) homespun cotton cloth
    d) a type of stick used by the British for crowd control

CHAPTER 5: THE POLITICS OF RIGHT MISTAKES

18. The 1920s witnessed the rise of the Hindu Mahasabha, an organization that promoted Hinduism. This contributed to the development of all of the following except
    a) Ali Jinnah's success in mobilizing the Muslim League to defend Muslim interests
    b) the widening of the divisions within the Congress party
    c) the intensification of riots between Hindus and Muslims
    d) the outlawing of the Hindu Mahasabha by the British government

19. In 1930 Gandhi was again imprisoned. This time he was arrested for
    a) inciting Bhagat Singh, a Sikh revolutionary, to murder British officials
    b) promoting civil disobedience in his campaign against the Salt Tax
    c) defiling Hindu temples in a campaign to ensure the admittance of Untouchables
    d) calling on Hindus to resist taunts by Muslims

20. Which of the following Muslim leaders did not belong to the League?
    a) Muhammad Iqbal
    b) Ali Jinnah
    c) Maulana Azad
    d) Syed Abu-l-ala-Maududi

21. In 1932 Gandhi decided to go on a hunger strike to protest a British decision to reserve 71 seats in provincial councils for Untouchables. He did so chiefly because he believed that
   a) Untouchables lacked the education to make legislative decisions
   b) Untouchables needed economic reform more than political representation
   c) the creation of separate political classes divided the Indian polity
   d) Untouchables deserved far more seats in the provincial councils

22. The Government of India Act of 1935 called for the establishment of reserved seats in provincial legislatures for Muslims, Untouchables, Christians, and representatives of industry, the landowners, the universities, labor, and women. Gandhi and Nehru opposed the Act as fracturing the Indian people, and Congress responded by
   a) endorsing the Act as a first step toward Indian independence
   b) calling for a boycott of the provincial elections and not accepting the decisions of legislatures elected by such a process
   c) putting Congress candidates up for election but insisting that they not take seats if elected
   d) encouraging Congress candidates to run for election under the names of other parties

23. Which party fared best in the provincial elections of 1936?
   a) none: the boycotted election was canceled
   b) Congress party
   c) Muslim League
   d) the party of the Sikhs

24. Ail Jinnah of the Muslim League became increasingly committed to the creation of a separate nation because he believed that
   a) British rule was becoming increasingly anti-Islamic
   b) Islamic law (*sharia*) should prevail in predominantly Muslim areas (shariat)
   c) a separate Islamic nation would be economically stronger
   d) Congress candidates, elected in 1936, took office and discriminated against Muslims in provincial governments

25. What, in Embree's view, were the "right mistakes" of the 1930s?
   a) Gandhi's cancellation of civil disobedience campaigns in 1922 and 1934, thereby postponing the final break from Great Britain
   b) Congress's refusal to form a coalition government after the 1936 elections
   c) Congress's neglect of the fears of Jinnah and the Muslim League
   d) all of the above

26. At the outset of World War II, Great Britain
    a) offered India immediate independence if it would side with the Allies
    b) proposed to divide India into two states, India and Pakistan
    c) declared that independence could not come until after the Axis powers had been defeated
    d) did all of the above

27. In the spring of 1942, as Japanese armies swept through China and Southeast Asia and neared India, Prime Minister Winston Churchill sent Sir Stafford Cripps to India with a proposal: Britain would retain control of India during the war but afterward would arrange for an elected Indian body that would draft a constitution. Congress leaders rejected the Cripps proposal because
    a) they had received a similar proposal during World War I and Britain had failed to deliver independence after the war
    b) the British Governors General and military officials would have excessive power during the war
    c) individual provinces could decide not to join the postwar Indian union
    d) all of the above

28. The "Quit India" campaign of 1942 was initiated
    a) by British leaders who thought money needed for the war was being wasted in India
    b) by Muslim League officials who called for partition
    c) by Congress leaders to demand immediate British withdrawal from India
    d) by all of the above

29. All of the following were consequences of the "Quit India" movement except
    a) the main leaders of Congress, including Gandhi and Nehru, were jailed
    b) widespread violence erupted in northern India
    c) Muslim League leaders became increasingly fearful of chaos in the wake of British withdrawal
    d) British efforts to stop the Japanese advance failed

30. Based on Map A (page 9), which of the following was NOT a princely state?
    a) Hyderabad
    b) Kashmir
    c) Bengal
    d) Mysore

31. Based on Map B (page 10), which of the following provinces did NOT have a Muslim majority?
    a) Baluchistan
    b) Sind
    c) Bengal
    d) Bombay

32. Based on Map B, which of the following provinces had the lowest percentage of Muslims?
   a) Hyderabad
   b) Punjab
   c) United Provinces
   d) Madras

33. Which one of the following colors is incorrectly matched?
   a) Islam/Green
   b) Hinduism/Yellow
   c) Communism/Red
   d) Irish nationalism/Blue

Sample Questions: *Sources of Indian Tradition, Volume 2*

34. Match the quotes that follow with their authors.
   <u>Leaders</u>
   1) Bankim Chatterjee
   2) B. G. Tilak
   3) Lajpat Rai
   4) Mohamed Ali
   5) Muhammad Iqbal
   6) Ali Jinnah
   7) Maulana (Abdul Kalam) Azad
   8) Gandhi
   9) Jawaharlal Nehru
   10) B. R. Ambedkar
   11) Manabendra Nath Roy
   12) Vinayak Damodar Savarkar

   <u>Quotations</u>
   A) Mother, I bow to thee!
   Rich with thy hurrying streams,
   Bright with thy orchard gleams,
   Cool with the winds of delight,
   Dark fields waving, Mother of might,
   Mother free.

   B) Our Essence is not bound to any place;
   The vigor of our wine is not contained
   In any bowl. . .
   We profess no fatherland
   Except Islam

C) Much as I wish for the advancement of socialism in this country, I have no desire to force the issue on the Congress and thereby create difficulties in the way of our struggle for independence. . . . But I shall do so stating my position frankly and hoping in course of time to convert the Congress and the country to [socialism], for only thus can I see it achieving independence. (1936)

D) The single *Gita* [Bhagavad Gita] religion, which preaches that the whole of one's life should be turned into a sacrifice contains the essence of the entire Vedic religion . . . . I now pray. . . at the end of this book that there should come to birth again in this our country such noble and pure men as will worship the Parameshvara according to this equable and brilliant religion of the *Gita*, which harmonizes devotion, spiritual knowledge, and energism. (1907)

E) It is extremely difficult to appreciate why our Hindu friends fail to understand the real nature of Islam and Hinduism. They are not religions in the strict sense of the word, but are, in fact, different and distinct social orders, and it is a dream that the Hindus and Muslims can ever evolve a common nationality . . . . Muslim India cannot accept any constitution which must necessarily result in a Hindu majority government. (1935)

F) Equally certain it is that whenever the Hindus come to hold a position whence they could dictate terms to the whole world—those terms cannot be very different from the terms which the *Gita* dictates or the Buddha lays down. A Hindu is most intensely so, when he ceases to be a Hindu; and [instead} exclaims: "My country? Oh brothers, the limits of the Universe—there the frontiers of my country life."

G) I think the people of Bengal ought to be congratulated on being leaders of that march in the van of progress. . . .They have begun the battle, they have begun the fight and they have begun it in right manly style. . . If the other Provinces of India will just follow their example, I say the day is not far from distant sights. . . .I am afraid that our record is extremely poor and extremely humiliating. If the people of India will just learn that lesson from the people of Bengal, I think the struggle is not hopeless.

H) [N]othing is further removed from the truth than to say that Indian Muslims occupy the position of a political minority. It is equally absurd for them to be apprehensive about their rights and interests in a democratic India. . . .I am a Musalman [Muslim] and am proud of that fact. . . .I am [also] proud of being an Indian. I am part of the indivisible unit that is Indian nationality.

I) Why should you remain in a religion that does not let you enter its temples? Why should you remain in a religion that does not let you get water to drink? Why should you remain in a religion that dishonors you at every step?

J) Warfare, according to the Quran, is an evil; but persecution is a worse evil, and may be put down with the weapons of war. When persecution ceases, and every man is free to act with the sole motive of securing divine goodwill, warfare must cease. These are the limits of violence in Islam, as I understand it. . . .But I have agreed to work with Mahatma Gandhi, and our compact is that as long as I am associated with him I shall not resort to the use of force even for purposes of self-defence. And I have willingly entered into this compact because I think we can achieve victory without violence. (1923)

K) I do want growth, I do want self-determination, I do want freedom, but I want all these for the soul. I doubt if the steel age is an advance upon the flint age. I am indifferent. It is the evolution of the soul to which the intellect and all our faculties have to be devoted. . . .I do not claim that nonviolence has penetrated the three hundred millions, but I do claim that it has penetrated deeper than any other message, and in an incredibly short time.

L) I do not make a secret of my determination of helping the organization of the great revolution which must take place in order to open up before the Indian masses the road to liberty, progress, and prosperity. The impending revolution is an historic necessity. Conditions for it are maturing rapidly. Colonial exploitation of the country creates those conditions. So, I am not responsible for the revolution, nor is the Communist International. Imperialism is responsible for it. My punishment, therefore, will not stop the revolution. (1931)

WRITTEN ASSIGNMENTS

Each player must submit **two** papers of a length prescribed by the instructor. The first must be submitted in writing on the date each faction's presentation is due to the British Governors General. The second is due on or before the final game session. Exception: the British Governors General will present their first paper, containing their set of recommendations (including maps), during Class 9. Groups, or multi-member factions, should coordinate their submissions to ensure that they have something substantive to say at every session. That is, they should use their first paper (and class presentations) to outline to the British Governors General, and to the other political leaders of the Indian subcontinent, what government they propose to put in place to replace the British. The second papers may be a response to the proposal of the Governors General, or they may make an argument of a different character.

India: A Chronology

INDIA'S POPULATION

100 A.D.	Approximately 100 million
1800	Approximately 125 million
1871	Approximately 250 million: 187 Hindu; 52 Muslim
1940	Approximately 400 million: 300 Hindu, 100 Muslim

PRINCIPLE EVENTS

1400s	Sikhs founded as religious order; sought to reconcile Muslim and Hindu doctrines; opposed caste restrictions; became military zealots.
1526-1761	**Mughal Dynasty (Muslim**, Akbar greatest leader); Sikhs/Mughal conflict: Sikhs crushed.
1690s	Hindu warrior, Shivaji, inflicts defeats on Mughals.
1700s	British East India Company makes incursions along Indian coastline; forces Mughal trading concessions; erodes Mughal power and suppresses it.
1757	British East India Company army defeats Mughal ruler at battle of Plassey; Company controls all of Bengal and much of India.
1800s	British extend education, railways, economic development throughout India.
1857	**Sepoy Mutiny** crushed.
1858	**Government of India Act:** India ruled directly as a British colony.
1885	INC founded.
1905	British Governor General proposes partition of Bengal and creation of a Muslim majoritarian state, East Bengal; Hindu protests.
1906	Muslim League founded in response.
1909	Government of India Act: franchise given to selected groups in India to choose representatives to the Governor's Executive Council.

1917	British adopt dyarchy: all branches of provincial administration divided, British/Indian.
1919	Gandhian *hartal* (work stoppage); protest to Rowlatt Acts; **Amritsar Massacre** (Gandhi suspends protests).
1920	Khilafat Movement (Muslim; Gandhi joins to unify).
1921	Peak of Gandhian non-cooperation movement.
1930	Gandhi leads **salt march** civil disobedience; Iqbal, Muslim writer, calls for separate Muslim state.
1932	British offer representation to **Untouchables**; Ambedkar approves; Gandhi protests.
1935	New **Government of India Act** passed by British parliament. End of dyarchy: Now Indians have sole control of provinces, although the British remain in control of the national government and all matters that pertain to it: the military, taxation, and defense. Accorded franchise to 35 million, and granted large measure of autonomy to Indian governments to rule provinces. The British, however, remain in firm control of the central government, controlling defense and the budget.
1937	Election: though ostensibly boycotting the election, Congress wins a majority in most provinces (seven) and the elected Congress officials did take office. The Muslim League, alarmed, mobilizes for separate Muslim state.
1942	Indian Nationalist leaders refuse to join war effort; call on Britain to "Quit India;" Congress leaders arrested and imprisoned for duration of war. British rule colony directly.
1945	Wavell, viceroy: deadlock between Muslim and Hindu leaders on interim government.

The historical outline that follows provides only a fundamental account of the historical context of this game. Students may wish to consult it before reading Embree's full account in *India's Search for National Identity*, in Appendix B.

During the 1600s, English merchants became a presence on the Indian subcontinent. The British East India Company, founded in 1600, established trading outposts in various Indian cities after 1619, seeking to sell Indian textiles in European markets.

At this time, India was ruled by the Mughals, Muslim warlords who imposed their rule on much of India in 1526 and extended it over the next two centuries. The Mughal emperors promoted cultural fusion with their far more numerous Hindu subjects. Lower caste Hindus were attracted to the Islamic profession of egalitarianism in fact, though the Muslims had a strong hereditary elite. The highest caste Hindus are known as Brahmans.

The British East India Company, often supported by Hindu merchants, encroached on the political authority and state revenues of the Mughal rulers and it backed up its economic encroachment with military might. In 1756, a Mughal ruler defeated a large force of Company soldiers and imprisoned them in Calcutta. Perhaps through neglect, scores of them suffocated in what became known as "the black hole of Calcutta."

1757: BRITISH EAST INDIA COMPANY DEFEATS MUGHALS

Company forces, backed by Britain, took their revenge by crushing the Mughal ruler at the battle of Plassey in 1757. Company officials soon obliged the Mughal emperor to cede all tax revenues of Bengal. Elsewhere, Company officials wrested land and revenues from other Mughal rulers, including the Nizam of Hyderabad. By 1800, many independent states had become indebted to the Company, which then annexed them outright. The Nizam of Hyderabad was among those princes who avoided outright annexation. In 1803 the British East India Company seized Delhi, bringing nearly all of northern India into Company dominion. Then the Company moved southward, finally defeating the Marathas in 1818.

By then, the only eighteenth-century kingdom not under the control of the Company was the Sikh Kingdom of Punjab, founded in 1790 by Ranjit Singh. Singh strengthened Sikh agriculture and commerce, the revenues of which built up his army. After Singh died in 1839, and the East India Company exploited subsequent Sikh divisions to defeat them in 1849. The Company then annexed the Punjab.

1857: THE SEPOY MUTINY

The British East India Company ruled through military despotism. In addition to British mercenaries, the Company increasingly relied on Indian *sepoys*, a corruption of the Urdu word for "soldier." By 1805, during the Napoleonic Wars, the British East India Company employed some 150,000 sepoys.

The political and military power of the Company had long drawn some criticism from London, especially from the parliamentarian and political thinker Edmund Burke, but the Company also brought considerable wealth to Great Britain. Cotton was the main cash export, followed by China tea and, later, opium. In general, the Company attended only to economic matters; it made little effort to transform Indian society or culture.

Revolts against Company rule were fairly commonplace; sometimes, too, the sepoys mutinied against Company officers. When rumors circulated in 1857 that the new rifle cartridges, which had to be bitten, were greased with cow and pig fat, Hindu and Muslim sepoys were appalled. The rumors held that such impure actions were part of a perfidious effort to devalue native religions and Christianize the sepoys. Thus began the great Sepoy Mutiny of 1857. Mutineers marched on Delhi and persuaded the elderly Mughal emperor to accept titular leadership of the revolt. Other revolts and mutinies flared up elsewhere in India, often spawned by anger at the British tax collectors. The Company force was divided between 40,000 British soldiers, and some 240,000 sepoys.

However, many of the sepoys were from the Punjab, and Sikh soldiers for the most part remained loyal to the British. Company forces eventually crushed the rebellion, but at a staggering cost of 50 million pounds (500 million rupees). The Company could not pay this debt. The Sepoy Mutiny was, to some, the "First War of Indian Independence."

1858: GOVERNMENT OF INDIA ACT: BRITISH DIRECT RULE COMMENCES

The Sepoy Mutiny forced London to take control of India. In 1858 Queen Victoria announced that the lands subject to Company rule would now be under the direct colonial administration of the British crown. The British Indian army and civil bureaucracy would be run by officials who ultimately reported to the Prime Minister in London. All upper echelons of the Indian bureaucracy would be staffed by British subjects; those officials would collect revenues formerly collected by the Company.

The Sepoy Mutiny engendered suspicion among many British officials toward Indian subjects. For a time, fewer Indians were allowed in the military and civil service. Many young Indians from middle or upper class backgrounds, who had previously been groomed for a government career, now found their options blocked. Some of them devoted their lives to criticizing British imperialism without repudiating Western and democratic concepts. They advocated Indian unity, promoted social and economic reform along Western lines within India, and expected the British to eventually grant

Indian self-government. This viewpoint can be found in the writings of Surendranath Banerjea, "Bengali moderate," in *Sources*, pages 97-102.

1885: INC (CONGRESS) FOUNDED

In December 1885, the Indian National Congress (or simply Congress) first met, in Bombay. At the time, the British military had nearly subdued native insurgents in Burma, completing its conquest of the subcontinent. Many of those present at the creation of the INC had been educated in the universities founded in 1857 by the British East India Company in a belated attempt to teach English to the native elites. But by the 1880s, few Indians had been admitted to the Indian Civil Service. During the early decades, Congress advocated liberalization of British rule. Progress toward this goal had been apparent in the rule of Lord Ripon, Governor General of India from 1880 to 1884. Ripon proposed reforms to grant increased participation of Indians within the ICS and to allow Indian judges to hear cases involving Europeans. These proposals were met with vehement opposition among the British living in India, and by the government in London. Ripon withdrew the reforms, and Congress was established partly in response.

The first Congress session consisted of 73 delegates from nearly every province in India. Of these, 54 were Hindu and only two were Muslim. Nearly all of the Hindu delegates were of the Brahman (highest) caste, and all spoke English. Despite the failure of Ripon's reforms, Congress leaders were optimistic that independence was inevitable and that when it came, the British would transfer power to Congress. (Half of the initial Congress delegates were lawyers.)

Though often sympathetic to Western values and inclined to support India's modernization, Congress nevertheless eschewed any campaign to reform or transform traditional social relationships such as the Hindu caste system. They sought a broad constituency, cemented by a belief in a vague Indian nationalism, endorsing few specifics apart from a demand for the immediate withdrawal of the British. Congress grew rapidly. In 1888, some 1250 delegates attended the annual meeting. Their position was best reflected in the writings of S. N. Banerjea (in *Sources*).

TILAK: A HINDU REVIVAL

The initially moderate (and somewhat ineffectual) nationalism of Congress was jolted into a new phase by the writings of Bal Gangadhar Tilak, "the father of Indian unrest." Tilak, editor of a weekly newspaper northeast of Bombay, published in both English and the Maratha local dialect, rejected the modern world and celebrated the traditions of Hindu village life. In the 1890s his newspaper championed honoring a Hindu god and Shivaji, a Maratha warrior who fought the Islamic Mughals. He mobilized opposition to the slaughter of cows and the eating of beef. His work inspired Hindu terrorists who assassinated British officials in 1897. (For examples of Tilak's writings, see *Sources*.)

Defining a Nation: India on the Eve of Independence, 1945

Tilak's work, which helped radicalize non-English-speaking Hindus in rural villages, alarmed India's Muslims. (Shivaji scored the last major victory of a Hindu over the Mughals.) A Congress leader, Tilak illustrated the militant possibilities of an Indian nationalism aligned to Hindu religious and cultural precepts. Tilak's radical nationalism proved increasingly influential among the younger Congress leaders. Some radicals joined secret societies that were active in Bengal and in Bombay, where Tilak's influence was greatest, and increasingly in the Punjab, where Lala Lajpat Rai was accused by the British of being a Hindu terrorist. (For the writings of Lala Lajpat Rai, "Lion of the Punjab," see *Sources*.)

MILITANT MUSLIMS

Throughout the British raj, disaffected Muslim elites longed to restore the Mughal dynasty or otherwise displace the British. But militant Muslims had little use either for the "Westernizing" liberals of Congress or for the reactionary Hinduism that was gaining force in the late nineteenth century. Islamic thinkers gained prominence like Sayyid Ahmad Khan, who visited Oxford and returned to India in 1875 to establish the Anglo-Muhammadan Oriental College (later, Aligarh Muslim University). He endeavored to combine Western science and Islamic culture. He specifically disapproved of Western "representative" democracies, which he thought incompatible with Indian traditions, Hindu as well as Muslim. Moreover, a representative government would ensure the subjugation of India's Muslims.

1905: PARTITION OF BENGAL

Lord Curzon, the Governor General of India from 1898 to 1905, was a central figure in the consolidation of the British administration of India. His talent was in strengthening the governmental apparatus, itself a precursor for national government. But he did much to alienate Indian nationalists, such as formulating measures to exert greater British control of Indian universities and to reduce the representation of Indians in the municipal government of Calcutta, a rapidly growing industrial city with horrendous slums.

Curzon's most controversial decision was to partition the province of Bengal, a vast region in east India inhabited by some 85 million people, including a high percentage of Muslims. Curzon proposed to divide Bengal into two new provinces, one of which would have a Muslim majority. Congress leaders denounced the partition as a British attempt to preserve its power by setting Muslims and Hindus against each other. Congress appeared to be opposed to Muslim rule even in those areas where Muslims were in the majority. Partition, Bengali Hindus insisted, was a means of removing Hindu leaders from governmental positions in East Bengal. Outraged Hindus protested this desecration of the "mother province" of India. Millions of Bengalis now joined Congress, filing petitions, marching in huge processions, and singing the "Bande Mataram" ("Hail to the Mother") anthem, whose words had been written by Bankim Chandra Chatterjee (see *Sources*.)

During the previous decades, too, Chatterjee's novels had attained great popularity, especially *Anandamath* ("The Abbey of Bliss," 1882). The *Anandamath* was set during a Hindu rebellion against the Mughal rulers of Bengal in the 1770s; the villains were the Muslim rulers, though the appeal to Hindu solidarity had obvious implications for Indian nationalism. Lord Curzon ignored the appeals for revocation of the partition of Bengal. In response, the defenders of "mother Bengal" initiated a campaign to boycott British-made textiles and to use only Indian-made (*swadeshi*) cottons. The movement spread throughout India. Congress now formally proclaimed *swaraj* (self-rule) as one of its demands. Increasingly, too, Hindu terrorists provided an alternative to the gradual approach of Congress. Tilak himself refused to rule out violence to depose the British. The struggle between the constitutional "moderates" in Congress and the militant "radicals" in Tilak's camp was forestalled in 1908, when the British imprisoned him for sedition. Terrorism intensified, especially in Bengal and Tilak's homeland northeast of Bombay. In 1911 London canceled the partition of Bengal.

1906: MUSLIM LEAGUE FOUNDED

The new radicalism of the Hindus caused many Muslims to look at Congress more warily. They regarded the Hindu criticisms of the partition of Bengal as evidence of a scarcely veiled Hindu agenda in opposition to any majoritarian Muslim province. Why, the Muslims asked, should the Hindus of Bengal be so alarmed by the fact of a Muslim majority province? Did not the Muslims constitute a minority in most of the other provinces of India? The politicization of the religious was reflected in the fact that while the Hindus protested partition, in eastern Bengal many Muslims agitated in **favor** of the measure. When Hindus there rioted against partition, Muslims often responded with anti-Hindu riots. Violence then fed on itself, exacerbating tensions between the groups.

Muslim nationalism thus emerged partly in response to the resurgence of a specifically Hindu nationalism associated with Congress. In 1906 the Muslim League first met in Dacca, capital of the newly created province of East Bengal. The 36 Muslim leaders declared their intention to "protect and advance the political rights and interests of Mussalmans [Muslims] of India." They also declared their "loyalty to the British government," affirmed their support of the Bengal partition, and denounced the boycott of English textiles. But in 1911, when London canceled the Bengal partition, the Muslim League was outraged. They insisted that the British had capitulated to Hindu terrorists.

WORLD WAR I

At the outset of World War I, most Indians supported the British. The hundreds of Indian princes of the "dependent" states volunteered to send men and money to support the British; Congress leaders including Tilak (recently released from prison) endorsed the war effort; Gandhi went so far as to urge rural Indians to support the war effort. The

Indian nationalists assumed that their support during the war would translate into an offer of independence afterward.

However, the Muslim League, which had been supportive of Britain **before** the war, shifted its position during the war. This was chiefly due to Islamic sympathy toward Turkey, the chief Islamic state and the home of the caliph, or chief religious leader, of the Muslim community throughout the world. Britain's invasion of Gallipoli, on the coast of Turkey, hammered home the British threat to Muslim Turkey.

World War I sent a shock wave through the Indian subcontinent. Wartime demand in Britain stimulated the production of Indian textiles and steel. As hundreds of thousands of British soldiers were swallowed up in the trenches of France and even on the coastline of Turkey (the result of a disastrous amphibious invasion conceived by Winston Churchill, then an admiralty official), the British recruited more soldiers from India. At the outset of the war, the Royal Indian Army consisted of 80,000 British soldiers and 230,000 Indians. During the war, over a million Indians were shipped to fight overseas; more than 100,000 were wounded, and 36,000 were killed in combat. (Nearly half of the combatants came from the Punjab, with a high Sikh representation.)

1919: GANDHI ARRIVES IN INDIA; THE AMRITSAR MASSACRE

The year 1857, the time of the Sepoy Mutiny, was one of the most significant years in modern Indian history. The year 1919 was nearly as important, for two reasons. The first was the emergence of Mohandas Gandhi as the most powerful apostle of Indian nationalism. Gandhi had recently returned from South Africa, where he had established a reputation for his defense of Indians and other minorities. Gandhi was a lawyer who manipulated the British legal system to defend clients and protect the rights of vulnerable minorities; he also lived in impoverished surroundings and adopted an ascetic lifestyle. He was drawn to a strain of Indian religion that contended that violence and hate poisoned the soul. He advocated challenging injustice through what he called *satyagraha*, nonviolent confrontation.

In 1919, Gandhi protested British laws (the Rowlatt Acts) that retained wartime censorship measures; those suspected of subversion—including, presumably, advocates of Indian nationalism—could be imprisoned without trial. In opposition to these laws, Gandhi in April called for a nationwide one-day *hartal*, or general strike. This resulted in massive protests, especially in the Punjab, where hundreds of thousands of Sikhs staged rallies. Amritsar, the sacred capital of the Sikhs, was the center for these protests. The British governor of the Punjab arrested the Sikh leaders and also Gandhi, who attempted to join them. More protests ensued, and British soldiers on two occasions opened fire to break them up. This resulted in rioting in Amritsar, the burning of banks and stores, and the murder of several Englishmen. When 10,000 protesters assembled inside the walled compound of the Jallianwalla Bagh (Garden), a British general ordered his troops to fire into the crowd, killing 400 and wounding 1,200 more.

The Amritsar massacre galvanized sentiment against the British throughout India. Moderates became would-be revolutionaries. Gandhi, stunned both by the riots among his followers and the bloody repression it provoked, called off the protests. The people of India, he declared, had been inadequately tutored on nonviolent resistance.

The British government in London was also shocked by the massacre. It enacted the Government of India Act of 1919, which greatly increased native Indian participation in administration. Several Indians were placed on the viceroy's Executive Council, and at the province level, Britain institutionalized dyarchy, or divided rule. British and Indian administrators would **together** administer the provinces: the British responsible for finances, police, and the courts, and the Indians for education, public health, public works, and agriculture. Some 5 million Indians—those owning property and holding education certificates—were allowed to vote.

1919-1924: KHILAFAT MOVEMENT

Amritsar marked a turning point for Gandhi, who now insisted that the British grant independence immediately. He called on Congress to boycott the elections and on its members to refuse to serve as Indian administrators in the dyarchy scheme. Then Gandhi, in an attempt to reach out to disaffected Muslims, came out in support of the Khilafat campaign, a worldwide Muslim effort on behalf of the caliph, the Islamic leader of Turkey (Khilafat=Caliph(at) Movement). (Turkey, formerly the Ottoman Empire, had been defeated in World War I, was stripped of its empire, and saw the caliph's authority sharply curtailed by Britain and the Allies.)

Gandhi next called on Congress to adopt *satyagraha*—a policy of non-cooperation with British rule "until the said wrongs are righted and *swaraj* is established." In 1920 Congress approved this program without explaining what, exactly, *swaraj* ("self-rule") entailed. Some Congress leaders regarded *swaraj* as an extension of democratic liberal practices to India, while others, especially adherents of Gandhi, regarded "self-rule" as a means of resurrecting Indian traditions and evading western industrialization and democratic politics. All Congress members sought to be free of British rule; whether they would replace it with the rural villages of the past or a modernizing society in the manner of western democracies was unclear.

Whatever its ultimate ends, Congress proceeded to lay the groundwork for a mass non-cooperation movement. Congress representatives organized small leadership groups, or cells, in nearly every village. These cells were in turn organized into local and regional councils. Congress established special colleges for students who had abandoned the government schools; these Congress colleges stimulated student engagement with the cause. Gandhi, too, appealed for people to forsake English manufactured cloth and instead wear *khadi,* the homespun cotton cloth produced by artisanal workers in most rural villages. Thus began the tradition of wearing a "Gandhi cap," a white cotton hat that became a symbol of Indian nationalism.

1922: GANDHI HALTS NATIONWIDE CIVIL DISOBEDIENCE

In 1921, the non-cooperation movement escalated to massive civil disobedience: a resistance to paying taxes and the Indian takeover of government buildings and offices. Gandhi insisted that the protesters pledge themselves to nonviolence, but in the United Provinces a police station was surrounded and set ablaze, burning alive several dozen policemen. Gandhi abruptly canceled the campaign: "God . . . has warned me . . . that there is not yet in India that nonviolent and truthful atmosphere which alone can justify mass civil disobedience." The decision astonished his lieutenants in the Congress party, who felt that the movement's momentum was irresistible. Congress now was in disarray.

During the 1920s, too, the Muslim League lost influence. In 1924 Mustafa Kemal Ataturk, the secularizing leader of Turkey, abolished the office of the caliph, and the Khilafat movement collapsed. Its demise weakened the appeal of Gandhi, and Congress, to India's Muslims.

1930: GANDHI'S SALT MARCH, THE BEGINNING OF SECOND CIVIL DISOBEDIENCE CAMPAIGN

In 1930 Gandhi resolved to recommence a civil disobedience campaign, but he scripted it more carefully. He chose to challenge the British tax on salt by marching several hundred miles from Ahmedabad in Gujarat to the seacoast. There they would "manufacture" salt by boiling salt water and sell it without the required tax. Gandhi was among those who were arrested for the protest.

As in 1922, the protests turned violent. Several Sikh militants murdered a political enemy; when they were hanged, riots erupted in the Punjab, resulting in hundreds of deaths. Gandhi deplored the violence but defended the actions of the Sikhs. "I would not flinch from sacrificing even a million lives for India's liberty," he declared.

1935: GOVERNMENT OF INDIA ACT

The Government of India Act in 1935 ended the system of dyarchy, where British and Indian officials jointly controlled the administration of the provinces. Indian officials now controlled nearly all aspects of provincial government, while the British remained in charge of the national government, which regulated taxation and defense. The law also extended the franchise to 35 million people, about 27 percent of the adult population, including women. But the act divided all voters into two categories: the "special classes" (meaning minorities) and the general classes (everyone else, i.e., Hindus). In the provincial legislatures and in the federal legislatures, a variable percentage was fixed for each voting group. Thus, of the 175-member Bombay provincial assembly, 114 seats were to be selected by voters of the "general classes" (Hindus), including 15 seats that could only be held by Untouchables. Of the remaining 61 seats, 29 seats were reserved for Muslims, and others among British voters, other Europeans, Christians, industry representatives, universities, labor, and women. The act also provided for two federal legislatures, one chosen from representatives of the Indian states (i.e., the princes).

Indian nationalists complained that this structure shattered India, giving the Indians power in the provinces but not at the federal level, which further fragmented the electorate into British India and the India of the princes and divided it once again into special electoral constituencies. The unified government of the raj had been similarly fractured, ensuring British domination and Indian weakness and vulnerability.

Congress denounced the act. It decided, however, to participate in the elections and to refuse to take office if elected. The plan was to destroy this British government by immobilizing its administration.

1937: PROVINCIAL ELECTIONS, CONGRESS WINS

Congress won the elections by unexpectedly large margins. Congress officials in several provinces, on being elected, now changed their minds. They accepted positions in seven provinces, including three of the most important: Madras, Bombay, and the United Provinces. From the time the Congress officials, most of them Hindu, began administering their predominantly Hindu provinces, Muslim officials complained of discrimination. This spurred Muslim fears of a Congress-dominated federal state. The Muslim League, formerly quiescent, now sprang to life.

1940: JINNAH CALLS FOR A MUSLIM STATE

The Muslim League, at its conference at Lahore, passed the following resolution:

> No constitutional plan would be workable in this country or acceptable to the Muslims unless it is designated on the following basic principles: that geographically contiguous units are demarcated into regions that should be so constituted . . . that the areas in which the Muslims are numerically in a majority (as in the North-Western and Eastern zones) should be grouped to constitute 'Independent States' in which the constituent units shall be autonomous and sovereign.

Now the Muslim League was calling specifically for the creation of a Muslim state, to be called "Pakistan," the name coming from the letters of the initial letters of the Muslim majority regions of India (Punjab).

In 1942, Gandhi and Congress called for a "Quit India" Movement; Congress leaders were imprisoned for duration of World War II.

Glossary

Adi Granth   Scripture of Sikhs, based on the teachings of Guru Nanak, compiled in the early 1600s.

ahimsa   Nonviolence.

Anandamath   A novel by Bankim Chandra Chatterjee.

"Bande Mataram"   "Salutation to the Mother," a song, originally about Bengal, for Hindu India.

dhamma   A way of life that inclines to virtue.

charkha   The spinning wheel, a symbol of the artisanal cotton-based economy of Gandhi.

dharma   A set of specific moral and religious obligations in Hinduism.

harijan   "Children of God," Gandhi's term for Untouchables.

hartal   A general strike, usually called for political purposes.

hindutva   Hindu essence or equivalency.

Indian Civil Service (ICS)   The bureaucracy of India, largely staffed by Indians under direction of British.

jati   An endogamous social group within Hinduism, assigned by birth according to varna.

jihad   A holy war; an effort to attain perfection, in Islam.

karma   The Hindu concept of reincarnation, where future births are based on current life.

khadi   A hand-woven cotton cloth, often associated with Gandhi.

Mahabharata   A classic Hindu text of ancient India.

Mahatma   "Great soul," applied to Gandhi.

mullah   An Islamic religious leader.

nizam A ruler.

Pandit A Hindu religious scholar; the title given to Jawaharlal Nehru of Congress.

Quaid "Great leader," title for Mohammad Ali Jinnah.

R.I.N. The Royal Indian Navy

raj A kingdom.

rupee The main unit of Indian currency.

sabha An association.

sati When woman who commits suicide by immolation on the funeral pyre of her husband.

satyagraha "Way of truth," Gandhi's strategy of nonviolent confrontation.

swadeshi "Of our own country," a phrase often applied to a preference for buying India-made goods.

swaraj Self–rule.

varna Literally, "color" in Hindi, but usually implying "caste," or the hierarchical arrangement of social groups.

Appendix A: Major Documents[DJ3]

MAHATMA GANDHI'S STATEMENT ON SATYAGRAHA (1919)

(Extract from a statement to the Hunter Committee on November 1, 1919, published in *Young India,* November 1919, pp. 11-13.)

For the past thirty years, I have been preaching and practicing Satyagraha. The principles of Satyagraha, as I know it today, constitute a gradual evolution. Satyagraha differs from Passive Resistance as the North Pole from the South. The latter has been conceived as a weapon of the weak and does not exclude the use of physical force or violence for the purpose of gaining one's end, whereas the former has been conceived as a weapon of the strongest and excludes the use of violence in any shape or form.

The term Satyagraha was coined by me in South Africa to express the force that the Indians there used for a full eight years and it was coined in order to distinguish it from the movement then going on in the United Kingdom and South Africa under the name of Passive Resistance.

Its root meaning is holding on to Truth, hence Truth-force. I have also called it Love-force or Soul-force. In the application of Satyagraha, I discovered in the earliest stages that pursuit of Truth did not admit of violence being inflicted on one's opponent but that he must be weaned from error by patience and sympathy. For what appears to be Truth to the one may appear to be error to the other. And patience means self-suffering. So the doctrine came to mean vindication of Truth, not by infliction of suffering on the opponent, but on one's self.

But, on the political field, the struggle on behalf of the people mostly consists in opposing error in the shape of unjust laws. When you have failed to bring the error home to the law-giver by way of petitions and the like, the only remedy open to you, if you do not wish to submit to error, is to compel him by physical force to yield to you or by suffering in your own person by inviting the penalty for the breach of the law. Hence Satyagraha largely appears to the public as Civil Disobedience or Civil Resistance. It is civil in the sense that it is not criminal.

The law-breaker breaks the law surreptitiously and tries to avoid the penalty; not so the civil resister. He ever obeys the laws of the State to which he belongs, not out of fear of the sanctions, but because he considers them to be good for the welfare of society. But there come occasions, generally rare, when he considers certain laws to be so unjust as to render obedience to them a dishonor. He then openly and civilly breaks them and quietly suffers the penalty for their breach. And in order to register his protest against the action of the law givers, it is open to him to withdraw his co-operation from the State by disobeying such other laws whose breach does not involve moral turpitude.

In my opinion, the beauty and efficacy of Satyagraha are so great and the doctrine so simple that it can be preached even to children. It was preached by me to thousands of men, women, and children commonly called indentured Indians with excellent results.

ON HINDU-MUSLIM RELATIONS

Muslim Resolutions at Dacca, 30 December 1906

That this meeting, composed of Mussalmans from all parts of India, assembled at Dacca, decides that a Political Association, styled the All-India Moslem League, be formed for the furtherance of the following objects: (a) To promote among the Mussalmans of India feelings of loyalty to the British Government and to remove any misconceptions that may arise as to the intentions of Government with regard to any of its measures; (b) to protect and advance the political rights and interests of Mussalmans of India and respectfully to represent their needs and aspirations to Government; (c) to prevent the rise among Mussalmans of India of any feelings of hostility towards other communities without prejudice to the other objects of the League.

That this meeting considers that partition is sure to prove beneficial to the community which constitutes the majority of the population, and that all such methods of agitation as boycotting shall be firmly condemned and discouraged.

M. A. Jinnah: Presidential Address, Patna Session of the Muslim League, December 1938

The Congress has now, you must be aware, killed every hope of Hindu-Muslim settlement in the right royal fashion of Fascism. The Congress does not want any settlement with the Muslims of India. As the Chairman of the Reception Committee has said in his address, the Congress wants the Muslims to accept the settlement as a gift from the majority. The Congress High Command makes the preposterous claim that they are entitled to speak on behalf of the whole of India, that they alone are capable of delivering goods. Others are asked to accept the gift as from a mighty sovereign. The Congress High Command declared that they will redress the grievances of the Muslims, and they expect the Muslims to accept declaration. I want to make it plain to all concerned that we Muslims want no gifts. . . .

As I have said before, there are four forces at play in this country. Firstly, there is the British Government. Secondly, there are the rulers and people of the Indian States. Thirdly, there are the Hindus and, fourthly, there are Muslims.

The Congress Press may clamour as much as it likes, they may bring out their morning, afternoon, evening and night editions, the Congress leaders may cry as much as they like that Congress is a national body. But I say it is not true. The Congress is nothing but a Hindu body. That is the truth and the Congress leaders know it. The presence of the few Muslims—the few misled and misguided ones and the few who are there with ulterior motives—does not, cannot make it a national body . . . .

Take next the case of Hindi-Hindustani. I need not add to what has already been said on the subject by the Chairman of the Reception Committee. Is there any doubt now in the mind of anyone that the whole scheme of Hindi-Hindustani is intended to stifle and suppress Urdu? (Voices: 'No doubt.')

Take next the Wardha scheme of education. Were the Muslims taken into confidence when the scheme was under preparation? The whole scheme was conceived and its details worked out behind the back of the Muslims. Who is the author of the scheme? Who is the genius behind it? Mr. Gandhi. I have no hesitation in saying that it is Mr. Gandhi who is destroying the ideal with which the Congress was started. He is the one man responsible for turning the Congress into an instrument for the revival of Hinduism. His ideal is to revive Hindu religion and establish Hindu raj in this country, and he is utilising the Congress to further this object.

The next question that you will have to consider is that of the Federation. Let the Congress continue to say that they will never accept the Federation. But I tell you I do not at all believe in the professions of the Congress. The Congress will tumble into it just as it tumbled into the Provincial part of the Constitution. . . . . The whole game of the Congress is and has been to get a substantial majority in this wretched, highly objectionable and rotten constitution which they want to enjoy. If they get a majority they will accept the Federation with utmost glee, and then they will begin to pursue their nefarious scheme of destroying the Muslim culture and organisation and to build up the Congress organisation as the one and only totalitarian organisation of the Fascist brand. And then they will be able to establish their ideal of Hindu raj in Hindustan.

Jinnah: Speech before the Assembly of the Muslim League, Lahore, 1940

ISSUES FOR THE FUTURE CONSTITUTION

Now, what is our position with regard to the future Constitution? It is that, as soon as circumstances permit, or immediately after the war at the latest, the whole problem of India's future Constitution must be examined de novo, and the Act of 1935 must go once and for all. We do not believe in asking the British Government to make declarations. These declarations are really of no use. You cannot possibly succeed in getting the British Government out of this country by asking them to make declarations. However, the Congress asked the Viceroy to make a declaration. The Viceroy said, 'I have made the declaration.' The

Congress said, 'No no, we want another kind of declaration. You must declare, now and at once, that India is free and independent, with the right to frame its own Constitution, through a Constituent Assembly to be elected on the basis of adult franchise, or as low a franchise as possible. This Assembly will of course satisfy the minorities' legitimate interests.' Mr Gandhi says that if the minorities are not satisfied, then he is willing that some tribunal of the highest character, and most impartial, should decide the dispute. Now apart from the impracticable character of this proposal, and quite apart from the fact that it is historically and constitutionally absurd to ask the ruling power to abdicate in favour of a Constituent Assembly—apart from all that, suppose we do not agree as to the franchise according to which the Central Assembly is to be elected, or suppose we, the solid body of Muslim representatives do not agree with the non-Muslim majority in the Constituent Assembly, what will happen? . . . Of course Mr. Gandhi says that the Constitution will decide whether the British will disappear and if so to what extent. In other words, his proposal comes to this: first give me the declaration that we are a free and independent nation, then I will decide what I should give you back.

Does Mr. Gandhi really want the complete independence of India when he talks like this? But whether the British disappear or not, it follows that extensive powers must be transferred to the people. In the event of there being a disagreement between the majority of the Constituent Assembly and the Musalmans, in the first instance, who will appoint the tribunal? And suppose an agreed tribunal is possible, and the award is made and the decision given, who will, may I know, be there to see that this award is implemented or carried out in accordance with the terms of the award? And who will see that it is honoured in practice, because, we are told, the British will have parted with their power, mainly or completely? Then what will be the sanction behind the award which will enforce it? We come back to the same answer; the Hindu majority would do it—and will it be with the help of the British bayonet or Mr. Gandhi's 'Ahimsa'? can we trust them any more? Besides, ladies and gentlemen, can you imagine that a question of this character, of a social contract upon which the future Constitution of India would be based, affecting 90 millions of Musalmans, can be decided by means of a judicial tribunal? Still, that is the proposal of the Congress.

. . . And now this is what Mr. Gandhi said on the 20 of March, 1940. He says:

> 'To me, Hindus, Muslims, Parsis, Harijans are all alike. I cannot be frivolous'—but I think he is frivolous—'I cannot be frivolous when I talk of Quaid-i-Azam Jinnah. He is my brother.'

The only difference is this, that brother Gandhi has three votes and I have only one vote!

> 'I would be happy indeed if he could keep me in his pocket.'

I do not know really what to say to this latest offer of his.

> 'There was a time when I could say that there was no Muslim whose confidence I did not enjoy. It is my misfortune that it is not so to-day.'

Why has he lost the confidence of the Muslim to-day? May I ask, ladies and gentlemen?

. . . . Why does not Mr. Gandhi honestly now acknowledge that the Congress is a Hindu Congress, that he does not represent anybody except the solid body of a Hindu people? Why should not Mr. Gandhi be proud to say, 'I am a Hindu, the Congress has solid Hindu backing'? I am not ashamed of saying that I am a Musalman. I am right I hope, and I think even a blind man must have been convinced by now, that the Muslim League has the solid backing of the Musalmans of India. Why then all this camouflage? Why all these machinations? Why all these methods to coerce the British to overthrow the Musalmans? Why this declaration of non-co-operation? Why this threat of civil disobedience and why fight for a Constituent Assembly for the sake of ascertaining whether the Musalmans agree or they do not agree? Why not come as a Hindu leader proudly representing your people and let me meet you proudly representing the Musalmans? That is all I have to say so far as the Congress is concerned.

AUTONOMOUS NATIONAL STATES

The problem in India is not of an intercommunal but manifestly of an international character, and it must be treated as such. So long as this basic and fundamental truth is not realized, any constitution that may be built will result in disaster and will prove destructive and harmful not only to the Musalmans, but also to the British and Hindus. If the British Government are really in earnest and sincere to secure the peace and happiness of the people of this Subcontinent, the only course open to us all is to allow the major nations separate homelands, by dividing India into 'autonomous national States.' There is no reason why these States should be antagonistic to each other. On the other hand, the rivalry and the natural desire and efforts on the part of the one (community) to dominate the social order and establish political supremacy over the other in the government of the country will disappear. It will lead more towards natural goodwill by international pacts between them (the states) and they can live in complete harmony with their neighbours. This will lead further to a friendly settlement all the more easily with regard to minorities by reciprocal arrangements and adjustments between the Muslim India and the Hindu India, which will far more adequately and effectively safeguard the rights and interests of Muslims and various other minorities.

It is extremely difficult to appreciate why our Hindu friends fail to understand the real nature of Islam and Hinduism. They are not religions in the strict sense of the word, but are, in fact, different and distinct social orders. It is a dream that the Hindus and Muslims can ever evolve a common nationality, and this misconception of one Indian nation has gone far beyond the limits, and is the cause of most of our troubles, and will lead India to destruction, if we fail to revise our notions in time. The Hindus and the Muslims belong to two different religious philosophies, social customs, and literature. They neither intermarry, nor interdine together, and indeed they belong to two different civilizations which are based mainly on conflicting ideas and conceptions. Their aspects on life and of life are different. It is quite clear that Hindus and Musalmans derive their inspiration from different sources of history. They have different epics, their heroes are different, and they have different episodes. Very often the hero of one is a foe of the other, and likewise, their victories and defeats overlap. To yoke together two such nations under a single State, one as a numerical minority and the other as a majority, must lead to growing discontent and the final destruction of any fabric that may be so built up for the government of such a State.

. . . . Muslim India cannot accept any Constitution which must necessarily result in a Hindu majority Government. Hindus and Muslims brought together under a democratic system forced upon the minorities can only mean Hindu Raj. Democracy of the kind with which the Congress High Command is enamoured would mean the complete destruction of what is most precious in Islam. We have had ample experience of the working of the provincial Constitutions during the last two and a half years; and any repetition of such a Government must lead to civil war and raising private armies, as recommended by Mr Gandhi to Hindus of Sukkur, when he said that they must defend themselves violently or nonviolently, blow for blow; and if they could not, they must emigrate.

Musalmans are not a minority, as it is commonly known and understood. One has only got to look round. Even today, according to the British map of India, 4 out of 11 provinces, where the Muslims dominate more or less, are functioning notwithstanding the decision of the Hindu Congress High Command to non-cooperate and prepare for civil disobedience. Musalmans are a nation according to any definition of a nation, and they must have their homelands, their territory, and their State. We wish to live in peace and harmony with our neighbours as a free and independent people. We wish our people to develop to the fullest our spiritual, cultural, economic, social, and political life in a way that we think best, and in consonance with our own ideals and according to the genius of our people. Honesty demands—and the vital interests of millions of our people impose a sacred duty upon us to find—an honourable and peaceful solution which would be just and fair to all. But at the same time, we cannot be moved or diverted from our purpose and objective by threats or intimidations. We must be prepared to face all difficulties and consequences, make all the sacrifices that may be required of us to achieve the goal we have set in front of us.

Gandhi: Extracts from **The Collected Works**

(SEVAGRAM, APRIL 1940; HARIJAN, 6-4-1940)

. . . . I do not believe that Muslims, when it comes to a matter of actual decision, will ever want vivisection. Their good sense will prevent them. Their self-interest will deter them. Their religion will forbid the obvious suicide which the partition would mean. The 'two nations' theory is an untruth. The vast majority of Muslims of India are converts to Islam or are descendants of converts. They did not become a separate nation as soon as they became converts. A Bengali Muslim speaks the same tongue that a Bengali Hindu does, eats the same food, has the same amusements as his Hindu neighbour. They dress alike. I have often found it difficult to distinguish by outward sign between a Bengali Hindu and a Bengali Muslim. The same phenomenon is observable more or less in the South among the poor who constitute the masses of India. [I didn't even know when I first met] Quaid-e-Azam Jinnah. For his name could be that of any Hindu. When I first met him, I did not know he was a Muslim. I came to know his religion when I had his full name given to me. His nationality was written in his face and manner. . . . Hindus and Muslims of India are not two nations. Those whom God has made one, man will never be able to divide.

And is Islam such an exclusive religion as Quaid-e-Azam would have it? Is there nothing in common between Islam and Hinduism or any other religion? . . .

[Here Gandhi quotes Jinnah's speech:]

> It is extremely difficult to appreciate why our Hindu friends fail to understand the real nature of Islam and Hinduism. They are not religions in the strict sense of the word, but are, in fact, different and distinct social orders. It is a dream that the Hindus and Muslims can ever evolve a common nationality, and this misconception of one Indian nation has gone far beyond the limits, and is the cause of most of our troubles, and will lead India to destruction, if we fail to revise our notions in time. The Hindus and the Muslims belong to two different religious philosophies, social customs, and literature. They neither intermarry, nor interdine together, and indeed they belong to two different civilizations which are based mainly on conflicting ideas and conceptions. Their aspects on life and of life are different. It is quite clear that Hindus and Musalmans derive their inspiration from different sources of history. They have different epics, their heroes are different, and they have different episodes. Very often the hero of one is a foe of the other, and likewise, their victories and defeats overlap. To yoke together two such nations under a single State, one as a numerical minority and the other as a majority, must lead to growing discontent and the final destruction of any fabric that may be so built up for the government of such a State.

He does not say some Hindus are bad; he says Hindus as such have nothing in common with Muslims. I make bold to say that he and those who think like him are rendering no service to Islam; they are misinterpreting the message inherent in the very word Islam. I say this because I feel deeply hurt over what is now going on in the name of the Muslim League. I should be failing in my duty, if I did not warn the Muslims of India against the untruth that is being propagated amongst them. This warning is a duty because I have faithfully served them in their hour of need and because Hindu-Muslim unity has been and is my life's mission.

(SEVAGRAM, APRIL 29, 1940; HARIJAN, 4-5-1940)

. . . . Time was when Hindus thought that Muslims were the natural enemies of Hindus. But as is the case with Hinduism, ultimately it comes to terms with the enemy and makes friends with him. The process has not been completed. And if nemesis had overtaken Hinduism, the Muslim League started the same game and taught that there could be no blending of the two cultures. . . .

Religion binds man to God and man to man. Does Islam bind Muslim only to Muslim and antagonise the Hindu? Was the message of the Prophet peace only for and between Muslims and war against Hindus or non-Muslims? Are eight crores of Muslims to be fed with this which I can only describe as poison? Those who are instilling this poison into the Muslim mind are rendering the greatest disservice to Islam. I know that it is not Islam. I have lived with and among Muslims not for one day but closely and almost uninterruptedly for twenty years. Not one Muslim taught me that Islam was an anti-Hindu religion.

Nehru: Against Pakistan

. . . If the economic aspects of separation are considered it is clear that India as a whole is a strong and more-or-less self-sufficient economic unit. Any division will naturally weaken her and one part will have to depend on the other. If the division is made so as to separate the predominantly Hindu and Moslem areas, the former will comprise far the greater part of the mineral resources and industrial areas. The Hindu areas will not be so hard hit from this point of view. The Moslem areas, on the other hand, will be the economically backward, and often deficit, areas, which cannot exist without a great deal of outside assistance. Thus the odd fact emerges that those who today demand separation will be the greatest sufferers from it. Because of a partial realization of this fact, it is now stated on their behalf that separation should take place in such a way as to give them an economically balanced region. Whether this is possible under any circumstances I do not know, but I rather doubt it. In any event, any such attempt means forcibly attaching other large areas with a predominantly Hindu and Sikh population to the separated area. That would be a curious way of giving effect to the principle of self-determination. I am reminded of the story of the man who killed his father and mother and then threw himself on the mercy of the Court as an orphan.

. . . It is clear that any real settlement must be based on the good-will of the constituent elements and on the desire of all parties to co-operate together for a common objective. In order to gain that any sacrifice in reason is worthwhile. Every group must not only be theoretically and actually free and have equal opportunities of growth, but should have the sensation of freedom and equality. It is not difficult if passions and unreasoning emotions are set aside, to devise such freedom with the largest autonomy for provinces and States and yet a strong central bond. There could even be autonomous units within the larger provinces or States, as in Soviet Russia. In addition to this, every conceivable protection and safeguard for minority rights could be inserted into the constitution.

All this can be done, and yet I do not know how the future will take shape under the influence of various indeterminate factors and forces, the chief of these being British policy. It may be that some division of India is enforced, with some tenuous bond joining the divided parts. Even if this happens, I am convinced that the basic feeling of unity and world developments will bring the divided parts nearer to each other and result in a real unity.

. . . In India, as elsewhere, we are too much under the bondage of slogans and set phrases deriving from past events and ideologies which have little relevance today, and their chief function is to prevent reasoned thought and a dispassionate consideration of the situation as it exists. There is also the tendency towards abstractions and vague ideals, which arouse emotional responses and are often good in their way, but which also lead to a woolliness of the mind and unreality. In recent years a great deal has been written and said on the future of India and especially on the partition or unity of India. And yet the astonishing fact remains that those who propose 'Pakistan' or partition have consistently refused to define what they mean or to consider the implications of such a division. They move on the emotional plane only, as also many of those who oppose them, a plane of imagination and vague desire, behind which lie imagined interest. Inevitably, between these two emotional and imaginative approaches there is no meeting ground. And so 'Pakistan' and 'Akhand Hindustan' (un-divided India) are bandied about and hurled at each other. It is clear that group emotions and conscious or subconscious urges count and must be attended to. It is at least equally clear that facts and realities do not vanish by our ignoring them or covering them up by a film of emotion; they have a way of emerging at awkward moments and in unexpected ways. Any decisions taken primarily on the basis of emotions, or when emotions are the dominating consideration, are likely to be wrong and to lead to dangerous developments.

It is obvious that whatever may be the future of India, and even if there is a regular partition, the different parts of India will have to co-operate with each other in a hundred ways. Even independent nations have to co-operate with each other, much more so must Indian provinces or such parts as emerge from a partition, for these stand in an intimate relationship to each other and must hang together or deteriorate, disintegrate, and lose their freedom. Thus the very first practical question is: what are the essential common bonds which must bind and cement various parts of India if she is to progress and remain free, and which are equally necessary even for the autonomy and cultural growth of those parts. Defence is an obvious and outstanding consideration, and behind that defence lie the industries feeding it, transport and communications, and some measure at least of economic planning. Customs, currency, and exchange also and the maintenance of the whole of India as an internally free-trade area, for any internal tariff barriers would be fatal barriers to growth. And so on . . . . There is no getting away from it whether we are in favour of Pakistan or not, unless we are blind to everything except a momentary passion.

. . . Thus we arrive at the inevitable and ineluctable conclusion that, whether Pakistan comes or no, a number or important and basic functions of the State must be exercised on an all-India basis if India is to survive as a free State and progress. The alternative is stagnation, decay, and disintegration, leading to loss of political and economic freedom, both for India as a whole and its various separated parts. As has been said by an eminent authority: 'The inexorable logic of the age present the country with radically different alternatives: union plus independence, or disunion plus dependence.' What form the union is to take, and whether it is called union or by some other name, is not so important, though names have their own significance and psychological value. The essential fact is that a number of varied activities can only be conduced effectively on a joint all-India basis.

. . . Before any . . . right of secession is exercised there must be a properly constituted, functioning, free India. It may be possible then, when external influences have been removed and real problems face the country, to consider such questions objectively and in a spirit of relative detachment, far removed from the emotionalism of today, which can only lead to unfortunate consequences which we may all have to regret later. This it may be desirable to fix a period, say ten years after the establishment of the free Indian States, at the end of which the right to secede may be exercised through proper constitutional process and in accordance with the clearly expressed will of the inhabitants of the area concerned.

Nehru, from *The Discovery of India*

Maulana Azad: Against Pakistan

President of Congress [Azad is a Muslim]
Document No. 92: PAKISTAN AGAINST MUSLIMS' INTERESTS
17 April 1946

As is well-known, Mr. Jinnah's Pakistan scheme is based on his two-nation theory. His thesis is that India contains many nationalities based on religious differences. Of them the two major nations, the Hindus and Muslims, must as separate nations have separate states. When Dr. Edward Thompson once pointed out to Mr. Jinnah that Hindus and Muslims live side by side in thousands of Indian towns, villages and hamlets, Mr. Jinnah replied that this in no way affected their separate nationality. Two nations, according to Mr. Jinnnah, confront one another in every hamlet, village and town, and he, therefore, desires that they should be separated into two states.

I am prepared to overlook all other aspects of the problem and judge it from the point of view of Muslim interests alone. I shall go still further and say that if it can be shown that the scheme of Pakistan can in any way benefit Muslims as such, I would be prepared to accept it myself and also to work for its acceptance by others. But the truth is that even if I examine the scheme from the point of view of the communal interests of the Muslims themselves, I am forced to the conclusion that it can in no way benefit them or allay their legitimate fears.

EFFECTS OF PARTITION ON MUSLIMS IN A HINDU STATE

Let us consider dispassionately the consequences which will follow if we give effect to the Pakistan scheme. India will be divided into two States, one with a majority of Muslims and the other of Hindus. In the Hindustan State there will remain three-and-a-half crores Muslims scattered in small minorities all over the land. With 17 percent in U.P., 12 percent in Bihar and 9 percent in Madras, they will be weaker than they are today in the Hindu majority provinces. They have had their homelands in these regions for almost a thousand years and built up most well-known centres of Muslim culture and civilization there.

They will awaken overnight and discover that they have become aliens and foreigners, backward industrially, educationally and economically; they will be left to the mercies of what would become an unadulterated Hindu Raj.

EFFECTS OF PARTITION ON MUSLIMS IN PAKISTAN

On the other hand, their position within the Pakistan State will be vulnerable and weak. Nowhere in Pakistan will their majority be comparable to the Hindu majority in the Hindustan State. In fact, their majority will be so slight that it will be offset by the economical, educational and political lead enjoyed by non-Muslims in these areas. Even if this were not so and Pakistan were overwhelmingly Muslim in population, it still could hardly solve the problem of

Muslims in Hindustan. Two states confronting one another offer no solution to the problems of one another's minorities, but only lead to retribution and reprisals by introducing a system of mutual hostages. The scheme of Pakistan, therefore, solves no problems for the Muslims. It cannot safeguard their rights where they are in a minority, nor as citizens of Pakistan secure them a position in India or world affairs which they would enjoy as citizens of a major State like the Indian Union.

EMOTIONAL FRENZY

It may be argued that if Pakistan is so much against the interests of the Muslims themselves, why should such a large section of Muslims be swept away by its lure? The answer is to be found in the attitude of certain communal extremists among the Hindus. When the Muslim League began to speak of Pakistan, they read into the scheme a sinister pan-Islamic conspiracy and began to oppose it out of fear that it foreshadowed a combination of Indian Muslims with trans-Indian Muslim States. This opposition acted as an incentive to the adherents of the League. With simple though untenable logic, they argued that if Hindus were so opposed to Pakistan, surely, it must be of benefit to Muslims. An atmosphere of emotional frenzy was created which made reasonable appraisement impossible and swept away especially the younger and more impressionable among the Muslims. I have, however, no doubt that when the present frenzy has died down and the question can be considered dispassionately, those who now support Pakistan will themselves repudiate it as harmful for Muslim interests.

CONGRESS FORMULA: IDEAL MODEL OF GOVERNMENT

The formula which I have succeeded in making the Congress accept secures whatever merit the Pakistan scheme contains, while all its defects and drawbacks are avoided. The basis of Pakistan is the fear or interference by the Centre majority areas, as the Hindus will be in a majority in the Centre. The Congress meets this fear by granting full autonomy to the provincial units and vesting all residuary power in the provinces. It also has provided for two lists of Central subjects, one compulsory and one optional, so that if any provincial unit so desires it can administer all subjects itself except a minimum delegated to the Centre. The Congress scheme, therefore, ensures that Muslim majority provinces are internally free to develop as they will, but can, at the same time influence the Centre on all issues which affect India as a whole.

The situation in India is such that all attempts to establish a centralized and unitary government are bound to fail. Equally doomed to failure is the attempt to divide India into two states. After considering all aspects of the questions, I have come to the conclusion that the only solution can be on lines embodied in the Congress formula which allows room for development both to the provinces and to India as a whole. The Congress formula meets the fears of the Muslim majority areas to allay which the scheme of Pakistan was formed; on the other hand, it avoids the defects of the Pakistan scheme which would bring the Muslims where they are in a minority under a purely Hindu Government.

I am one of those who consider the present document of communal bitterness and differences a transient phase in Indian life. It firmly holds that they will disappear when India assumes the responsibility for her own destiny. I am reminded of a saying of Mr. Gladstone that the best cure for a man's fear of the water was to throw him into it, for he would then learn to swim and realize that it is not so dangerous as it had seemed to his imagination. Similarly, India must assume responsibility and administer her own affairs. When India attains her destiny, she will forget the present document of communal suspicion and conflict and face the problems of modern life from a modern point of view.

Differences will no doubt persist, but they will be economic not communal. Opposition among political parties will continue but it will be based not on religion but on economic and political issues. Class and not community will be the basis of future alignments and policies will be shaped accordingly. If it be argued that this is only a faith which events may not justify, I would say that in any case the nine crores of Muslims constitute a factor which nobody can ignore, and, whatever the circumstances, they are strong enough to safeguard their own destiny.

From *The Selected Works of Maulana Abul Kalam Azad,* Volume II (1943-1946). Ed. Dr. Ravindra Kumar (New Delhi: Atlantic Publishers & Distributors, 1991), 161-163.

V. D. Savarkar's Presidential Address at the 20th Session of the All-India Hindu Mahasabha, 1938

Before we proceed to indicate the easiest remedy to capture the political power and disable the Congress from doing any practical harm to the Hindu Sanghatan movement, let us declare in unmistakable terms that we are not out to spite the Congress Institution itself, nor the leaders and followers thereof. Mr. Jinnah is quite correct in stating that the Congress has been since its inception down to this day a Hindu body manned mostly by the Hindu brains, Hindu money, and Hindu sacrifice. Even today some of them are noble patriots. They are erring but cannot be wicked and almost all of them are our own kith and kin. The few Moslems there, although they are allowed to boss the Congress policy at times through the suicidal folly of the Hindu leaders, are but nonentities, are kept there merely as figureheads to run the poor show of a 'United Indian Nation.' We are out not to spite the Congress as an institution but to chastise its anti-Hindu policy, to cure it of the intolerable hypocrisy which is all the more harmful for its strutting about under the mask of Truth. Truth absolute and nothing but Truth, with its lathi charges and English bayonets going merrily hand in hand with nonviolence, nonviolence absolute and nothing but nonviolence in thought, word and deed!

So under the present circumstances the Congress has compelled us to disown it and divest it of all power to represent the Hindus in any aspect or capacity whatsoever. They have foolishly challenged the Hindu Community and the Hindu Mahasabha and we must take up the challenge.

Just think, oh Hindu Sanghatanists, on what meat does this Congress feed that it has grown so great? Only remember that the Congress draws all its supplies—men, money and votes, from the Hindus. Then cut off those supplies and the position which the Congress has taken against the Hindu and which seems to be so impregnable will be untenable in no time.

... A truly Indian National electorate cannot be divided as Moslem one and non-Moselm one or Christian one, and non-Christian one, special and general. A truly Indian National electorate must be only an 'Indian' electorate pure and simple without the least mention of the Un-national and unreasonable difference of race and religion. If our Congressites are true and conscientious Indian Nationalists they ought to refuse forthwith to stand as candidates to elections under this communal electoral roll and resign their seats forthwith which are tainted with these communal labels. Is there a single Congress Minister or member ready to resign and run that ordeal? None, none! Next election when they come to your Hindu doors to beg for votes tell them in all honesty and humility, "Sirs Congressmen you are Indian Nationalists; but I am a Hindu and this is a Hindu Electorate. Then how can you accept a vote so tainted by communalism? Please go to a truly "Indian Nationalist electorate," to beg for votes wherever you may find it; and if you find it nowhere in the world today please wait till a pure and simple and truly "Indian Electorate," comes into being!' Do you think you will find a dozen Congress candidates honest enough to do so? None, none!

Gandhi: On Assam and Grouping Proposal, 15 December 1946

"The British cannot interfere with the working of the Constituent Assembly. Supposing the vast majority, including the Muslims and others, form a constitution, you can defy the British Parliament if it seeks to interfere. Power is in your hands. Some such thing happened in Ireland only recently. And De Valera is no nonviolent fighter. The position of India is far better than that of Ireland. If we have not the penetration we will lose the advantage we have, as it is apparently being lost today."—said Mahatma Gandhi in an interview given by him to two Assam Congressmen, Shri Bijaya Chandra Bhagwat and Shri Mohdendra Mohan Choudhury, who saw him on behalf of Sj. G. N. Bardoloi, Premier of Assam, on December 15.

"Rightly or wrongly, the Congress has come to the decision that it will stand by the judgment of the Federal Court. The dice are heavily loaded. The decision of the Federal Court will go against the Congress interpretation of Grouping as far as I can make out for the simplest reason that the Cabinet have got advice which upholds their decision.

"The Federal Court is the creation of the British. It is a packed court. To be consistent, the Congress must abide by its decision whatever it may be. If Assam keeps quiet, it is finished.

"No one can force Assam to do what it does not want to do. It is autonomous to a large extent today. Assam must not lose its soul. It must uphold it against the world."

"Asked for guidance in regard to the question of Grouping as there was no clear lead from the Congress Working Committee to Assam, Mahatma Gandhi replied: "I do not need a single minute to come to a decision, for on this I have a mind. . " I told Bardoloi that if there is no clear guidance from the Congress Working Committee, Assam should not go into the Section. It should lodge its protest and retire from the Constituent Assembly. It will be a kind of satyagraha against the Congress for the good of the Congress.

"It must become fully independent and autonomous. Whether you have that courage, and conviction, I do not know. You alone can say that. But if you can make that declaration, it will be a fine thing.

"As soon as the time comes for the Constituent Assembly to go into Sections, you will say, 'Gentlemen, Assam retires.' For the independence of India, it is the only condition. Each unit must be able to decide and act for itself. I am hoping that in this, Assam will lead the way. I have the same advice for the Sikhs.

"But your position is much happier than that of the Sikhs. You are a whole province. They are a community inside a province. But I feel every individual has the right to act for himself, just as I have."

Question: "But we are told that the framing of the constitution for the whole of India cannot be held up for the sake of Assam. Assam cannot be allowed to block the way."

Answer: "There is no need to do that. That is why I say I am in utter darkness. Why are not these simple truths evident to all after so many years? If Assam retires, it does not block but leads the way to India's independence."

Question: "The British Government has said that the constitution framed by the Constituent Assembly cannot be imposed on unwilling units. So if some parts do not accept it, the British Parliament won't accept it."

Answer: "Who is the British Government? If we think independence is going to descend on our heads from England or somewhere, we are greatly mistaken. It won't be independence. We will be crushed to atoms. We are fluctuating between independence and helpless dependence. The Cabinet Mission's plan lies in between."

"If we act rightly there will be the full-blown flower of independence. If we react wrongly the blossom will wither away. Mind you, the League standpoint is quite correct. If they stand out, the Constituent Assembly cannot impose its Constitution on an unwilling party. The British Government has no say in the matter, one way or the other.

"If Assam takes care of itself the rest of India will be able to look after itself. What have you got to do with the constitution of the Union Government? You should form your own constitution, that is enough. You have the basis of a constitution all right even now.

"I have never despised the 1935 constitution. It is based on provincial autonomy. It has the capacity for fullest growth, provided the people are worthy of it. The hill people are with you. Many Muslims are also with you. The remainder can be too, if you act squarely.

"You will have to forget petty jealousies and rivalries and overcome your weaknesses. Assam has many weaknesses as it has much strength, for I know my Assam."

"With your blessing we can even go outside the Congress and fight," the Assam Congressman interposed.

Gandhiji replied that in 1939, when there was the question of giving up the Ministry, Subhas Babu opposed it as he thought Assam's was a special case. "I told Bardoloi that there was much truth in what Subhas Babu had said, and although I was the author of that scheme of boycott I said Assam should not come out of it if it did not feel like it. But Assam did come out. It was wrong."

The Assam Congressman said that Maulana Saheb had then said that exception could not be made in the case of Assam.

Gandhiji replied: "Here there is no question of exception. Assam rebelled and that civilly. But we have that slavish mentality. We look to the Congress and then feel that if we do not follow it slavishly something will go wrong with it.

"I have said that not only a province but even an individual can rebel against the Congress and by doing so save it, assuming that he is on the right. I have done so myself. Congress has not attained the present stature without much travail.

"I remember, in 1928 I think there was the provincial conference of the Congress workers of Gujarat at Ahmedabad. The late Abbas Tyabjee Saheb was in the chair. All the old guards were there. The Ali brothers had not yet joined hands with me fully then, as they did later on. The late Shri Patel was there, and I moved the non-co-operation resolution. I was a non-entity then.

"A constitution question arose. Could a provincial conference anticipate the decision of the Congress? I said, 'Yes.' A provincial conference and even a single individual could anticipate the Congress for its own benefit. In spite of the opposition of old hands, the resolution was carried. That paved the way for the Congress to pass a similar resolution at Calcutta. India was dumb-founded at the audacity of a provincial conference passing the revolutionary resolution.

"We had formed a satyagraha sabha outside the Congress. It was joined by Horniman, Sarojini Devi, Shankarlal, Umar Sobhani and Vallabhbhai. I was ill. The Rowlatt Act was passed. I shook with rage. I said to the Sardar, I could od nothing unless he helped me. Sardar was willing. And the rest you know. It was rebellion but a healthy one. We celebrate the 6th of April to the 13th. You have all these historical instances before you.

"I have given you all this time to steel your hearts, to give you courage. If you do not act correctly now, Assam will be finished. Tell Bardoloi, I do not feel the least uneasiness. My mind is made up.

"Assam must not lose its soul. It must uphold it against the world. Else, I will say that Assam had only manikins and no men. It is an impertinent suggestion that Bengal should dominate Assam in any way.

Asked if they could tell the people that they have rebelled against the Congress with Gandhiji's blessings, Gandhiji said: "Talk of God's blessings. They are much richer. Tell the people: even if Gandhi tries to dissuade us we won't listen."

From A. C. Banerjee, *The Constituent Assembly* 1947, pp. 266-270.

ON THE UNTOUCHABLES

B. R. Ambedkar on the Depressed Classes, at the Indian Round Table Conference, 1 January 1931

Mr. Chairman, I am sure you will readily agree that the task which has fallen upon me to represent the case of the Depressed Classes is. . . really an enormous one . . . .

The first observation that I will make is this, that although there are various minority communities in India which require political recognition, it has to be understood that the minorities are not on the same plane . . . .They differ in the social standing which each minority occupies *vis-à-vis* the majority community. We have, for instance, the Parsee community, which is the smallest community in India, and yet, *vis-à-vis* its social standing with the majority community, it is probably the highest in order of precedence.

On the other hand, if you take the Depressed Classes, they are a minority which comes next to the great Muslim minority in India, and yet their social standard is lower than the social standard of ordinary human beings.

Again, if you take the minorities and classify them on the basis of social and political rights, you will find that there are certain minorities which are in enjoyment of social and political rights, and the fact that they are in a minority does not necessarily stand in the way of their full and free enjoyment of those civic rights. But if you take the case of the Depressed Classes, the position is totally different. They have in certain matters no rights, and, where they have any, the majority community will not permit them to enjoy them.

My first submission to this Committee, then, is that it should realise that although, to use an illustration, the minorities are all in the same boat, yet the most important fact to remember is that they are not all in the same class in the same boat; some are travelling in 'A' class, some in 'B' class and some in 'C,' and so on. I have not the slightest doubt in my mind that the Depressed Classes, though they are a minority and are to that extent in the same boat as other minorities, are not even in 'C' or 'D' class but are actually in the hold.

Starting from that point of view, I agree that, in some respects, the position of the Depressed Classes is similar to that of the other minorities in India. The Depressed Classes, along with the other minorities, fear that under any future constitution of India by which majority rule will be established—and there can be no shadow of a doubt that that majority rule will be the rule of the orthodox Hindus—there is great danger of that majority with its orthodox Hindu beliefs and prejudices contravening the dictates of justice, equality and good conscience, there is a great danger that the minorities may be discriminated against either in legislation or administration or in the other public rights of citizenship, and therefore it is necessary to safeguard the position of the minorities in such a manner that the discrimination which is feared shall not take place.

Take the case of employment in the Police or in the Army. In the Government of India Act it is provided that no subject of His Majesty shall be deprived of the right of being employed in any public service by reason of his caste, creed or colour. Having regard to that, it is obvious that every member of the Depressed Class community who is capable, who is in a position to satisfy the test laid down for employment in any public department, should have the right to enter that public department. But what do we find? We find this. If a Depressed Class man applied for service in the Police Department to-day, he is told point blank by the executive officers of the Government that no member of the Depressed Classes can be employed in the Police service, because he is an untouchable person. In the case of the Military the same situation obtains. Up to 1892 practically the whole of the Madras Army and the whole of the Bombay Army consisted of members drawn from the Depressed Classes . . . .Yet in 1892 a rule or regulation was made which debarred the Depressed Classes from entry into the military service, and even to-day, if you ask a question in the Legislative Council as to why this is done, the answer is that the bar of untouchability does create insuperable difficulties in the recruitment of these classes.

I can cite many other cases. For instance, there is the difficulty the Depressed Classes find in getting themselves accommodated in a public inn when they are travelling, the difficulty they find in being taken in an omnibus when travelling from one place to another, the difficulty they find in securing entry to public schools to which they have themselves contributed, the difficulty they find in drawing water from a well for the building of which they have paid taxes, and so on. But I need not go into all these cases. The one circumstance which distinguishes the position of the Depressed Classes from that of the other minorities is that they suffer from civic disabilities which are as effective as though they were imposed by law.

. . . We propose the following safeguards. First of all, we want a fundamental right enacted in the constitution which will declare 'untouchability' to be illegal for all public purposes. We must be emancipated, so to say, from this social curse before we can at all consent to enter into the constitution; and secondly, this fundamental right must also invalidate and nullify all such disabilities and all such discriminations as may have been made hitherto . . . .

. . .Now, on the question of granting of representation of the Depressed Classes, we are absolutely unanimous that that representation shall be by election and not by nomination. The system of nomination has produced, in the case of the Depressed Classes, results which we all say are abominable. The system has been abused in a manner in which it was never expected that it would be abused, and it has never given the Depressed Classes the real and independent representation which they must have as their safeguard. Under no circumstances, therefore, will the Depressed Classes accept representation by nomination.

. . . Now regarding the question of the number of seats, it is not possible, of course, for us to state definitely what that number should be, except to state that we will not tolerate any invidious discrimination. We insist upon equality of treatment. . . . The first observation that I will make is this—that we, the Depressed Classes, demand a complete partition between ourselves and the

Hindus. That is the first thing. We have been called Hindus for political purposes, but we have never been acknowledged socially by the Hindus as their brethren. They have taken to themselves all the political advantage which our numbers, which our voting strength, have given to them, but in return we have received noting. All that we have received is a treatment which is worse than the treatment that they themselves have accorded to other communities whom they do not call Hindus. . . .

Excerpts from *Gandhi and Gandhism* by B. R. Ambedkar

GANDHI'S FAST

From B.R. Ambedkar, *Gandhi and Gandhism*, Punjab: Bheem Patrika Publications (1970).

. . . I need hardly say that I was astounded to read the correspondence between Mahatma Gandhi, Sir Samuel Hoare and the Prime Minister, which was published recently in the papers, in which he has expressed his determination to starve himself unto death till the British Government of its own accord or under pressure of public opinion revise their opinion and withdraw their scheme of communal representation for the Depressed Classes. The unenviable position, in which I have been placed by the Mahatma's vow of self-immolation, can easily be imagined.

It passes my comprehension why Mr. Gandhi should stake his life on an issue arising out of the communal question which he, at the Round Table Conference, said was one of a comparatively small importance. Indeed, to adopt the language of those of Mr. Gandhi's way of thinking, the communal question was only an appendix to the book of India's constitution and not the main chapter. It would have been justifiable, if Mr. Gandhi had resorted to this extreme step for obtaining independence for the country on which he was so insistent all through the R.T.C. debates. It is also a painful surprise that Mr. Gandhi should single out special representation for the Depressed Classes in the Communal Award as an excuse for his self-immolation. Separate electorates are granted not only to the Depressed Classes, but to the Indian Christians, Anglo-Indians, Europeans, as well as to the Mahomedans and the Sikhs. Also separate electorates are granted to landlords, labourers and traders. Mr. Gandhi had declared his opposition to the special representation of every other class and creed except the Mahomedans and the Sikhs. All the same, Mr. Gandhi chooses to let everybody else except the Depressed Classes retain the special electorates given to them.

The fears expressed by Mr. Gandhi about the consequences of the arrangements for the representation of the Depressed Classes are, in my opinion, purely imaginary. If the nation is not going to be split up by separate electorates to the Mahomedans and the Sikhs, the Hindu society cannot be said to be split up if the Depressed Classes are given separate electorates. His conscience is not aroused if the nation is split by the arrangement of Special Electorates for classes and communities other than the Depressed Classes.

I am sure many have felt that if there was any class which deserved to be given special political rights in order to protect itself against the tyranny of the majority under the Swaraj constitution it was the Depressed Classes. Here is a class which is undoubtedly not in a position to sustain itself in the struggle for existence. The religion to which they are tied, instead of providing for them an honourable place, brands them as lepers, not fit for ordinary intercourse. Economically, it is a class entirely dependent upon the high-caste Hindus for earning its daily bread with no independent way of living open to it. Nor are all ways closed by a reason of the social prejudices of the Hindus but there is a definite attempt all throughout the Hindu Society to bolt every possible door so as not to allow the Depressed Classes any opportunity to rise in the scale of life. Indeed it would not be an exaggeration to say that in every village the caste Hindus, however divided among themselves, are always in a standing conspiracy to put down in a merciless manner any attempt on the part of the Depressed Classes who form a small and scattered body of an ordinary India citizen.

In these circumstances it would be granted by all fair-minded persons that as the only path for a community so handicapped to succeed in the struggle for life against organised tyranny, some share of political power in order that it may protect itself is a paramount necessity.

I should have thought that a well-wisher of the Depressed Classes would have fought tooth and nail for securing to them as much political power as might be possible in the new Constitution. But the Mahatma's ways of thinking are strange and are certainly beyond my comprehension. He not only does not endeavour to augment the scanty political power which the Depressed Classes have got under the Communal Award, but on the contrary he has staked his very life in order to deprive them of the little they have got. This is not the first attempt on the part of the Mahatma to completely dish the Depressed Classes out of political existence. Long before, there was the Minorities Pact. The Mahatma tried to enter into an agreement with the Muslims and the Congress. He offered to the Muslims all the fourteen claims which they had put forth on their behalf, and in return asked them to join with him in resisting the claims for social representation made by me on behalf of the Depressed Classes.

It must be said to the credit of the Muslim delegates that they refused to be a party to such a black act, and saved the Depressed Class from what might as well have developed into a calamity for them as a result of the combined opposition of the Mahomedans and Mr. Gandhi.

From B.R. Ambedkar, *Gandhi and Gandhism*, Punjab: Bheem Patrika
Publications (1970).

... As a second piece of evidence [of Gandhi's being more anxious to placate
the Hindus than to help the Depressed Classes] I would refer to what is known as
the Kavitha incident. Kavitha is a village in the Ahmedabad District in Gujarat.
In 1935, the Untouchables of the village demanded from the Hindus of the
village that their children should be admitted in the common school of the
village along with other Hindu children. The Hindus were enraged at this
outrage and took their revenge by proclaiming a complete social boycott. The
events connected with this boycott were reported by Mr. A. V. Thakkar, who
went to Kavitha to intercede with the Hindus on behalf of the Untouchables.
The story told by him runs as follows:

"The Associated Press announced on the 10th inst. that the Caste Hindus of
Kavitha agreed to admit Harijan boys to the village school in Kavitha and that
matters were amicably settled. This was contradicted on the 13th instant by the
Secretary of the Ahmedabad Harijan, Sewak Sangh, who said in his statement
that the Harijans had undertaken (privately of course) not to send their children
to the school. Such an undertaking was not given voluntarily, but was extorted
from them by the Caste Hindus, in this case the Garisias of the village, who had
proclaimed a social boycott against poor Harijans—weavers, chamars, and
others, who number over 100 families. They were deprived of agricultural
labour, their animals of grazing in the pasture land, and their children of
buttermilk. Not only this, but a Harijan leader was compelled to take an oath by
Mahadev that he and others would not hereafter even make an effort to reinstate
their children in the school. The so-called settlement was brought about in this
way.

"But even after the bogus settlement reported on the 10th and the complete
surrender by poor Harijans, the boycott was not lifted up to the 19th and partly
up to the 22nd from the weavers. It was lifted somewhat earlier from the head of
the chamars, as Garasias themselves could not remove the carcasses of their dead
animals, and thus had to come to terms with the Chamars earlier. As if the
enormities perpetrated so far were not enough, kerosene was poured into the
Harijan's well, once on the 15th instant and again on the 19th instant. One can
imagine what terrorism was thus practised on poor Harijans because they had
dared to send their children to sit alongside of the 'princely' Garasia boys. . .
Harijan boys are thus practically banned from the village school with nobody to
help them. This has caused despondency among the Harijans to such an extent
that they are thinking of migrating in a body to some other village."

This was the report made to Mr. Gandhi. What did Mr. Gandhi do? The
following is the advice Mr. Gandhi gave to the Untouchables of Kavitha:

"There is no help like self-help. God helps those who help themselves. If the Harijans concerned will carry out their reported resolve to wipe the dust of Kavitha off their feet, they will not only be happy themselves but they will pave the way for others who may be similarly treated. If people migrate in search of employment how much more should they do so in search of self-respect? I hope that well-wishers of Harijans will help these poor families to vacate inhospitable Kavitha."

Mr. Gandhi advised the Untouchables of Kavitha to vacate. But why did he not advise Mr. Thakkar to prosecute the Hindus of Kavitha and help the Untouchables to vindicate their rights? Obviously, he would like to uplift the Untouchables if he can but not by offending the Hindus. What good can such a man do to promote the cause of the Untouchables? All this shows that Mr. Gandhi is most anxious to be good to the Hindus. That is why he opposes satyagraha against the Hindus. That is why he opposed the political demands of the Untouchables as he believed that they were aimed against them. He is anxious to be so good to the Hindus that he does not care if he is thereby becoming good for nothing for the Untouchables. That is why Mr. Gandhi's whole programme for the removal of Untouchability is just words, words and words and why there is no action behind it.

FROM DR. BABASAHEB AMBEDKAR, WRITINGS AND SPEECHES, VOLUME 5 Compiled by Vasant Moon, Education Department, Government of Maharashtra, 1989; Chapter 25: Gandhi and His Fast.

. . . It is my firm conviction that for the Untouchables to merge in the Congress or for the matter of that in any large political party cannot but be fatal for them. The Untouchables need a movement if they are to remain conscious of their wrongs and if the spirit of revolt is kept alive amongst them. They need a movement because the Caste Hindus have to be told that what is tragedy of the Untouchables is their crime. The Congress may not be a red-blooded Hindu body so far as the Musalmans are concerned. But it is certainly a full-blooded and blue-blooded Hindu body inasmuch as it consists of Caste Hindus. A movement of the Untouchables must mean an open war upon the Caste Hindus. A movement of the Untouchables within the Congress is quite impossible. It must mean an *inter necine* within the party. The Congress for its own safety cannot allow it.

The Congress has strictly forbidden the Untouchables who have joined the Congress to carry on any independent movement of the Untouchables not approved of by the High Command. The result is that in those Provinces where the Untouchables have joined the Congress the movement of the Untouchables is dead.

The Untouchables must retain their right to freedom of speech and freedom of action on the floor of the Legislature if they are to ventilate their grievances and obtain redress of their wrongs by political action. But this freedom of speech and action has been lost by the representatives of the Untouchables who have joined the Congress. They cannot vote as they like, they cannot speak what they think. They cannot ask a question, they cannot move a resolution and they cannot bring in a Bill. They are completely under the control of the Congress party Executive. They have only such freedom as the Congress Executive may choose to allow them. The result is that though the tale of woes of the Untouchables is ever-increasing, the untouchable members of the Legislature are unable even to ask a question about them. So pitiable has their condition become that the Congress party sometimes requires them to vote against a measure that may in the opinion of the Untouchable members of the Legislature be beneficial to the Untouchables. A recent instance of this occurred in Madras. Rao Bahadur Raja, a member of the Madras Legislature, brought in a Bill to secure the entry of the Untouchables into Hindu Temples in the Madras Presidency. The Congress Government had promised to support it at first. Subsequently the Congress Government in Madras changed its opinion and opposed the measure. It was a dilemma for the Untouchable members of the Madras Legislature. But they had no choice. The whip was applied and they in a body voted against the measure. The representatives of the Untouchables were supposed to be watch-dogs of the Untouchables. But by reason of having joined the Congress they are muzzled dogs. Far from biting, they are not even able to bark. This loss of freedom of speech and action by these Untouchable members is entirely due to their having joined the Congress and subjected themselves to the discipline of the Congress.

ON THE FUTURE OF THE INDIAN ECONOMY

Jawaharlal Nehru's Presidential Address at the Lucknow Session of the National Congress, 12 April 1936 (Pro Socialism)

The real problem for us is, how in our struggle for independence we can join together all the anti-imperialist forces in the country, how we can make a broad front of our mass elements with the great majority of the middle classes which stands for independence.

. . . Most of you must know my views on social and economic matters for I have often given my expression to them. Yet you chose me as president. I do not take that choice to mean an endorsement by you all, or by a majority, of those views, but I take it that this does mean that those views are spreading in India and that most of you will be indulgent in considering them at least.

I am convinced that the only key to the solution of the world's problems and of India's problems lies in socialism, and when I use this word I do so not in a vague humanitarian way but in the scientific, economic sense. Socialism, is, however, something even more than an economic doctrine; it is a philosophy of life and as such also it appeals to me. I see no way of ending poverty, the vast unemployment, the degradation, and the subjection of the Indian people except through socialism. That involves vast and revolutionary changes in our political and social structure, the ending of vested interests in land and industry, as well as the feudal and autocratic Indian States system . . . . Some glimpse we can have of this new civilization in the territories of the USSR. Much has happened there which has pained me greatly and with which I disagree, but I look upon that great and fascinating unfolding of a new order and a new civilization as the most promising feature of our dismal age. If the future is full of hope it is largely because of Soviet Russia and what it has done, and I am convinced that, if some world catastrophe does not intervene, this new civilization will spread to other lands and put an end to the wars and conflicts which capitalism feeds.

*   *   *

Socialism is thus for me not merely an economic doctrine which I favor: it is a vital creed which I hold with all my head and heart. I work for Indian independence because the nationalist in me cannot tolerate alien domination: I work for it even more because for me it is the inevitable step to social and economic change. I should like the Congress to become a socialist organization and to join hands with the other forces in the world who are working for the new civilization. But I realize that the majority in the congress, as it is constituted today, may not be prepared to go thus far. We are a nationalist organization and we think and world on the nationalist plane. It is evident enough now that this is too narrow even for the limited objective of political independence, and so we talk of the masses and their economic needs. But still most of us hesitate, because of our nationalist backgrounds, to take a step which might frighten away some vested interest. Most of those interests are already ranged against us and we can expect little from them except opposition even in the political struggle.

*   *   *

How does socialism fit in with the present ideology of the Congress? I do not think it does. I believe in the rapid industrialization of the country and only thus I think will the standards of the people rise substantially and poverty be combated. Yet I have co-operated whole-heartedly in the past with the khadi programme and I hope to do so in the future because I believe that khadi and village industries have a definite place in our present economy. They have a social, a political, and an economic value which is difficult to measure but which is apparent enough to those who have studied their effects. But I look upon them more as temporary expedients of a transition stage rather than as solutions of our vital problems. That transition stage might be a long one, and in a country like India, village industries might well play an important, though subsidiary, role even after the development of industrialism. But though I co-operate in the village industries programme my ideological approach to it differs considerably from that of many others in the Congress who are opposed to industrialization and socialism.

The problem of untouchability and the Harijans again can be approached in different ways. For a socialist it presents no difficulty, for under socialism there can be no such differentiation or victimization. Economically speaking, the Harijans have constituted the landless proletariat and an economic solution removes the social barriers that custom and tradition have raised.

Report on the Gandhi-Inspired Wardha Education Scheme, 1939

The following is a summary of the main conclusions reached at the meeting of the Committee:

1. The scheme of 'basic' education should first be introduced in rural areas.
2. The age range for compulsion should be 6 to 14 years, but children can be admitted to the 'basic' schools at age 5.
3. Diversion of students from the 'basic' school to other kinds of schools should be allowed after the 5th class or about the age of 11 . . . . Pupils wishing to join other schools at the end of the 5th class should be granted a leaving certificate (see #13).
4. The medium of instruction should be the vernacular of pupils.
5. A common language for India is desirable. This should be Hindustani with both the Urdu and Hindi scripts. Option should be given to children to choose the script and provision should be made for teaching them in that script. Every teacher should know both scripts . . . . Some members of the Committee suggest that the adoption of Roman script might prove a solution to the language difficulty and greatly minimise the work of both scholar and teacher.
6. The Wardha scheme is [based on] the principle of learning by doing. . . . This activity should be of many kinds in the lower classes and later should lead to a basic craft, the produce from which should be saleable and the proceeds applied to the upkeep of the school.
7. Certain elements of cultural studies, which cannot be correlated with the basic craft, must be taught separately.
8. The training of teachers should be reorganised and their status raised.
9. No teacher should recieve less than Rs. 20 per mensem.
10. Efforts should be made to recruit more women teachers and to persuade girls of good education to take up teaching.
11. English should not be introduced as an optional subject in basic schools.
12. The State should provide facilities as at present for every community to give religious teaching when so desired, but not at the cost of the State.
13. No external examinations need be held. At the end of the basic school course a leaving certificate based on an internal examination should be given.

Report of the Committee of the Central Advisory Board of Education, 1939 in C. H. Philips, ed., *Select Documents on the History of India and Pakistan,* Volume IV. London: Oxford University Press: 1962. 770-771.

The Communist Party of India

MANIFESTO OF THE COMMUNIST PARTY OF INDIA, MARCH 1940
The tenth anniversary of Independence Day takes place in the midst of the second imperialist war, a war which signifies the deeper crisis of imperialism, a war which is daily extending and drawing millions into its devastating orbit . . . .

Amidst chaos and carnage, amidst world-wide clash of arms, new forces are arising in every land, challenging the very system that bred the war; forces that by battling against countless terror are daily gathering strength. In every imperialist country engaged in war the masses are already raising the Red banner of Revolt. In every country in bondage the people are preparing for decisive battles with their enslavers.

At the head of these forces stands the Soviet Union, the land of victories, Socialism, the citadel of world Revolution. Afraid of the tremendous Revolutionary role of the Soviet Union, the forces of reaction are planning an assault against it. Finland has already become the outpost of international revolution...

Undreamt of possibilities have opened up for fulfilling our pledge that we took ten years back for striking a decisive blow for our own freedom and against the most powerful bulwark of world reaction, for making our most effective contribution—the creation of a new world order.

If that opportunity is wasted. . .we shall commit a crime against our national movement, a crime against humanity. History will never forgive that crime.

Never were we as powerful as we are today. Never was our enemy so weak. With the power that the Congress has achieved during the last ten years, with the tremendous advance that the working class, peasants and States, Peoples' Movements have registered, with the unity that has been forged in numerous struggles, we are to-day in a position to launch an attack that Imperialism will not be able to resist.

Let this truth be carried to the millions of our countrymen on Independence Day. Let the people be made conscious of the glorious opportunity which history has placed before us. Let us Congressmen realise that we stand upon the threshold of victory.

Obstacles that today seem formidable, obstacles created by communalist agencies, obstacles that the policy of compromise and inaction have encouraged to grow, will vanish in thin air when the nation's indignation is directed against the main enemy, against Imperialist Rule.

Struggling against the economic distress caused by the war, struggling against the suppression of political liberties, the masses are already moving on the path of action. Aided and led by the Congress, these struggles will draw millions of our countrymen into organised assault on the very citadel of imperialism.

For a democratic Republic with a Peoples' Army.

For the eight-hour day and a living wage.

For freedom from Rack-renting, and debt-slavery.

. . . Let tens of thousands of workers come out on the street and place themselves at the head of the demonstrations. Let the peasant masses hold gigantic rallies all over the country and organise marches. Let the students actively participate in the Day's celebrations. Let Congress Committees everywhere work for making Independence Day a day of mobilisation of the national forces for the battle of freedom.

It must be a day that gives Imperialism a fore-taste of the coming struggle, a day that creates deathless determination in our people, a day that inaugurates a new period of advance.

The Communists Quit the Congress: P. C. John's statement, Indian Annual Register, 1945

As a protest against the 'new attitude taken by the Congress towards the Communists,' the Communist Party Headquarters in India called upon all communists—with the exception of the Communist members of the A.I.C.C.—to resign from the Congress. A statement issued in this connection from Bombay on 5 October 1945 by the General Secretary of the Communist Party, Mr. P. C. Joshi, explains that the Communist members of the A.I.C.C. have been asked not to resign in order that they may remain to answer the charges made against them by the Congress Working Committee 'as the decision of the Congress will concern not only the past but the future of our common national movement.'

It may be recalled that Pandit Jawaharlal Nehru stated in Bombay recently that a sub-committee appointed by the Working Committee had presented the Communist members of the A.I.C.C. with the charge sheet that they had acted against the Congress's declared policy and that a time limit of 15 days had been given for a rejoinder as to why disciplinary action should not be taken against the Communist members concerned. Mr. P. C. Joshi, in his statement, says:

'We Indian Communists had great hopes that the leaders of the Congress, our foremost patriotic organisation, would rally the whole country behind a democratic plan for realising Indian freedom in alliance with progressive forces all over the world. We made their release the central plank of our agitation for the last three years, but the Congress leadership after release is not doing serious thinking and demonstrating sectarian arrogance. Instead of a plan to win Indian freedom and build Indian democracy, they have in the last A.I.C.C. meeting committed the organisation to a course which will only divide and disrupt the freedom forces themselves.'

The Hindu Mahasabha's Economic Plan, 1931

(a) We shall first of all welcome the machine. This is a Machine age. The handcrafts will of course have their due place and encouragement. But National production will be on the biggest possible machine scale.

(b) The peasantry and the working class form literally the chief source of National wealth, health, and strength as well; for, a stalwart army also has for its recruitment to depend chiefly on these very classes which supply the Nation with the first two requisites. Therefore, every effort will be made to reinvigorate them and the villages which are their cradle. Peasants and labourers must be enabled to have their share in the distribution of wealth to such an extent as to enable them to have not only a bare margin of existence but the average scale of a comfortable life. Nevertheless it must be remembered that they too being a part and parcel of the Nation as a whole must share obligations and responsibilities and therefore can only receive their share in such as away as is consistent with the general development and security of the National Industry, manufacture and wealth in general. . . . (d) If an industry is flourishing, the profits will be shared in a large portion by the labourers. But on the contrary if it is a losing concern, not only the Capitalist but to a certain extent even the Labourer will have to be satisfied with diminishing returns so that the National Industry as such may not altogether be undermined by the overbearing attitude of the selfish class interests of either the capitalists or labourites. In short the claims of capital and labour will be so co-ordinated from time to time as to enable the Nation as a whole to develop its National Industry and manufacture and make it self-sufficient. (f) In some cases some of the key industries or manufacturers and such other items may be altogether nationalised if the National Government can afford to do so and can conduct them more efficiently than private enterprise can do. (g) The same principle applies to cultivation of land. We should so co-ordinate the interest of the landlord and the peasant that the National agricultural production may on the whole be developed and does not suffer owing to any selfish tussle between the class interests of the landowner or the tenants or the tiller. (h) In some cases the Government may take over the land and introduce State cultivation if it can serve to train up the peasant class as a whole with the use of big machines and agriculture on a large and scientific scale. (i) All strikes or lockouts which are obviously meant or inevitably tend to undermine and cripple National industry or production in general or are calculated to weaken the economic strength of the Nation as a whole must be referred to State arbitration and get settled or in serious cases quelled. (j) Private property must in general be held inviolate. (k) And in no case should there be on the part of the State any expropriation of such property without reasonable recompense. Every step must be taken by the State to protect National industries against foreign competition.

I have hurriedly lined out the above items to serve as illustrations only. The National economical strength must grow and the Nation must be made economically self-sufficient; those two form the pivot of the Policy.

A special feature of no less importance of this Hindu Sanghatanist [Unity] economics must of course be to safeguard the economical interests of the Hindus wherever and whenever they may be threatened by the economical aggression of the non-Hindus as happens today of a set policy in the Nizam State, in the Punjab, in Phopal, in Assam and in several other parts of India. Hind Sabhas in all localities should make it a point to see that the Hindu peasants, the Hindu traders, the Hindu labourers do not suffer at the hands of non-Hindu aggression while the conflicting class interests amongst the Hindus themselves should be solved in light of the above general principles.

Appendix B: Embree, *India's Search for National Identity*

Ainslie T. Embree, *India's Search for National Identity* (Revised edition, 2005).

PREFACE TO THE REVISED EDITION

The original version of this book was written in India at a time when great changes were taking place in the political system, as there are at the present time when it is being republished. It seemed to me then, as it does now, that beyond those changes were the enduring patterns of a dynamic society characterized by an ability to fit incongruous and discordant elements into an immensely complicated mosaic. Accounts of India often stress that it possesses an ancient civilization with a remarkable ability to absorb other cultures. This is to some extent a misleading reading, for while India has, of course, a very ancient past, what has endured is not so much material artifacts, splendid though so many of them are, as ideas, values, and customs. Foreigners are sometimes astonished at how new, almost impermanent, the cities of India are, in comparison with, say, the old cities of Europe. That the survivals of the past are in the lives and consciousness of the people is part of the fascination of India, but it means that more than most countries, India lives always with the heavy burden of the past. And to emphasize that India has absorbed other cultures is to miss a fact of enormous significance for modern India: other cultures were not absorbed, but they continued to exist side by side with each other and with the dominant culture. What was produced was not a synthesis but patterns of culture quite unlike those that developed elsewhere in the world. Modern history has introduced peculiar stresses into the fabric of those patterns, and this essay attempts to trace the development of some of these, particularly those having to do with the contradiction between claims for representative government based upon an aggregation of individuals and those based upon the claims for group representation. The contradictions in these opposing claims are now visible in many parts of the world, but they had been very little examined in the period when Indian leaders were engaged in their momentous task of defining a nation. In the Middle East, Northern Ireland, and, of course, in India itself, the claims are often made in terms of a religious faith, and while there is no gainsaying its importance, beyond religion is the group, not the nation, as the source of one's identity. For three or four generations before Independence, Indian nationalists asserted the primacy of identification with the nation, not a group.

If India was the first major country to come to terms with those conflicting claims in its search for national identity in the context of foreign rule, so it may be one of the first to find a politically viable solution to a problem that now haunts the world. Even in countries like Great Britain and the United States, with long established political systems based upon the rule of the majority, the claims of minority groups for special recognition challenges the theory and practice of representative government as it developed in the nineteenth century.

This book, then, is not so much a history of modern India as an interpretation of that history during a period when a nationalist ideology was being formulated in the context of foreign political domination and the conscious reassertion of indigenous values and traditions. Concentration on this theme has meant that many aspects of modern Indian life have been either ignored or touched upon very lightly and that most attention has been given to political events and decisions. The assumptions that underlie much of the book are sketched in the first chapter. One is the importance of the creation of a modern structure of administration for the development of the complex of ideas that we call nationalism; another is the crucial role, particularly significant in India, of leaders whose personal identities became involved with the quest for nationality. Many of the questions asked about Indian nationalism have arisen out of the European historical experience, and it is hoped that, while Indian nationalism is illuminated by these questions, they will in turn suggest questions about the origins and development of nationalism elsewhere.

This book was written with a specific audience and purpose in mind: to provide American university students, who were not specializing in South Asian Studies, with materials for a comparative study of nationalism. It has been found useful for that purpose, and I am pleased that Longman Publishers are making it available once more. The details that were included for the previous audience will be familiar to Indian readers, but it is hoped that this attempt to interpret nationalism in South Asia in a way that will invite comparison with nationalist movement elsewhere may be of interest to them.

In the preface to the original edition, I noted that in writing even a small book, one incurs many debts of gratitude, but I especially recorded my thanks to old friends: B. R. Nanda, V. C. Joshi, Sourin Roy, and Sugata Dasgupta. They are thanked once more, and, in addition, all those other friends in India who through the years have helped me through both agreeing and disagreeing with my ideas. Professor Mark Carnes of Barnard College, Columbia University, is editor for the "Reacting to the Past" series that will make use of this book. As editor of a series on nationalism in which this book first appeared, my colleague Professor Eugene Rice of Columbia provided an introduction which set its themes in a larger context of modern world history; and it is republished here with its vivid reminder that "for good or ill the world has begun to live a single history."

Ainslie T. Embree
Columbia University, November 1987

INTRODUCTION

One of the intellectual virtues of our time is a willingness to recognize both the relativism of our own past and present beliefs and the civilizing value of the study of alien cultures. Yet, in practice, as every teaching historian knows, it is immensely difficult to construct a viable course in world history; and almost as difficult to include satisfactorily unfamiliar, and especially non-Western, materials in the traditional Western Civilization survey course. The reason for this difficulty is that until very recently mankind had no common past. The pre-Columbian civilizations of America attained their splendor in total isolation from the rest of the world. Although the many different ancient peoples living around the Mediterranean were often in close touch with one another, they had little knowledge about civilizations elsewhere. The Chinese knew accurately no other high civilization. Until the nineteenth century, they regarded the ideals of their own culture as normative for the entire world. Medieval Europe, despite fruitful contact with the Islamic world, was a closed society; medieval Western historians identified their own past with the history of the human race and gave it meaning and value by believing that this past was the expression of a providential plan.

The fifteenth-century European voyages of discovery began a new era in the relations between Europe and the rest of the world. Between 1500 and 1900, Europeans displaced the populations of three other continents, conquered India, partitioned Africa, and decisively influenced the historical development of China and Japan. The expansion of Europe over the world gave Western historians a unifying theme: the story of how the non-Western world became the economic hinterland, political satellite, and technological debtor of Europe. Despite an enormously increased knowledge of the religions, arts and literatures, social structures and political institutions of non-Western peoples, Western historians wrote a universal history that remained radically provincial. Only their assumptions changed. Before 1500, these assumptions were theological; by the nineteenth century, they were indistinguishable from those of intelligent colonial governors.

The decline of European dominance, the rise to power of hitherto peripheral Western countries such as the United States and the Soviet Union and of non-Western ones such as China and Japan, and emergence of a world economy and a state system embracing the planet have all created further options and opened wider perspectives. Historians of the future will be able to write real world history because for good and ill the world has begun to live a single history; and while this makes it no easier than before to understand and write the history of the world's remoter past, contemporary realities and urgencies have widened our curiosity and enlarged our sympathies and made less provincial our notions of what is relevant to us in the world's past.

One viable way to overcome the ethnocentric provincialism of an exclusively Western perspective is to deal with both Western and non-Western civilizations on a comparative basis. The comparative procedure has a double advantage. On the one hand, it describes a culture different from our own and makes clear to us that in order to understand it we must scan its history with humility and sophistication, abandoning implicit analogies with our own civilization and leaving aside some of our most fundamental assumptions about time, space, causality, and even about human nature itself. On the other hand, it encourages us to make explicit those very assumptions of our own tradition we now recognize to be different or unique. By studying comparatively an alien civilization we learn something about it—a good in itself— and at the same time sharpen our understanding of ourselves.

Professor Embree's book serves these purposes admirably, for it is at once an excellent introduction to the modern states of India and Pakistan and a fascinating study of how nationalism has flourished in a non-Western setting. In 1880 India had no physical, political, social, religious, or linguistic unity; and it was ruled by foreigners. In 1947 the entire subcontinent—not one of whose many languages, Gandhi once remarked, had a word for "independence" intelligible to the masses—was free of foreign rule, free and independent, but not united. For in India the heady consciousness of national identity had spread in a society that attached primary importance to religious identification. Nationalism therefore accentuated rather than minimized the division of Hindu and Muslim and produced not a single nation state, but two: India and Pakistan. Professor Embree's account of India's search for national identity between 1880 and 1947 is rich in irony and instruction. He gives us important comparative evidence about nationalism: what it is and how it works. The Indian experience he describes helps explain the relation between a growth of national sentiment and the progress of administrative unification and between nationalism and political ideology, allied at one time and place with the struggle for civil liberty, at another to militarism and reaction. The Indian experience makes us see more familiar stories of national unification, those of nineteenth-century Germany and Italy, for example, in a new and fruitful perspective. And finally, the Indian experience underlines one of the critical paradoxes of contemporary history: the diffusion of doctrines, which have come to seem to many Europeans and Americans to be symptoms of disease in the body politic rather than of health, among non-Western peoples who have made them the novel foundation of their sense of individual dignity, a call for social revolution, and the hope and motor of movements of national liberation around the globe.

Eugene Rice
Columbia University

CHAPTER 1. ONE GREAT NATION?

In 1888 Sir John Strachey, one of the ablest of the British administrators of India in the nineteenth century, with an excellent knowledge of the country's political and social history, made this judgment:

> This is the first and most essential thing to learn about India— that there is not, and never was an India, or even any country of India, possessing, according to European ideas, any sort of unity, physical, political, social or religious. . . . That men of the Punjab, Bengal, the North-Western Provinces, and Madras should ever feel they belong to one great nation, is impossible.[1]

This may seem silly looking at India now, but he was responding to a nascent nationalist movement which he regarded as a threat to the system of law and order he had helped to create. He was expressing a genuine conviction based upon what seemed to be an unbiased reading of the obvious facts of Indian history. On the basis of the same facts, but from a different perspective, the great Victorian reformer John Bright had argued thirty years earlier that the lack of any common nationality within India would prevent the endurance there of British rule. He believed that a country with twenty different nations and twenty languages could never be consolidated into one compact and enduring empire.

What these observers were emphasizing was that India lacked the elements generally regarded as the essential ingredients of nationality: a common language, a common religious tradition, and a historical experience shared by the majority of the people. India seemed, in fact, to be peculiarly fragmented precisely where unity and cohesion were demanded. Strachey and the others were mistaken in their belief that nationalism in the nineteenth century depended upon the cultural homogeneity characteristic of England or France. The variety and complexity of the manifestations of nationalism throughout the world have prevented any wholly satisfactory generalizations to explain this phenomenon, but one feature that does appear to be common to the development of nationalism in many countries is the prior creation of a modern structure of administration. This is the point made by Carl Friedrich when he asserts, after a survey of the growth of nationalism, "the building of the state comes first, and it is within the political framework of the state that the nation comes into being, or at any rate to fruition."[2] In this analysis, the modern state, with its mechanisms for organizing and controlling social activity, is seen as the producer, not the product, of nationalism.

Origins of Indian Nationalism

This insight has special relevance to the Indian situation, where nationalists reject as a reflection of Western chauvinism the argument that their nationalism is a Western import, unknown before British rule. They are incorrect, insofar as a nationalist movement necessarily draws its inspiration and vitality from the indigenous cultural tradition. But British rule did contribute that pattern of

administrative organization characterized as "Western" or "modern."
This political modernization was the base in India for the development of the
variegated and powerful sentiments that make up what we call "nationalism."

Benjamin Disraeli defined a nation as "a work of art and a work of time,"
gradually created by "a variety of influences—the influence of original
organization, of climate, soil, religion, laws, customs, manners, extraordinary
accidents and incidents in their history and the individual character of their
illustrious citizens."[3] Out of such forces came the dominant political idea of
modern times: The nation, however defined, demands complete allegiance
from all those who live within its territorial boundaries and takes precedence in
its claims over such other centers of loyalty as religious institutions, class, and
family. The groups of people constituting the nation are regarded as bound
together in a common destiny. In the nineteenth century constitutional
government and representative institutions were generally accepted as the
political forms most conducive to national well-being; but transcending the
commitment to any particular political pattern was always the emphasis on
the uniqueness inherent in being German or American or French.

One new and supremely important political consequence of this definition of the
state in terms of nationality was the insistence that the rulers and the ruled
should share a common nationality. In India's past, as in the rest of the world,
the rulers frequently had been alien in culture and race. A related characteristic
of nationalism of significance for India in the late nineteenth century was the
sense that "individual identity hinges on the existence of a national identity."[4]
The leaders in the search for nationhood identified their own needs and
aspirations with those of the society as a whole. In the beginning of a nationalist
movement there may be great disparity between the aspirations of the leaders
and of the masses, which was the case in India, as the British never wearied of
pointing out. But the triumph of nationalism comes when the masses share some
of the sense of correlation between national and personal identity.

In the second half of the nineteenth century the nationalist sentiment then
operating so powerfully in Europe became part of the thinking of important
segments of the Indian intelligentsia. The national movements that had ended in
the unification of Italy and Germany were well known to them, and Mazzini's
writings were popular in translations in both English and Indian languages.
Such analysts of the political process as John Stuart Mill, Herbert Spencer, and
Auguste Comte were familiar to the intellectuals in the great new urban centers
of Bombay, Calcutta, and Madras, and the intellectuals had memorized in school
Shakespeare's patriotic speeches and Milton's defense of political liberty.
English literature and European history thus provided Indian nationalists with
their illustrations and metaphors. Using European models, they created out of
India's past what John Stuart Mill called the strongest cause for the rise of a
sense of nationality: "the possession of a national history, and consequent

community of recollections, collective pride and humiliation, pleasure and regret, connected with the same incidents in the past."[5]

The development of such a sense of nationality was everywhere complex and haphazard, but there were especially complicating factors in the Indian situation. One factor was that the changes in political institutions and the whole process of national unification had to take place in the context of a vital traditional society whose economic and social structures were different or in a different stage of development from those in which European nationalism had flourished. The other was the inescapable fact that the instrument of political transformation was an alien government.

Many attempts have been made to analyze the effects of British rule on India, but, whether the judgments are friendly or harsh, they have often been misleading because of the assumption that British rule in India is a component that can be isolated from the fabric of Indian society. British rule and Indian nationalism both were organically related to the society in which they operated, and the antithesis often made between them is false. As already emphasized, the apparatus of the modern state was the framework that made the growth of nationalism possible, and in India this framework was provided by the administrative structures created by the British. British rule was, in the common phrase, "imposed" on India, but its manifestations—political, social, and economic—were inextricably blended into Indian life. The technology, commercial methods, and political institutions introduced into India were British or, at least, Western; but once they were accepted by large segments of the Indian population, they ceased to be "British" and became simply aspects of modernity shared by India and the rest of the world. At the same time there were many levels of Indian life, especially those relating to religion and the family, that were scarcely touched by the Western intrusion.

Because of the mingling of modern and traditional elements, the search for national identity in India is marked by paradoxes and ambiguities that make possible conflicting interpretations of its historical development. The struggle for independence against an alien invader can be seen as the dominant theme, with emphasis on the dynamic role of the Indian National Congress from its founding in 1885 to the moment of triumph in 1947 when India became free. It is also possible to read the story as the classic example of Western imperialism, with India's agricultural resources serving the ends of capitalistic, industrialized Great Britain. Or Hindu-Muslim tensions can be seen as the central motif of the period, with the partitioning in 1947 of the united India created in the nineteenth century as the proof of an irreconcilable division within the social fabric. From a quite different standpoint, modern Indian history may appear as an exercise in Western trusteeship. The growth of constitutionalism and responsible government is, in this version, not the achievement of the nationalist movement but of British administrators and civil servants.

All these interpretations deal with the same sets of facts, and they share an overestimation of the uniqueness and the power, for good or evil, of the British presence in India. What is important is not that the rulers were British, but that they were the bearers of the institutions of political modernization. The specific concern of this book is the interaction of these institutions with an increasingly articulate expression of nationalist sentiment underlying modern Indian history.

Profile: 1880s

Almost any point in the nineteenth century could be chosen for a starting point of an examination of this process of interaction. In the very early years Ram Mohan Roy (1772-1833) and others in Calcutta saw the advantages that might accrue from an intellectual association with the British, who were "advocates of liberty and promoters of knowledge."[6] Or 1835 is symbolic as the point at which the government began to support the use of English as the medium of higher education. This meant that English, not an Indian language, was to be the vehicle of Indian nationalism. Somewhat like Latin in the Middle Ages in Europe, English was to be the language of the learned, providing a common medium of expression for people with diverse linguistic backgrounds. It also made accessible to India the ideas of the West, including nationalism itself. The uprisings of 1857 are also a landmark as an unsuccessful attempt by representatives of the old political and social order to overthrow the new power. But 1880 has been chosen for the purposes of this study because by that time the political, economic, and intellectual forces of both British power and traditional Indian society had interacted to produce a society that had many of the characteristics of the modern nations of the Western world and that differed sharply from preceding Indian political structures. A rough profile of India in the 1880s is perhaps the best way to illustrate this.

ADMINISTRATION

By 1880 all of the Indian sub-continent had been brought under either the direct control of the central government located in Calcutta or indirect control through Indian rulers who acknowledged the supremacy of the British crown. Although direct rule was exercised in only three-fifths of the area, that area included almost four-fifths of the population, all the great cities, the seaports, and the Indo-Gangetic plains, one of the most populous and fertile regions of India. Beyond India proper, the government of India controlled such outposts as Aden on the Arabian coast and, by the end of the decade, the whole of Burma. Throughout this vast area there was not then, or indeed at any time, unbroken peace. But what impressed observers was the general stability of the region. To a considerable degree this was the result of the physical force that the government of India was able to apply, but it also indicated widespread acceptance of British rule. For the British it was this passive acceptance that sanctioned their rule, making them the legitimate successors of the previous rulers.

The major instruments of the government's power were the army and the civil bureaucracy. The Indian army had about 200,000 men, of whom 60,000 were British, the rest Indian. There were about 2,000 officers of commissioned rank—all British. In 1880, by the standard of contemporary European armies, it was neither very efficiently organized nor well armed; but in the Indian context, both in relation to the neighbouring countries and to any possible internal armed uprising, its superiority was axiomatic. The factors that had given the British their military success for a century still obtained: modern weapons, discipline, mobility, and efficient arrangements for military supplies. Perhaps the most important difference between the Indian army in 1880 and that of any earlier Indian ruler was that the army was under direct and immediate control of the central authority. Lack of such control previously had allowed local officials and military commanders to build up centers of power to be used against central administration. Furthermore, while army officers frequently occupied high posts in the Indian bureaucracy under the British, especially in the early period, the principle of civilian control was never seriously challenged. The civilian authorities were the rulers of India, and the army was their instrument, never their master. The army was part of the governmental structure, performing a defined role; it was not a potential rival for political power.

In 1880 the location of that power in India was without question the governor general and the Indian Civil Service. While ultimate authority was vested in the British crown, India was governed from Calcutta, not London. The principal function of the home government was not to direct the administration itself, but to evaluate and monitor actions taken by the Indian governments and to guide those governments in their future actions. The government of India to a large degree was autonomous, functioning at all levels in much the way any government would have, given the suppositions and powers of its particular ruling class.

[The bureaucratic structure of this government, however complicated in detail, was relatively simple in outline. At the top were the governor general and the six members of his council, appointed by the British crown. For legislative purposes this council was enlarged by twelve members appointed by the governor general, two or three of whom were Indians. The powers and functions of this legislative body were very modest, but despite all disclaimers by the British, it was regarded by an increasing number of Indians as foreshadowing a parliamentary structure, and the line of development between the present Indian parliament and the Legislative Council is direct and unmistakable. Much of the power of the central government was delegated to provincial administrations. There were seven of these, differing somewhat in organization, but in general duplicating the central structure, with a governor, an executive council, and a legislative council. The provinces were in turn divided into districts, each with a population of about a million people.

The actual work of administration, whether at the central, provincial, or district level, was in the hands of the Indian Civil Service, a body very different in power and composition from the civil services of other governments. The Indian Civil Service in 1880 had only about one thousand members, of whom all but a half dozen or so were British. Since they held all the key administrative posts—including the crucial positions of collectors, as the heads of districts were usually known—the civil servants, not the governor general, were the real rulers of India. With their long tenure, superior knowledge of the administration, and a very strong awareness of their indispensability to the maintenance of British power in India, they had a kind of power not enjoyed by many other ruling groups in the nineteenth century. It was in recognition of its position in the power structure that the early nationalist leaders made admittance of Indians to the Civil Service a central part of their demands. In 1880 Indians were not formally barred from the Civil Service, as they had been at any earlier date, but racial prejudice combined with educational restrictions to prevent the entry of any but the most gifted and the most persistent.

Although the government of India in the 1880s was a despotism, its functions were limited, and it did not seek to bring about any widespread social or economic changes. As far as social change was concerned, one of the conclusions the British in India had drawn very early, and which had been reinforced by the uprisings of 1857, was that it was best not to attempt to interfere in social and religious customs. For this reason, the government of India was even less innovative in the second half of the nineteenth century than it had been in the first half. The general assumption that the Indians did not care who ruled them, provided they were left undisturbed in their customary ways of life, made for a profoundly conservative attitude on the part of officials. In the economic sphere, however, the government's policy was more ambiguous. It was notably active in the creation of the whole new system of communications, and irrigation projects opened up new areas for agriculture and increased yields elsewhere.]

In outline, this structure of administration does not differ radically from that of the Indian empire of the Turkish Mughals; the territorial divisions, especially at the local level, were often identical with divisions of the Mughal provinces, and the functions of the officials were also analogous. Indeed, the basic pattern was the one used by the Mauryas in the third century B.C. and by successive imperial rulers. The British themselves were fond of making this analogy, perhaps because it gave a kind of historical legitimization to their rule. But there were differences that were more important than the similarities, and it was these that helped to make India in the 1880s a modern state, with unique possibilities of development.

COMMUNICATION

One difference has already been stressed in connection with the army: the control exercised by the central authority. The possibility of such control was in large measure the product of the technological achievements in communication that occurred, quite fortuitously, with the expansion of British power in India. The importance of the railway and telegraph were recognized almost at once by the government of India, and by the 1880s India had a remarkably complete communications system. Railways linked the interior of the country to the seaports; the Grand Trunk Road stretched from Calcutta to Lahore; telegraph lines reached into areas served by neither railways nor good roads; and an efficient postal service operated almost everywhere. We have no studies analyzing in detail what this rapid expansion of new systems of communications meant for India, but it must have made people in different parts of the country aware of each other and their common interests, thus providing a base for building a sense of nationality. There is a measure of irony in this, since the British officials responsible for these changes insisted on the impossibility of unity among India's people.

ECONOMY

The centralization of political power and the general improvement in communications made it profitable for the first time to transport agricultural products to distant areas within India as well as to foreign markets. India had been a center of trade since time immemorial, but the goods involved had been mainly those classifiable as luxury items, light in weight and small in bulk, such as spices, textiles, indigo, and ivory. The basis of the new trade was entirely different. By 1880 wheat was one of India's main exports, with the farmers of Punjab no longer raising crops only for local consumption, but also for a competitive world market. Other products, including hides, jute, raw cotton, tea, oilseeds, and rice, experienced the same expansion.

Throughout this period India had a favorable balance of trade, exporting far more than she imported; for example, in 1883 the value of exports exceeded imports by 186 million rupees. Most of the imports were manufactured goods; nearly 80 percent of them came from Great Britain. This excess of raw material exports over imports became a central theme in the Indian nationalist interpretation of the effect of British rule on India, the argument being that India was drained of her natural wealth to support the industrial power of Great Britain. Although the argument in this form needs qualification, there can be little doubt that the emphasis in the late nineteenth century on the production of agricultural products for export to foreign markets, as well as to new markets within India itself, profoundly affected the course of India's economic development. The increase in external trade alone, aside from internal trade developments, which were probably equally great, was very large—about eightfold since 1800. But this was not reflected, as might have been expected, in the growth of industrialization or large-scale urbanization. India continued overwhelmingly to have an agricultural economy, but one that was open to the influence of world markets.

POPULATION GROWTH

Changes in the size and distribution of the population that were clearly visible by 1880 also underscored the transformation taking place in economic and political structures. Although the evidence is admittedly fragmentary, it is estimated that the Indian subcontinent had a population of about 100 million in the first century A.D. and that growth was very slow until 1800, when the figure was about 125 million. There were undoubtedly fluctuations within this period, both over the whole area and within different regions, but no radical changes seem to have taken place until the nineteenth century. The population growth then accelerated, slowly at first, rapidly after 1850; and when the first census was made in 1871 there was a population of about 250 million. Although this was an enormous increase in absolute terms, the growth rate was not higher than that of many other areas of the world, including Europe, in the nineteenth century. What is of greatest importance is that population growth took place not in the context of industrialization and urbanization as in Europe, but in an economy that was still overwhelmingly agricultural and rural. Of the total population in 1881, 9 percent was urban, and this proportion had probably not changed much since 1800. But if the degree of urbanization had not altered, the location and function of the great cities had changed radically. The three largest cities— Bombay, Calcutta, and Madras—were all new; two hundred years before they had been at best small villages. Delhi, Agra, and Lahore, the great court cities of the Mughals, probably had fewer inhabitants than they had in the seventeenth century, and they had lost their old importance. The new cities were, almost without exception, centers of trade and industry. They were also centers for the law courts and educational institutions, two other aspects of change that marked off the new India from the old and helped to define her as a nation state.

LAW

In the nineteenth century most British officials would have argued without hesitation that the greatest change that had been brought about by British control in India was the introduction of what they liked to call the "rule of law." The suggestion implicit in this claim—that before the coming of the British India did not have a system of law—is obviously untenable, since no civilization could survive without a framework of law. Nevertheless they were probably correct in their general assessment of the importance of the system of law they had introduced. The innovative influence of the new system came from both the laws promulgated by various legislative bodies and the law courts where they were administered. A remarkable change had taken place in that for the first time there was a large body of legislation applicable everywhere in India and actually enforced. This law was universal both in the sense that it was effective throughout British India (but not in the Indian states) and that it had equal application to all citizens, irrespective of civil or religious status. Both the criminal and commercial codes were based wholly on Western law, with little in them to suggest any kind of continuity with India's past. The Evidence Act of 1872 completed the process of making all aspects of legal procedure conform to British practice. The Western origin of so many of the laws, combined with their universality of application, moved Indian society away from some of its traditional moorings.

A very important exception in regard to the universalization of law was made, however, in regard to personal law, that is, in areas relating to such matters as marriage, divorce, adoption, and inheritance. Here, in line with the general principle of not interfering in religious customs and beliefs, laws were applicable according to the religious group to which a person belonged. This made for an extremely complicated legal system, for the nature and possibilities of divorce proceedings would depend, for example, on whether one was Hindu, Christian, or Muslim. The Government was, in effect, enforcing through law the customs of particular religious communities. This practice had its analogue in that of Western countries, including Great Britain, where it was assumed that the divorce laws reflected Christian beliefs. There were, however, a number of differences in the Indian situation. The government was not only legalizing a variety of belief systems, but within those systems, particularly in the Hindu but also, although to a lesser extent, within the Islamic, there was no recognized consensus on such matters. There does not seem to have been much discussion of the advisability of the diversity of personal law at the time, or a recognition that a modern nation-state would move towards the demand for a common personal law for all its citizens. That the existence of a variety of personal laws should have been so readily accepted in the 1880s but later became a subject of intense and divisive debate illustrates one of the transformations made by the formulations of a nationalist ideology and the difference between an imperialist political power and a nation-state.[7]

But no matter what kind of legal case was involved—criminal, commercial, or religious—the system of courts in which they were heard was one that was derived from Western practice. Perhaps in no other area of Indian life was so complete an institutional change affected as in the judicial process, with its network of courts extending from the high courts in each of the provinces, through civil and criminal district courts, down to local courts. These courts, with their common body of law, their uniform procedures, and their interlocking structures, were an integral ingredient in the process of making a social change, although the nature of that change is not without great ambiguity. On the one hand, the use of precedents in the law courts probably tended to give customs that had been purely local and perhaps of no great antiquity, the status of law, and so to make for greater rigidities in Indian society; on the other hand, the possibility of getting a decision through a court of law made it possible to introduce new conventions into the society. Cases dealing with the position of castes in the society provide examples of both, with groups going to court to claim higher status than had traditionally been accorded them. The courts dealt with many matters of this kind which in British courts would not have been considered legal issues.

By 1880 important changes had also taken place in the field of education. India had had its own systems of education for the transmission and preservation of the traditional culture, but in the nineteenth century new content and new institutional forms were introduced. In general, as in the case of the legal system, the direction was towards uniformity and universality so that curricula and methodologies were remarkably similar throughout India. This was as true of government schools where the medium of instruction was an Indian language as it was of those where the medium was English.

Universities modeled on the University of London, that is, a parent examining body for numerous teaching colleges, had been established in Calcutta, Bombay, and Madras in 1857. The universities themselves were government-sponsored, but the colleges were operated by both government and private interests, often foreign missionary societies and churches. English was the medium of instruction for higher education, and the curriculum was almost wholly Western in content: European history, English literature, and Western philosophy. An important aspect of this Western-oriented curriculum was that it was believed by many of those responsible for it that it would communicate not only factual knowledge but that in itself Western learning, particularly English literature, would have an elevating effect on the morals of the students.[8] In government institutions as well as in missionary ones, it was fondly hoped that exposure to the great literature of the West would weaken the hold of Hinduism and Islam on the lives of the students and lead them to an acceptance of true religion. Actual conversions even in missionary schools were extremely rare, but that English literature, including the Bible, was shaping the thinking of Indian intellectuals by the 1880s seems clear from their writings.

Primary and secondary schools were neither free nor everywhere available. As with the colleges, they were operated partly by official bodies and partly by private groups, among which foreign missionary organizations were most conspicuous for the number and quality of their institutions. The regional languages were used in the schools, but a knowledge of English was mandatory for everyone who sought university admission.

Any analysis of the impact and penetration of education into the fabric of Indian society is at best impressionistic because of the lack of suitable data, but the census materials for 1881 and 1891 provide some clues as to what was happening. One familiar fact is the very high rate of illiteracy: 95 percent of the population, in the 1881 census, was unable to read or write. But this figure is misleading because it conceals facts of profound importance for the social and political history of India. One of these was the literacy differential between men and women. Over the age of twenty-five, 14 percent of the men were literate, but only 0.47 percent of the women were. Even more striking were the enormous variations in literacy between different classes and castes. Agricultural workers and artisans, who made up 75 percent of the population, had a male literacy rate of only about 5 percent. Groups that can be identified very loosely as "professional" or trade, who made up about 12 percent of the population, had a male literacy rate of about 27 percent. Figures for literacy by caste tell a confirming story. The Brahmans in Madras had a male literacy rate of 72 percent; in Bombay, 65 percent; and in Bengal, 50 percent, despite the fact that large numbers lived in rural areas.

In relation to the total population, the number of people who knew English was negligible, but they were overwhelmingly high caste, urban, and Hindu, with 80 percent of the English-knowing population coming from such groups. Since they provided the leadership at almost every level of national life—in education, the professions, journalism, and the bureaucracy itself—their importance is obvious.

Another aspect of educational development of great importance for Indian nationalism was the difference between the responses of Hindus and Muslims to Western-style education. Overall the differences were not very significant: the Hindus had a literacy rate in the 1880s of slightly less than 5 percent and the Muslims, a little more than 4 percent. But in regard to higher education, which included a knowledge of English, the differences were very striking: the proportion of Hindu students was far greater than the population ratio of Hindus to Muslims. The position is dramatically illustrated by figures from the Rajshahi district in northern Bengal. Muslims made up 75 percent of the population, but in the one college in the district 80 percent of the students were Hindus. These figures do not reflect, as has often been suggested, a fundamentally different attitude between the two religious communities toward the new Western-oriented educational system, but rather the lack among the Muslims of classes, corresponding in size and influence to those of the Hindus, whose livelihood, either in trade and commerce or in government service, had traditionally been dependent on literacy. It was from these classes among the Hindus that the English-knowing, Western-educated groups were drawn.

These figures taken together lead to the inescapable conclusion that the new educational system and the new ideas that went with it made their impact largely on those classes that had traditionally been literate in India and had provided leadership in every sphere of social and religious life. The Western intrusion had not, therefore, led to the creation of new classes or any fundamental shifts in social power and prestige but had reinforced in most cases the prevalent pattern of society. An important exception to this statement is the loss of power and prestige by the Muslim upper classes, who had lost their place as the dominant political group. But their position, like that of the British in the nineteenth century, had always been somewhat artificial, a temporary function of political power, not an integral part of the structure of society throughout the subcontinent. Leadership would come, with few exceptions, from the Hindu upper-caste groups that had always provided it. The approximately fifteen hundred students per year who received university degrees of some kind during the 1880s were an infinitesimal percentage of the total population, but they were an important part of an influential segment, a vital fact that was often missed by the British officials, who dismissed them as a group so small and so unrepresentative of the whole population that their views need not be seriously considered.

RELIGION

In drawing this impressionistic profile of India in 1880, only passing reference has been made to religion. The importance of religious attitudes and allegiances in Indian society is a truism that needs no special emphasis, but it would be misleading to attribute to religious groups roles that are the same as, or even analogous to, those in Western society. Within traditional Indian society one did not identify oneself as a Hindu; this is a broad category imposed by outsiders. Instead identity was in terms of a particular caste or other group within the society. The same pattern was true of the Muslims, who also tended to think of themselves not in the general category of Muslims, but as members of a particular social class, involvement in which defined to a large extent the perimeters of social life. One of the changes, however, that was taking place with considerable rapidity in the 1880s was a new self-conscious awareness of religious differences and distinctions. This self-consciousness was both a function and a cause of the nationalist movement, and one of the fundamental changes observable between the India of 1880 and the India of 1947 is the increasing importance of what became known as "communalism," that is, the definition of social and political interests through primary reference to religious communities. The largest of these communities was Hindu, although it must be emphasized that this term covers such a range of belief and practice that the general designation at times conceals more than it reveals of the intellectual beliefs and social practices of those subsumed under it. About 187 million people were classified as Hindus in 1881, and the second largest group was the Muslims with about 52 million.

A number of factors must be taken into account when discussing the relative size of the religious communities in India in the 1880s in relation to political leadership. One is that, for reasons suggested above, there was a larger Hindu middle class than there was a Muslim one, even though that term must be loosely used for India of the time. That educated members of the middle class have provided leadership for nationalist movements throughout the world is a truism, and India is no exception. Almost by sheer logic of numbers the leadership of Indian nationalism would come then from Hindus. And this middle-class Hindu intelligentsia had memories of the past that were peculiarly suited for a nationalist ideology. A fundamental aspect of nineteenth-century Indian intellectual history was the discovery of the greatness of ancient India in religion, philosophy, art, and literature, with great symbols of cultural and political unity furnished by the Maurya and Gupta empires. Literature from the 1880s suggests how potent such memories were in providing the framework for a nationalist ideology. The lack of hostility to British ideas, values, and institutions on the part of the early Indian nationalists has seemed odd to some observers, but there was no reason to be hostile since many of the nationalist leaders found these same qualities in their own tradition. This may not have been a justifiable reading of the evidence, but the content of historic memories is more important than textual criticism in the making of a nation.

On a more mundane level, another factor that is of importance in looking at the relative size of the religious communities is their distribution throughout India. Hindus were 73 percent of the population as a whole, but they constituted 90 percent of the great province of Madras and only 43 percent of Punjab. Muslims made up 20 percent of the total population, but they were concentrated overwhelmingly in the northwest and northeast, with about 50 percent of the population of Punjab and Bengal being Muslims. Distribution of communal groups, rather than their total numbers, was to become a crucial factor in Indian history.

*   *   *

Such then was India in outline in 1880. The materials for a nationalist ideology were present in the form of well-articulated social institutions, highly sophisticated literary and artistic traditions and religious systems that provided satisfactory answers to life's hard questions. To these had been added in the nineteenth century many of the necessary forms of a modern nation-state: a well-organized bureaucracy, educational institutions for the transmission of the ideas and values of modernization, and the infrastructure of modern communications. The next stage, an attempt by Indian groups to participate in the political direction of the new state, was entered into hesitantly and without anticipation of the many factors involved in the undertaking. An essential preliminary for such participation was that the Indian groups should be able to state their interests and their demands in terms significant to both Indian society and the British rulers. The formulation of this statement of nationalist aspirations, centering on various political events and drawing vitality from social and religious movements, constituted the essential feature of Indian history in the last two decades of the nineteenth century.

NOTES

1. Sir John Strachey, *India* (London: Kegan Paul, 1888), 5-8.
2. Carl Friedrich, *Man and His Government* (New York: McGraw-Hill, 1963), 547.
3. Quoted in Karl W. Deutsch, *Nationalism and Social Communication* (Cambridge: Massachusetts Institute of Technology Press, 1967), 21.
4. Lucian Pye, *Politics, Personality, and Nation Building* (New Haven: Yale University Press, 1968), 4.
5. John Stuart Mill, *Representative Government*, quoted in Deutsch, *Nationalism and Social Communication*, 19.
6. Ram Mohan Roy, *The English Works of Ram Mohan Roy* (Allahabad: Panini Office, 1906), xxiii.
7. Ainslie T. Embree, "Religion and Politics" in *India Briefing, 1987*, edited by Marshall Bouton (New Delhi: Oxford University Press, 1987), examines this issue.
8. Gauri Viswanathan, *Masks of Conquest: Literary Study and British Rule in India* (New York: Columbia University Press, 1989) is a detailed study of this aspect of education.

CHAPTER 2. VOICES OF INDIA

In his presidential address to the Indian National Congress in 1890, Sir Pherozeshah Mehta reminded his listeners of Thomas Babington Macaulay's prediction in 1833:

> The public mind of India may expand under our system till it has outgrown that system; that by good government we may educate our subjects into a capacity for better government; that having become instructed in European knowledge they may in some future age demand European institutions.[1]

That day had come, Mehta said, because an educated class existed in India that was ready and able to share in the maintenance—not the destruction—of British rule. Since the Congress was the only group that could articulate opinions, its voice was the voice of India. Mehta insisted that educated Indians had "not learnt the lessons of history so badly as to demand the introduction of full-blown representative institutions." What they wanted was participation in the existing structures of the government in order to make that government responsive to the needs of India as they interpreted them.

Lord Curzon opposed this demand of the Indian National Congress to be recognized as the voice of India when his term of office as governor general ended in 1905. He contended that a genuine, articulate public opinion did not exist in India, but only "a manufactured public opinion . . . which was barren and ineffective because it merely represented the partisan views of a clique."[2] The real Indians were, he concluded, "the Indian poor, the Indian peasant, the patient, humble, silent millions, the eighty percent who subsist by agriculture, and who know very little of policies."[3] Who then spoke for these silent millions? Underlying all Curzon's rhetoric was the assumption that it was the British rulers of India who knew best the needs of these millions, not the vocal, English speaking intellectuals whom he contemptuously dismissed as a "microscopic minority."

In quantitative terms Curzon was correct, but he was ignoring the realities of the Indian situation that made this small, articulate minority in fact the traditional spokesmen for India. Early in the nineteenth century Sir John Malcolm, who had helped to consolidate British power in Western India, showed his awareness of a vital aspect of Indian society when he noted that the Brahmans and other high castes, although for ages nominal servants, had been actually the masters of those in power. Because of the dominance of these groups in Indian society, he argued, any serious challenge to British rule would come from them, not from the military tribes, who were turbulent and bold, but too ignorant and superstitious to threaten the British. The accuracy of Malcolm's observation is suggested by the fact that in 1880 almost all the graduates of Calcutta University were from the Brahman and other small high-caste groups that had traditionally assumed leadership in Bengali society.

By and large, members of these groups had played a dominant role in British rule in India throughout the nineteenth century. The actual physical power of the government was based on its army, composed mostly of Indians, and civilian police forces, virtually all of whom were Indian. The highest paid and most responsible jobs in the bureaucracy were held by Europeans, but these numbered, in all kinds of government employment, only about six thousand. The hundreds of thousands of other jobs were held by Indians. It was not force alone that held India, but "the collaboration of Indians who helped to fulfill the purposes of the British."[4] No adverse moral judgment is implied; all governments, alien or indigenous, despotic or democratic, depend upon groups in the society actively identifying their interests with those of the rulers. In India, aside from the soldiers, these collaborators were the landlords and the commercial groups, especially in the new cities, and above all those who, having been educated in the new schools and colleges, had found careers in government, educational institutions, and the new professions, such as medicine, law, and journalism. The whole orientation of Indian nationalism was determined by the fact that its leadership came from these groups, whose members were involved with the new political and economic order.

Finally, the opposition of these particular groups to the numerous unsuccessful uprisings against British rule is of special importance in assessing their role in articulating a nationalist ideology. The failure of these uprisings, especially those in 1857, had lasting consequences for the development of nationalism. The English educated, urban elite had supported the British in 1857. They believed that their own future—and the future of India—was bound up with British rule and what it represented. Being protagonists for the social and political changes they saw coming from Western influence, they had no sympathy with the insurgents' attempt to restore such symbols of the past as the Mughal emperor. The British, although their victory reinforced their feeling of superiority, feared another uprising. Public statements do not always make it clear that after 1857 the government was extremely careful not to antagonize any of the groups of north India—the orthodox religious, the landlords, the old ruling groups—that had participated in the uprisings. As late as 1902 Lord Kitchener, the commander in chief, complained that the Indian army was deployed to protect India not from its external enemies, who he was convinced were the Russians, but from uprisings of the people. The other side of this fear of a repetition of 1857 was respect for those groups likely to fight again, and contempt, or at least mild scorn, for the Bengali businessmen and intellectuals who had supported the government during the uprisings. The result was that when the educated, Western-oriented Indian groups began to seek participation in the structures of power at the end of the century, the process of alienation between them and the British rulers was well under way, although still concealed.

First Responses to the West

The first tentative expression of the involvement of the Indian elite had begun very early—almost simultaneously with the consolidation of British power in Bengal. Early in the nineteenth century many of the distinctive features of the Indian nationalist movement made their appearance: the use of a political vocabulary infused with religious and moral overtones; an emphasis on the social concerns of the urban elite; and a desire to introduce Western norms of political and social behavior. The great figure in this early period is Ram Mohan

Roy, an eloquent spokesman for an interpretation of Indian history and culture that is of great importance in the intellectual development of modern India. Roy accepted the harsh criticisms made of many aspects of Hindu society by Europeans, but he argued that these were the superstitious excrescences of a degraded age. If one returned to the most ancient sources of Hindu religion, the Vedas, he believed, one would find a pure morality and simple deistic faith identical with the highest reaches of Christian thought. Roy and his followers urged their fellow Hindus to abandon such practices as child marriage; sati, the burning of widows on their husbands' funeral pyres; and the worship of idols. At the same time they encouraged the spread of Western education, demanding that the government give its support to the use of English as the medium of instruction in the new colleges that were being set up at that time, rather than the classical languages of the Hindus and Muslims—Sanskrit, Arabic, and Persian.

Roy's ideas were later institutionalized in the Brahmo Samaj, a quasi-religious society that sought to provide a spiritual home for those who were dissatisfied with the cultic practices of Hinduism. It provided an important service in giving Indian intellectuals a standing ground during the early years of the Western impact, but it was too apologetic for what it considered the weaknesses of Indian society, and too anxious to make Hinduism conform to current Western norms, to provide a satisfactory rationale for a nationalist movement.

Other movements met more adequately the need for a national consciousness to be rooted in a self-confident assertion of its own virtues. One was the Arya Samaj, founded by Swarai Dayananda Saraswati (1824-1883). According to Dayananda, India had need of nothing from the West, for her own spiritual inheritance contained all the truths of science and religion. Like Roy he denounced idol worship and other current practices as late superstitions, but unlike Roy he refused to make common cause with Christianity and Islam. The apologetic note was gone; he did not argue, as had Roy, that all religions shared a common truth, but rather that religions were as opposed to each other as night and day. Christianity and Islam, he argued, were absurdly superstitious. Much of the appeal of Dayananda's movement came from this positive, self-assertive attack on other religious groups, but he was equally scornful of the practices and customs of orthodox Hinduism, especially the emphasis on caste purity, idol worship, and the treatment of women.

Dayananda has been called "The Luther of India" by his admirers, an appellation which, while it is too enthusiastic in assessing his historical role, aptly describes the vigor of his arguments. He made no direct attack on foreign rule, but instead he castigated the Hindus for their lack of discipline and patriotism, which had led in the past to India's defeat by foreigners. The implication was plain: The cultivation of discipline and patriotism would lead to the revival of India.

The Arya Samaj emphasized that the true Indians were the Aryas, or "the noble ones," the descendants of the ancient peoples who had come into India in the remote past bearing the pure Vedic religion. The Aryas once ruled India, but dissensions led to their destruction and conquest by enemies; a return to moral purity would mean the restoration of their power. Dayananda found his most receptive audience in the Punjab, probably because there the Hindus were more conscious of themselves as a group, since they were surrounded by Muslims and Sikhs. His message, with its combination of religious reform and patriotic appeal, gave them an incentive to assert their claims for leadership.

Another union of religion and nationalism, very different in tone and spirit from the Arya Samaj, grew up in Bengal in the 1860s and 1870s. Young writers who had been deeply influenced by modern Western literature and political ideas began to express themselves in poetry, plays, and novels. Their themes were often drawn from India's past, especially from stories of the heroic deeds of the Rajput warriors in their battles against the invading Muslims. The casting of Muslims in the role of villains probably did not rise as much from anti-Muslim feelings as from the frustrations of a generation resentful of foreign domination and conscious of its own weakness. An important aspect of the movement was an undertone of religious mysticism, an exaltation of selfless devotion to Kali, the mother-goddess whose cult was widely popular in Bengal. Kali is a representation of the dark, vital forces of nature, the slayer of demons whose cult involved blood sacrifices and whose worship demanded passionate commitment. The identification of this mother-goddess figure with India, the motherland, was an easy step.

Anti-Muslim sentiment and a passionate religious nationalism found their most influential statement in the novels of Bankim Chandra Chatterji (1838-J894). Possibly he used Muslims as villains in *Anandamath*, his best-known novel, as a thinly veiled allegory in which the British were really intended to take the role of oppressor; but it seems more likely that his desire for national purity and unity took the form, as in other nationalist movements, of a revulsion against all alien elements in the society. The British could have filled this role, but Chatterji was not anti-Western in the sense that Dayananda was, and he saw Western ideas as having a creative role in Indian life. His combination of Indian religious symbols with Western concepts of patriotism is shown in a striking manner in his famous poem "Bands Matram" in the novel *Anandamath*. One of the characters in the poem invokes the goddess Kali as both deity and motherland.

> Mother, to thee I bow.
> Who hath said thou art weak in thy lands,
> When the swords flash out in twice
> Seventy million hands,
> And seventy million voices roar
> Thy dreadful name from shore to shore.[5]

The singer went on to tell the hero, a young man, that the way to drive out the intruder is to use the intruder's method—violence. This mystical nationalism, building on concepts deeply rooted in Indian life, is of great importance for modern India. It is often overlooked because of the later emphasis on nonviolence in the Gandhian period, but its romantic appeal provides the background for many later developments.

Role of Regional Languages

The social and intellectual ferments that found expression in Bankim Chandra's novels were not confined to Bengali literature. Throughout India the creation of new forms of literary expression through the use of regional languages was one of the most striking and contradictory developments in the search for national self-identity. The role of English as a unifying and vitalizing factor in the growth of Indian nationalism has rightly been stressed, but probably this new literature in the regional languages was equally significant. Everywhere in India in the nineteenth century the regional languages gained a new vitality and a new prestige. The classical languages—Sanskrit in the older Indian tradition, Persian for the Muslims—had been replaced by English as the official language and as the medium of higher education. But secondary schools were conducted in the regional languages, as was the day-to-day business of local courts. English missionaries in Bengal at the very beginning of the nineteenth century had shown the possibilities of using Bengali prose—a new literary creation—for communication with the masses and had published not only religious works, but also newspapers and other secular works. Newspapers in all the major regional languages soon became commonplace, with every city and large town having at least one. None of them had large circulations—around five hundred seems to have been the norm—and many of them were short-lived. But every copy probably reached at least ten people, and their ideas would spread far beyond that number. The newspapers were frequently sharply critical of the government, but the fact that they were in regional languages and often published in obscure places meant that they had a freedom of expression that, as officials frequently complained, bordered on the seditious. In 1878 a government official concluded, after a survey of his district, "the great political fact of the day" was that "a feeling of nationality, which formerly had no existence . . . had grown up," and that the press could now for the first time "appeal to the whole Native Population of India against foreign rulers."[6]

Other forms of literary activity in the regional languages also contributed to this new sense of self-conscious identity about politics and society. Social evils were attacked in plays and novels; histories were written for the first time in the local languages; poetry expressed a concern with the ordinary life of the time. These trends were visible in a dozen languages, giving a new self-awareness to regional cultures. The persistence of these regions as cultural and political entities constitutes one of the fundamental facts of Indian historical experience, for they were far more enduring than the great empires. This modern development ran counter to the all-India nationalism, just as the possibility of regionally based political power had always constituted a challenge to imperial structures. From this point of view, the cultivation and encouragement of regional literatures in the nineteenth century were divisive forces that increased the strains on the fabric of national unity in modern India, as did the identification of religious symbols with nationalism. But it is difficult to see how, without either a religious or a regional emphasis, an Indian nationalism could have been created that would have had any vitality, for religious and linguistic preferences provided the basis for the emotional as well as much of the intellectual appeal of nationalism.

Nationalist Organizations

The proliferation of associations and organizations of all kinds was another crucial aspect of the development of public opinion and national identity. The nineteenth-century British pattern of voluntary public associations to achieve some desired end through publicity, discussion, and pressure on authorities was taken over with remarkable success by the Indian elite. The National Association was formed in 1851 in Calcutta. It was open to all classes and creeds, and its aims were "to assert our legal rights by legitimate means" and "to apply for any amendment or reform . . . either to the Local Government or to the authorities in England."[7] This was soon transformed into the British Indian Association, possibly because the word "national" suggested disloyalty to the regime. Its aims were modest: Indian representation on the legislative councils that advised the governor general and the provincial governors and admission of Indians to the Civil Service. The Indian Association, formed in 1876 under the leadership of S. N. Banerjea, listed among its aims the creation of a strong body of public opinion and the inclusion of the masses. It also made a direct appeal for student membership and support. The extent of student response is indicated by an official's complaint that "the current of opinion among the educated natives of Bengal is . . . largely swayed by the views held by schoolboys."[8]

In Madras the Mahajana Sabha addressed itself to more specific issues: the economic condition of the peasants, the working social self-government, and the efficiency of the judicial system. In the Bombay Presidency, the Poona Sarvajanik Sabha emphasized the need for Indian representation at all levels of government, including members in the British Parliament. Such sentiments are not revolutionary in the sense that they indicate a desire to overthrow the established order by force, but their fulfillment would certainly have undermined the government of India as it was constituted at the time.

Ilbert Bill

Sir Richard Temple, the lieutenant governor of Bengal surveying the activities of the political associations in 1876, remarked, "they indicate a stir of thought and movement in the national mind."[9] How justified Temple was in his use of the phrase "the national mind" was demonstrated in the early 1880s after the appointment of Lord Ripon as governor general (1880-1884). Ripon was known to be sympathetic on moral ground with Indian aspirations, but he was also convinced that unless steps were taken to unite their interests with those of the government there would be increasing bitterness and estrangement, making British rule impossible. The reforms that Ripon proposed as a way of granting some measure of participation were moderate, but all were important to Indian public opinion.

The proposed reforms centered on four issues: the Vernacular Press Act, the Arms Act, rules for entrance into the Indian Civil Service, and right of Indian judges to hear criminal cases involving Europeans. The Vernacular Press Act of 1878 had made provisional the censorship of journals published in Indian languages and had been a direct response to the growing criticism of the government in newspapers that had proliferated throughout the country. The Act had been regarded as an illiberal measure in England as well as in India, as it seemed like such a clear denial of the freedom of speech which was regarded as a hallmark of British life. Ripon's government announced its intention of abandoning the Act, but in subsequent years other administrations had to modify the commitment to a free press. Freedom of the press had been an issue through the nineteenth century, and many thoughtful observers argued that a genuinely free press was possible only in a society where people had the right to change their governors, not in a country like India where the government's power could not be challenged. That the press was as free as it was in India is one of the curiosities of British rule, for far more latitude was allowed to newspapers than is the case in many independent countries today. The essential nature of Indian nationalism can be explained to a considerable extent by the possibility of public opinion finding expression even when there were no institutions of responsible government. The Arms Act, which also dated from 1878, required that all firearms be licensed except those owned by Europeans. One might have supposed that it would have been of much less interest to educated Indian opinion, but in fact it was widely criticized by speakers and writers, many of whom probably had little interest in either hunting or self-defense. What they found especially distasteful about both the Vernacular Press Act and the Arms Act was that they revealed a widespread mistrust of Indians dating from the uprisings of 1857 and a pervasive racism that was increasingly characteristic of the attitudes of many Englishmen towards Indians. Racism is not an invention of the late nineteenth century, but there is no doubt that it finds more frequent expression then than at any previous time in the relationship between Europeans and Indians, and it is of peculiar importance in the context of the Indian demand for participation in political power. So symbolic was the Arms Act of this racism that Ripon was not able to amend it. Another issue that was of enormous interest to Indians who had been educated under the new system of university education were proposals for changes in the rules governing entry into the Indian Civil Service, the locus of power within the political structure. Technically it was possible for Indians to be admitted into the Civil Service, but since the examinations were given in England, and based on a wholly British curriculum, the hurdles for Indians were so great that it is surprising that by the 1880s even a few had managed to make it. Again, it seems clear that racism and fear of sharing power with Indians were major factors. So strong was the opposition that even the slight concession of raising the age limit to give Indian candidates a better chance to prepare for the examinations could not be made.

The proposed measure of reform that created the greatest furor was the Ilbert Bill, named after the Law Member who was its author. The issue was the existing rule that if Europeans were brought to trial in a criminal court they had the right to be tried by a European judge. The Ilbert Bill was intended to remove this distinction between British and Indian judges.

From the beginning of his term of office it was apparent that Ripon would be faced with great opposition in his attempts to extend the principles of British liberalism to India. It came from the members of the India Council in London, the advisers of the secretary of state, who were opposed to the liberalism of the Gladstone ministry; from the Civil Service in India; but overwhelmingly from the British business community residing in India. The Ilbert Bill was the special target of attack. Much was made of the untrustworthiness of Indians and especially the danger confronting an Englishwoman brought before an Indian judge. All of this can be seen as the attempt by a minority to maintain their privileges or as an expression of racism, which indeed it was. But there was more than this involved in the issue: The British community in India was exhibiting what can be thought of as a different sort of nationalism. The British were making claims for themselves as rulers in the same fashion that white settlers in Rhodesia and Algeria have done in our own time. At this time there were only 89,798 Europeans in India, of whom 55,760 were in the army; but the few thousand businessmen, planters, and professional people manifested a fierce passion against Indian participation in the administration. Much of their anger was directed against the British government for betraying them, and there was even talk of the settlers setting up an independent Indian state, which would be the true guardian of British interests.

In the end the outcry against the Ilbert Bill from the British community was so great that Ripon felt compelled to withdraw it. The Anglo-Indians, as the British residents in India were called, had shown it was possible to control the government of India from India itself as well as from England. This was what an Indian editor had in mind when he thanked the British residents in India "who in one short year taught their Indian fellow subjects that determination and sustained action in support of a cause deeply felt could be invincible."[10]

Seen against this background, the decision in 1885 to organize the association that became the Indian National Congress was a logical expression of the sense of national identity of the Indian educated classes. The need was obvious for a central organization of some kind to coordinate the activities of the hundreds of local associations formed throughout the country to discuss politics and to mobilize their members for more effective pressure on the government. From the very start there was a curious sense of destiny, a belief that the Congress marked a new day in Indian life. The president of the Congress called it "the first National Assembly ever yet convened in India," stressing that "not only were all parts of India represented, but also most classes; there were barristers, solicitors, pleaders, merchants, landowners, bankers, medical men, newspaper editors and proprietors; principals and professors . . . religious teachers and reformers."[11] A critic might have noticed the absence of members of the urban working class or peasants, but then they would also have been absent from any similar gathering almost anywhere else in the world in 1885. The Congress was a remarkably representative cross-section of educated India, and that was what it claimed to be.

The successes and failures of the Congress, which has one of the longest records of continuous existence of any political party anywhere in the world, are rooted in its origins. Since the beginning its leaders sought not so much a consensus as the identification of issues that would be of interest to a wide spectrum of opinion, and they endeavored to find a formula that would not alienate any specific groups. For this reason social reforms did not occupy a significant place in the Congress platform. The complexities of the political society have always been obvious; the problem has been to give those complexities an expression that would present actual possibilities of political action. In 1885 this involved defining a program that would appeal to the social and intellectual groups interested in politics, almost all of whom, as emphasized earlier, were in some sense "collaborationists," in that they were involved in the new political and economic society associated with British rule in India. They were "modern" men, in that they preferred the Western, or modern, forms of political institutions to those of traditional India. It was this preference, not servility, that made Dadabhai Naoroji declare that the Congress, so far from being a nursery for sedition or rebellion against the British government, was "another stone in the foundation of the stability of that Government."[12]

That the nationalists had no desire to replace the political arrangements created by the British with those that had existed previously highlights the ambiguities and dilemmas of Indian nationalism. The nationalists were espousing the values of the foreign rulers' political system, not opposing them. Their criticism of the British was that they had not extended these values in full measure to India. Nor were they as wholehearted in the acceptance of their own past as nationalists often are. Most of them were very critical of many aspects of their society, and their criticisms were frequently the same as those made by Westerners. In addition to this intellectual and emotional acceptance of the value of Western rule, they were convinced that the only way to move toward participation was

Defining a Nation: India on the Eve of Independence, 1945

through granting of their requests by the English, since they did not have the power to demand them or to take them by force.[13]

The resolutions passed by the Indian National Congress in 1885 and at its annual meetings throughout the next ten years sum up the particular concerns of the groups constituting political India. They asked for an installment of representative government through an increased Indian representation in the legislative councils of the governor general and the governors. They wanted the Civil Service to be made more accessible to Indians through examinations held in India as well as in London. The government's expenditure on military operations outside India and in frontier wars was condemned, but at the same time a plea was made for Indians to have the right to become officers in the army. The poverty of the masses was always stressed, with its causes located in the economic policies of the government, especially the high tax on land and the free-trade policy, which deprived Indian industry of all protective duties.

These interpretations of India's needs represented the areas of agreement among the diverse elements for which the leadership of the Indian National Congress spoke. They concealed growing tensions, both in the nationalist movement itself and in the fabric of Indian society. While rooted in Indian social and political life, these were, in the particular forms in which they manifested themselves in the last years of the nineteenth century, the direct product line of the Congress' success in creating, however tentatively, a nationalist ideology. Two areas of tension were of immediate concern. One was the result of the emergence of B. G. Tilak (1856-1920) to a position of leadership in the Congress; the other was the tentative formulation of a rival Muslim nationalism by Syed Ahmad Khan (1817-1898) and other Muslim leaders.

B. G. Tilak

B. G. Tilak's place in modern Indian history is based on his use of religion and regional loyalties as vitalizing forces for the nationalist movement. He was regarded by many of his contemporaries as a reactionary religious revivalist, rejecting the modern world in favor of the world of the past. But in the perspective of nationalist movements elsewhere and of later Indian political life itself, Tilak can be seen as being more open to the forces that were shaping the future than the liberal leaders—men like S. N. Banerjea, Naoroji, and his great rival in Bombay, G. K. Gokhale. Tilak understood, as they did not, that, to be effective, nationalism had to be grounded in the emotions and needs of the people and that it must squarely identify and challenge its enemy.

His main weapon—journalism in Marathi, the language of his region—was the product of the new age, but there were many sides to his crusades to create a patriotism colored by Indian, not Western, assumptions. Striking use was made of the traditional Hindu religious festivals as occasions for patriotic speeches and political education. Tilak saw that these old institutions could be made to serve nationalist aspirations in an effective way. If instead of starting new associations, he wrote, "we give a more or less new turn to the old institutions, then they will in all probability become popular and soon they will be permanent."[14]

This shrewd understanding of the possibilities of using old forms for new political purposes was also seen in his support of the Cow Protection Societies. The cow in India, contrary to the common label, is not regarded as "sacred." She is, however, the symbol and touchstone for many of the deepest emotions of Hindu experience. As a symbol of fertility and of the bounty of nature, the cow was inextricably bound up with religious emotions, becoming not so much sacred, at least in the Western sense, as a mother symbol. All killing is deprecated, and an orthodox Hindu would see little more reason to kill and eat a cow than to practice cannibalism. The cow was an accessible symbol for Hinduism, which is very amorphous and hard to define. The cow protection movement was a call to protect Hindu society from its enemies, who were, in effect, the same as the enemies of the cow— the British and the Muslims. The same complex appeal to religion and sentiment was apparent in Tilak's emphasis on the allegory of Sivaji, the Maratha chieftain who had waged a successful war against the Mughal Empire in the seventeenth century. As Sivaji drove out the Muslims, so could the Indians drive out the British.

Tilak's nationalism was not only anti-British, it was also by implication, if not always directly, anti-Muslim. Emphasis on the greatness of the past, a common feature of all nationalist movements, meant the Hindu past—a bitterly anti-Muslim past—with Sivaji as hero. Such an emphasis in itself would be enough to create uneasiness or hostility among Muslims, and the proof of this was the growing number of outbreaks of violence between Hindus and Muslims. But aside from this, many Muslim leaders had, almost from the beginning, regarded the Indian National Congress as a threat to their own hopes and aspirations.

Muslim Movements

MILITANT ISLAM

The rigidities of Islamic intellectual conventions had never precluded intellectual ferment, and a number of movements of great importance had been at work in the Muslim community of India long before the formal expression of modern nationalism. During the decay of the political power of the Mughals in the eighteenth century, Shah Wali Ullah (1703-1762) had sought to unite all Muslims in a common loyalty to their faith. He emphasized the centrality of the Koranic teachings and traditions that all Muslims shared and stressed the need for religious unity in a time when political power was no longer a dependable defense. His son Shah Abdul Aziz (1746-1824) spelled out the implications for Muslims of the British conquest. India had ceased to be Dar-al-Islam, the "Home of Islam," and had become Dar-al-Harb, the "Home of War," where Muslims could no longer practice Islam in peace. The duty of pious Muslims was, therefore, to restore Islam by driving out the non-Muslim rulers. His spiritual successors carried on *jihad*, or holy war, from bases on the northwest frontier, first against the Sikh rulers of the Punjab, then, after their defeat, against the British. While they were not able to organize an effective challenge to the British, they kept alive a sense of Islamic separatism and, through nostalgia for past glories, a hope for the future restoration of Islamic rule.

Such Islamic movements were fiercely opposed to any accommodation, political or intellectual, with the new order. Their belief in a return to the primal purity of Islamic faith and their insistence that Islam could only develop in a state where Islamic religion and political power were one made any cooperation with the British impossible. In other contexts a group so firmly grounded in an ideological position might have been expected to serve as a vital organizing force for a nationalist movement that could have challenged foreign rule. They could not fulfill this function in India because of their inability to make any alliances with the other sources of leadership and power within Indian society. The aims of militant Islam had as little place for the liberals of the Indian National Congress as for the extremists of Hindu revivalism. The uprising of 1857 had shown how tenuous were the common interests of the different groups. The failure of the uprisings had further embittered the Muslim leaders and added to their frustrations: Not only were the British secure, but in many areas power was passing to the Hindus, notably to the Bengalis.

ISLAMIC MODERNISM

This leads to a fundamental point for understanding the content and character of the new Muslim nationalism: the change in the position of the Muslims relative to the Hindus. Statistically it is possible to show that in north India Muslims had more than their share of government jobs in proportion to their numbers. But the emotional reality is that the Muslims saw the tide beginning to turn. Public opinion among Muslims represented the views of a small group that realized Muslims everywhere were losing their old positions of leadership. They wanted, in other words, neither proportional power nor parity; they wanted to restore their lost heritage. It is in the complexities of this situation that Syed Ahmad Khan did his seminal work

Syed Ahmad Khan was a member of the old official class of the Mughal Empire. He had entered the service of the British regime as a legal officer, and he gained recognition for his support of the government during the uprisings in 1857. Convinced that the only hope for a tolerable future for Indian Muslims, especially for those of the class to which he belonged, was to come to a reasonable compromise with the British, he tried, on the one hand, to persuade the British that the Muslims were not compelled by religious and historical sentiment to oppose British rule. On the other hand, he tried to persuade the Muslim leadership that they must adjust themselves to the new patterns of administration and government. Both goals could be accomplished by the same method: the acceptance of Western education. This would show the

British that Muslims intended to accept the changed conditions of society, and at the same time it would restore Muslims to their place of authority and prestige.

Syed Ahmad Khan argued that such an accommodation entailed no denial of Islamic doctrine. Like Rani Mohan Roy he believed the seeming conflicts between religion and the new learning were caused by corruptions that had been added to the pure original traditions, and a major part of his apologetic was to urge the rejection of many Islamic practices and beliefs then current on the grounds that they did not find support in the Koran. The way to the future was to combine the science of Europe with the learning and culture of Islam. This advocacy of accepting the best of both worlds was institutionalized in the new college he founded at Aligarh, which soon became an important training center for Muslims who sought freedom from the frustrations of a defeated society through involvement in the new order.

Such freedom was not to be found, Syed Ahmad Khan warned his followers, through participation in the nationalist movement represented by the Indian National Congress. His objection was fundamental: The aims and objectives of the Congress were "based upon an ignorance of history and present-day realities; they do not take into consideration that India is inhabited by different nationalities." These nationalities spoke different languages, professed different religions, followed different customs, and had different historical traditions. This explicit denial of the Congress' faith in one nation carried with it further challenges to the whole nationalist position. He denied that representative political institutions could find root in India's soil, since they were completely alien to her traditions, Hindu or Muslim. India needed a strong, autocratic government to maintain order between the contending nationalities, and this role was admirably fulfilled by the British. Representative rule meant majority rule: the subjection of the Muslim minority to the Hindu majority. But this would lead to suffering for more than the Muslims, for, he said, "Muslims are prone to take the sword in hand when the majority oppresses them."[15]

On the surface Syed Ahmad Khan's deference to the British resembles the Indian National Congress leaders' insistence on their loyalty and devotion, but there is an important difference. Men like Dadabhai Naoroji supported British rule because of their conviction that it promised representative, constitutional government for India. Syed Ahmad had no such vision for India; he was an authoritarian aristocrat, believing in strong paternal rule. A. O. Hume's accusation that Syed Ahmad and his fellows "in their hearts hate British rule"[16] sounds absurd in the light of their almost obsequious praises of the British, but it contains an interesting insight.

In much writing on British rule, it is frequently asserted that the British got along better with Muslims than they did with Hindus, and there is a tedious repetition of the comparison between the "manly" Muslim, especially on the Frontier, and the intellectualized and "effeminate" Bengali Brahman. There is remarkably little evidence, however, from Muslims that they returned this high regard. To take an example from a later stage of nationalism, Jinnah was far more bitter in his comments on the British than was Nehru. Sir Syed in his writings, in a guarded way, sometimes expresses what must have been his own real feeling for the English. He notes that Muslim officials in government service, when they are forced to put up with abuse from arrogant British superiors, exclaim to themselves, "Oh, that I could gain my living otherwise, cutting grass by the wayside were better than this."[17]

The aristocratic class accepted the inevitability of British rule as a political fact, but, consciously or not, they must have hoped for a restoration of Muslim power. Nothing went so certainly against the grain of such a hope as the Congress demands.

Syed Ahmad Khan's rejection of majority rule had been foreshadowed in a controversy, in which he and other Muslim leaders had long been involved, between Hindi, the most commonly used language of the northern Hindus, and Urdu, the language most commonly used by the Muslims. Urdu was widely used in the law courts of north India, but in 1867 an agitation started for its replacement by Hindi. The argument was that Hindi, written in the Devanagri script, not Urdu, using the Arabic script, was the language known to the majority of the people. The differences between the two languages themselves was not very great, but the two scripts were totally different. Devanagri was associated with Sanskrit and Hindu culture; the Arabic script with Muslim rule and culture. The demand for Hindi was thus part of the general resurgence of Hindu culture, and when the government of Bengal responded by making Hindi the official language in the courts of the Bihar districts, Muslims objected strongly. They saw that more was involved than just prestige: The replacement of Urdu meant loss of employment for Muslims and an increase in the employment of Hindus. Syed Ahmad Khan's conclusion was that it was no longer possible for the two nations to be "partners with each other in any common enterprise."[18]

TRADITIONAL ISLAM

A very different approach came from a group of Muslims associated with a school for Islamic studies that had been founded at Deoband, a small town north of Delhi, after the 1857 uprisings. The scholars there maintained a traditional Islamic training that aimed, not at reconciliation with the modern world, but freedom from it. The hopelessness of armed revolt had been demonstrated in 1857, but the alternative was not acceptance of the conqueror. The Deoband school disagreed profoundly with Syed Ahmad Khan and the other modernizers who argued that the salvation of Islam was in rapprochement with the British. For this reason, when Syed Ahmad Khan denounced the Indian National Congress and urged Muslims not to participate in it, the Deoband leaders issued a *fatwa*, a formal statement based on religious law, contradicting him. In secular affairs, it argued, cooperation with Hindus was permissible. Thus a curious situation developed in which the Aligarh group, who followed policies in many ways very similar to those of the liberals who had founded the Congress, were estranged from it, while the traditionalists, so antithetical in their religious and social views, if they did not actually support the Congress, at least did not oppose it. In the end it was the spiritual descendants of the Aligarh movement who favored the creation of Pakistan, while the Deoband group opposed it.[19]

*   *   *

At the end of the century the various internal tensions necessary to a definition of nationality in the Indian context had thus become active, demanding attention and consideration. Virtually every stand that constitutes the fabric of present-day Indian political life was clearly visible: the "moderates" arguing for compromises phrased according to the vocabulary of Western constitutionalism; the "extremists" insisting on solutions that recognized the cultural dominance of the Hindu tradition; and, finally, the anxieties of Muslims, still unfocused, but powerful in their negative statements. All of these reacted to what may be thought of as an external force: the responses of the government of India, and beyond it, the British government. Out of this amalgam came the shifting, uncertain search for nationality in the first two decades of the new century.

NOTES

1. Pherozeshah Mehta, "Presidential Address," 1890, in *The Indian National Congress* (Madras: G.A. Natesan, 1909), 86.

2. Sir Thomas Raleigh, ed., *Lord Curzon in India* (London: Macmillan, 1906), 486-487.

3. Ibid., 585.

4. Anil Seal, *The Emergence of Indian Nationalism* (Cambridge: Cambridge University Press, 1968), 9.

5. Bankim Chandra Chatterji, *Anandamath*, in *Sources of Indian Tradition*, William Theodore de Bary et. al., eds. (New York: Columbia University Press, 1958), 709-714.

6. Quoted in Seal, *Emergence of Indian Nationalism*, 147.

7. Quoted in B. B. Majumdar, *Indian Political Associations and Reform of Legislature (1818-1917)* (Calcutta: Firma K.L. Mukhopadhyay, 1965), 34.

8. Quoted in Seal, Emergence of Indian Nationalism, p, 217.

9. Ibid., p, 205.

10. Quoted in Christine Dobbin, "The Ilbert Bill: A study of Anglo-Indian Opinion in 1883," *Historical Studies: Australia and New Zealand*, Vol. 12 (1965), p. 122.

11. Report of the First Indian National Congress Held at Bombay on 28, 29, and 30 December 1885 (Lucknow, 1886).

12. Dadabhai Naoroji, "Presidential Address," 1886, in *The Indian National Congress*, 7.

13. Ainslie T, Embree, "Pledged to India : The Liberal Experiment, 1885-1909," in *The Political Culture of Modern Britain; Studies in the Memory of Stephen Koss*, edited by Malcolm Bean (London: Hamish Hamilton, 1987), is an examination of the relationship of the Indian nationalist leadership to British Liberalism.

14. Quoted in Stanley Wolpert, *Tilak and Gokhale* (Berkeley: University of California Press, 1961), 68.

15. de Bary, *Sources of Indian Tradition*, 68.

16. Quoted in I. H. Qureshi, *The Struggle for Pakistan* (Karachi: Karachi University Press, 1965), 25.

17. Sir Syed Ahmed Khan, "The Causes of the Indian Revolt," in Sir Sayyid Ahmed Khan, *History of the Bijnor Rebellion*, translated by Hafeez Malik and Morris Dembo (East Lansing: Asian Studies Centre, Michigan State University, n.d.) 141.

18. Quoted in Hafeez Malik, *Moslem Nationalism in India and Pakistan* (Washington: Public Affairs Press, 1963), 210.

19. This issue is studied in Barbara Daly Metcalf, *Islamic Revivalism in British India, 1860-1900* (Princeton: Princeton University Press, 1982) and in David Lelyveld, *Aligarh's First Generation: Muslim Solidarity in British India* (Princeton: Princeton University Press, 1982).

CHAPTER 3. SEARCH FOR A CENTER

The first phase of the nationalist movement ended with challenges to the compromises of the moderates from two directions: the resurgent Hindu nationalism represented by Tilak and the Muslim reaction led by Syed Ahmad Khan. The second phase, from 1898 to 1917, was marked by an increasing articulation of the tensions within Indian society and, to counter this, a search for positions that could replace the compromises of 1885. In this search for a center the government of India was a more active participant than it had been in the first period.

In nationalist rhetoric the imperial power is often seen as a wholly negative force, whose contribution to nationalism is primarily the provision of an antagonist, compelling the nationalist leaders to harden their positions and redefine their goals. This view ignores the creative potential in the existing political structure actually to shape the form and content of nationalist activity. This potential existed in India, especially in the period from 1898 to 1917. The first date marks the beginning of the seven-year administration of Lord Curzon as governor general and the second, the announcement in August 1917 that Britain's aim in India was the establishment of responsible government. Within these limits a number of government actions gave nationalist opinion new causes and new motivations, but at the same time the political life of India was subjected to modifications that provided what was in effect a new framework for nationalist agitations. Some of these changes, such as the partition of Bengal, are associated primarily with Curzon's administration, whereas the constitutional reforms of 1909 reflect the interplay of Indian nationalism, the government of India, and the responses of the British government in London.

Curzon Era

At the end of Lord Curzon's term of office as governor general, a spokesman for the moderate, liberal group in the Indian National Congress referred to Curzon with distaste as an "Asiatic Viceroy." "He has forgotten English methods of ruling India and is daily growing in love with Asiatic ways of ruling. . . . This Viceroy will leave the country the most odious and hated."[1] It is curious that an Asian nationalist should denounce a foreign ruler because that ruler was behaving according to the political customs of Asia, not of England, but it is indicative of the orientation of the liberal nationalists.

The irony of Curzon's reputation with the nationalists is that many of the goals for which he had worked were precisely those necessary for a country moving toward nationhood. The record of his administration justifies his claim that his policy had been one of the payment of due regard to Indian authority in the determination of India's needs. Insistence on the autonomy of the government of India led to clashes with the British government in which he was the loser on two notable occasions. One was his assertion of the influence of the government of India over Tibet, which was disavowed by the British government; the other was his quarrel with Lord Kitchener over the powers of the commander in chief of the army. When he was not supported by the British Cabinet, Curzon resigned, arguing that any weakening of civilian control over the armed forces could lead to military dictatorship.

But in his emphasis on bureaucratic efficiency, Curzon had neither sympathy nor understanding for the nationalist demand for Indian participation in the governmental process. The result was a series of administrative changes that combined with his contemptuous dismissal of Indian democratic aspirations to deepen the growing cleavage between the government and the nationalist leaders. At the same time the reaction to the Curzon policies tended to make more visible the divisions within Indian society itself. Three of these policy decisions were of particular importance in activating Indian political life. One of these decisions involved the municipal boards set up by Lord Ripon in 1882 to introduce an element of self-government and elected representation to many towns and cities. The boards worked with varying success and often were dominated by government officials, but in the great cities the elected members had gained considerable power. This was especially true in Calcutta, where members of the Indian National Congress were strongly represented. The Calcutta municipal corporation might have justified itself as an exercise in self-government, but Calcutta had already become one of the most unmanageable cities in the world, with vast areas of slums unserved by even minimal municipal services. Curzon blamed this on the inefficiency and irresponsibility of the elected members, and in 1899 he had an act passed cutting the elected membership from 66 percent to 50 percent and giving the major share of the power to British officials. The plea of the nationalists that Indians should have a major voice in the government of their own city was answered with quick brutality by a European member of the Legislative Council.

> Commerce made Calcutta. By Commerce I mean European commerce. . . . The history of Calcutta shows it to have been little more than a mud bank until European merchants settled there. The present Bengali population who clamour for the Government of Calcutta are not for the most part natives of the place. . . . The interests of Government and of Foreign Commerce are more important than all other interests put together. [2]

Given this attitude on the part of the Europeans, it is no wonder that Indian members of the Legislative Council regarded the act as a threat to an orderly advance toward responsible government.

Another political decision of the Curzon regime that angered the nationalists was the reorganization in 1904 of the governing bodies of the Indian universities. The universities were largely self-governing through senates made up of representatives of colleges, most of whom were Indian and many of whom identified with the nationalist movement. The Universities, like the other measures, aimed at tightening British control and giving the government a larger share in management. Again this act was denounced by Indian leaders as a direct attack on the educated classes. The moderates were in despair, with their faith in British intentions increasingly undermined, much to the satisfaction of their extremist opponents.

The administrative action of Curzon's regime that had the most far-reaching effect, however, was undoubtedly the partition of Bengal into two provinces in 1905. For a number of years there had been complaints from officials that it was too large to be administered as a separate province. With a population of 78 million, it was larger than most countries, as it included what is now West Bengal, Bangladesh, Bihar and Orissa. The origin of the province was the *suba* of the Mughal empire which the East India Company had acquired in 1765 and to which other territories had been added as they were annexed in the early years of the nineteenth century. The reorganization, in which Bengal lost about eleven million of its population to the new province of East Bengal and Assam, could be viewed, therefore, as a sensible administrative measure. The Indian nationalist leaders, however, saw it as a peculiarly sinister action on the part of the British to weaken nationalism in general and Bengali nationalism in particular. Responding to the increasing frustration of even the moderate leaders as they failed to win concessions from the British, as well as to the militant revolutionary fervor that was building up in Bengal and elsewhere, the agitation against petition by the leaders of the Indian National Congress helped to alter the temper and direction of the nationalist movement. Nowhere else in India was there such a close identification of geographic area and nationalist sentiment, and the partition seemed to be a rending of that motherland of which Bankim Chandra Chatterji had sung in *Bande Mataram*. It was also a blow to the dominance of the Calcutta intelligentsia—the teachers, the lawyers, the journalists, the novelists and poets—who had made the city the intellectual capital, not just of the vast hinterland of Bengal, but of all India. And finally, although this was not always made explicit in the denunciations of the partition, the new East Bengal would have a Muslim majority, and many of the nationalists were Hindus who had their ancestral ties there. By this time there was a growing suspicion that the British administration were encouraging the Muslims to see the Indian National Congress with its nationalist ideology as a threat to the Muslims in the community. From this point on, the argument that the British used the Muslims in a strategy of "Divide and Conquer" becomes an essential ingredient of that ideology. The reaction on the part of Muslim leaders to this Congress attack on the partition of Bengal was almost inevitable: they saw it as proof that the Congress was unwilling to give Muslims an opportunity for political control.

Curzon had a clear perception of the political consequences of partition: an inevitable clash between the imperial power and the nationalists. He had no doubt of the outcome or of its desirability. The government believed that the agitation against partition represented only the small Western-educated minority in Calcutta and argued that "it cannot be for the lasting good of any country that public opinion or what passes for it should be manufactured by a comparatively small number of people at a single center and should be disseminated thence for universal adoption." The very strength of the opposition to the partition by the articulate Hindu upper classes underlined its value for some officials. It would restrict Nationalist areas of influence, while providing the Muslims opportunity to regain some of the status they had lost through Hindu economic and intellectual domination based in Calcutta. The Muslims, it was assumed, would reciprocate by showing a firm attachment to the government.

Partition put new vitality into the nationalists' cause by providing an opportunity for a defiant challenge to imperial power. There were many sources of this challenge, not all of which were coordinated, and some of which worked at cross-purposes. Numerous secret societies, which amalgamated religious devotion and nationalist fervor, had been formed in the last years of the nineteenth century. Most of them were in Bengal, but there were a number in Bombay, where B. G. Tilak's influence was strong, and in Punjab, where the British suspected the eminent Indian National Congress leader, Lala Lajpat Rai, of being involved in terrorist activities.

New Radicalism

Indian nationalists began to wonder if India might not also be stirred by a Japanese defeat of Russia in 1905. Now that a great Western power had been humiliated by a small Asian nation, Indians—and not just Bengali revolutionaries—began to wonder if India might not be able to repeat the Japanese experience and use force to defeat Great Britain. The dreams of the revolutionaries were also fed by the militant religious nationalism of Aurobindo Ghose and his followers, and for the first time since 1857 the government was faced with political assassinations and acts of sabotage. The secret societies responsible for these activities probably never enrolled more than a few thousand members, most of whom were young students, but they provided a genuine alternative to the political gradualism of the Indian National Congress.

An interesting aspect of the 1905 movement, and one that was supported by many people who had no sympathy for the terrorists, was a campaign to replace British goods of all kinds with those manufactured in India. The emphasis on *swadeshi*, things belonging to India, which was intended to strengthen the Indian economy while at the same time hurting the British, indicates a concern to give the nationalist movement a more indigenous base. The *swadeshi* movement and the boycott were concrete manifestations of an economic interpretation of modern Indian history that by this time was widely accepted by nationalists. In barest outline, the argument was that the poverty of India had been caused by British rule. Aside from the historical accuracy of this judgment, its value to a nationalist movement is obvious: The poverty and economic backwardness of

India were due not to anything inherent in Indian society, but to the foreign intrusion. It was especially important to the early nationalist leaders because they had so genuinely accepted what may be called the nineteenth-century political interpretation of Indian history: The British had saved India from anarchy and chaos and given her peace and order. Thus it was no accident that the most telling criticisms of the economic effect of British rule came from Dadabhai Naoroji and R. C. Dutt, to both of whom, in Dutt's phrase, "the Indian Empire was the grandest of human institutions." Naoroji popularized the idea of "The Drain," the idea that Indian wealth flowed to England in the form of high salaries paid to the governing class and in the great excess of India's exports over her imports. In the previous forty years £500 million worth of goods had been drained to England, he estimated in 1901. Here was the remedy for all of India's economic ills: Let her keep what she produces; let her use her own raw materials, instead of shipping them out of the country and then buying them back as finished goods. Like Naoroji, Dutt backed the arguments in his survey of nineteenth-century economic history with an impressive array of statistics, coming to the conclusion that because of British policies India was given "peace but not prosperity: . . .the manufacturers lost their industries; . . . the cultivators were ground down by a heavy and variable taxation; . . . the revenues were to a large extent diverted to England; and . . . recurring famines swept away millions of the population."[4]

The *swadeshi* movement in 1905 was thus an assertion of both spiritual and material independence, based on a reasoned, although perhaps fallacious, understanding of the working of economic forces. The extremists, contemptuous of the caution of the moderates, pressed for an unequivocal statement of support from the Indian National Congress for *swadeshi* and the idea of self-rule. The old liberal leadership compromised in 1906 by accepting a resolution that gave limited support to the boycott of British goods and the *swadeshi* ideals, but they insisted on reserving the right of interpretation of the meaning of the resolution. The Congress, Gokhale said, had "no aspirations except such as may be realized within the British Empire." This may have been true for the majority of the leadership, but the restless dynamism of the new nationalism spoke for the younger intelligentsia and the students, who by this time had become, in modern terms, politicized. "We have perceived one fact," Tilak declared, "that the whole of this administration, which is carried by a handful of Englishmen, is carried on with our assistance. . . . The point is to have the entire control in our hands."[5] A confrontation with imperial power was necessary, but this could be achieved through a boycott, without recourse to arms. Violence was not ruled out as a possible future weapon, but it was accepted that British power was too strong to be challenged. This belief in British invulnerability is a very important factor in explaining the quiescence of India.

The open clash between the moderates and the extremists came at the meeting of the Indian National Congress at Surat in 1907. The members of the New Party, as Tilak's followers were called, were ousted by the moderates, who demanded a pledge of loyalty to the old program of strictly constitutional action for reform of the existing administration. Tilak's followers did not form a separate organization as they still hoped to gain control of the Congress, but Tilak's imprisonment on a charge of encouraging sedition deprived them of their most experienced leader. The price the Congress paid for the formal unity imposed by the moderates was, however, a loss of vitality.

At the same time the tensions that had generated the divisions in the Indian National Congress itself were having repercussions on Muslim leaders. The new radicalism, with its scarcely veiled appeal to violence as the most effective road to Indian freedom, and the quasi-religious vocabulary in which it expressed its aspirations, caused disquiet among Indian Muslims. Syed Ahmad Khan's forebodings that the nationalist movement pointed toward Hindu domination seemed confirmed, for an important element in the fierce antagonism aroused by the partition of Bengal was the charge by the Indian National Congress that the government had created a province in Eastern Bengal with a Muslim majority. The denunciation of the partition by the Congress, whose leadership was overwhelmingly Hindu, had been countered by Muslims in Eastern Bengal with expressions of support for the measure and in some areas by anti-Hindu riots. These outbreaks frequently had roots in the economic grievances of the peasants, but since the peasants were largely Muslim and the landlords were Hindus, the outbreaks easily assumed a religious character. Added to this sentiment of the economically disadvantaged was the dislike by members of the Muslim upper classes of Hindu political and social power. This latter group formed in 1906 the Muslim League, which challenged the claims of the Congress to speak for the nation by insisting that Muslims constituted a separate nationality.

Muslim League

The importance of the Bengal partition for Muslim sentiment has been bluntly stated by I. H. Qureshi, one of the most influential historians of modern Pakistan: "The Hindu attitude during the anti-partition agitation had convinced the Muslims of the futility of expecting any justice or fair play from the Hindu majority."[6] This harsh judgment has been challenged on the grounds that it is not based on sufficient evidence of Hindu behavior and that it ignores the government's policy of "divide and conquer," but these criticisms are irrelevant since Qureshi's statement reflects quite accurately how many Muslims appraised the situation. This anti-Hindu element was probably as essential for the development of Muslim nationalism in India as was the more positive expression of identity between religious and patriotic values within the Congress for Indian nationalism itself.

The founders of the Muslim League were not the Muslim counterparts of the founders of the Indian National Congress, for they represented the landlords and the old Muslim ruling classes rather than the new professions created by the Western impact. As already stressed, this was a reflection of differences between Hindu and Islamic social organization. The Muslims who formed the League had prided themselves on staying out of politics, and their activity in 1906 was an indication that political activity could no longer be avoided. It was precisely this kind of political action that had been anathema to the older generation of Muslim leaders represented by Syed Ahmad Khan, who had envisaged ideal government in terms of rulers acting benevolently for the welfare of the people, not as a process of negotiating demands and applying pressures. The formation of the League indicated the conversion of the Muslim leaders to the new style of political life.

The objectives of the Muslim League as outlined in 1906 indicate the groping of the Muslim leaders for new policies for dealing with the government and the Hindu majority. Their desire "to promote among the Mussulmans of India feelings of loyalty to the British Government and to remove any misconceptions that may arise as to the intentions of Government" was a tacit recognition that both British suspicions of Muslims and Muslim dislike of British rule had to be eradicated. The protection and advance of the political rights and interests of Indian Muslims and their representation to the government expressed the conviction that Muslims must assert their special status. They were not a minority, but a nation. A final objective was "to prevent the rise among Mussulmans of India of any feelings of hostility towards other communities." A curious saving rider was attached to this: "without prejudice to other objects of the League."[7] The phrasing is ambiguous, but it probably recognizes that the assertion of Muslim rights might lead to Hindu-Muslim strife, and if so, the claiming of rights could not be forgone for the sake of communal harmony.

Constitutional Reforms

A conflict of interest was always latent in the Indian National Congress demand for representative institutions, and it became of central importance when the government announced the constitutional changes known as the Morley-Minto Reforms (after the governor general, Lord Minto, and the secretary of state for India, John Morley). These were embodied in the Government of India Act of 1909, one of the landmarks of Indian constitutional history.

The government denied that the constitutional changes were a response to nationalist agitation. Minto was still insisting as late as 1906 that nationalism in India was "altogether peculiar." In Europe national leaders had the support of the great majority of their fellow countrymen, but in India "there is no popular movement from below. The movement, such as it is, is impelled by the leaders of a class very small indeed in comparison to the population of India, who, if by some miracle they obtained the reins of Government, are totally incapable of ruling and would not for an instant be tolerated by the people of India as a whole."[8] Yet despite these protestations the aim of the reforms was to ensure that Indian cooperation which made the Indian administration possible. A number of the longstanding demands of the Indian National Congress were met, at least in a partial fashion, by the Government of India Act. The legislative councils were enlarged to permit increased Indian representation; an Indian was appointed to the governor general's Executive Council, and the members were allowed to discuss the budget. The principle of election was conceded by giving the franchise to certain groups and organizations—chambers of commerce, landowners, trade associations, local governments, and universities. This was far from a democratic suffrage, but Indian opinion regarded it as the first installment of representative government. The Congress, securely controlled by moderates, expressed its thanks in 1908 for the promise of "a large and liberal installment of the reforms needed to give the people of this country a substantial share in the management of their affairs."[9]

The Government of India Act contained concessions acceptable not only to the moderate leaders of the Indian National Congress, but also to the rival Indian nationalism represented by the Muslim League. The objection by the Muslim leaders to any form of representative government was answered by the provision of special constituencies for Muslims that guaranteed them places in the central and provincial legislative councils. The Muslim League welcomed the application of what they termed the principle of separate racial representation. The use of the word "racial" is interesting, for even if the League did not intend to suggest that Muslims constituted a separate "race" in India, at least it implies that something more than religious preferences separated them from the rest of the population. The full meaning of this position was not spelled out for many years, but logically it could only lead either to a bi-national state or to partition.

Although the moderate leaders who controlled the Indian National Congress had at first welcomed the reforms of 1909, they soon denounced the provision of special representation for Muslims as subversive of Indian nationhood. That no representation was guaranteed the Hindu minorities in East Bengal, where the Muslims were in a majority, also rankled. Almost imperceptibly, the defense of Indian nationality was transformed in the discussions of 1910 into a defense of Hindu rights with regard to new Muslim privileges. The moderates, who had for so long refused to let any religious distinctions color their concept of India's nationhood, now found themselves driven to arguing in communal terms. As one speaker summed up this situation at the Congress meeting in 1910, it was not his intention to "say a word of discord. . . . At the same time . . . it will be sheer hypocrisy to deny the facts. . . . The Muhammedans have got an over-representation."[10] The proof adduced was that in the central Legislative Council there were thirteen Hindus and eleven Muslims, while the ratio in the general population was four Hindus to one Muslim.

The growing tension between Hindus and Muslims did not mean that all Muslims followed the leadership of the Muslim League. Sectarian conflicts within Islam itself were betrayed by the charge that the Muslim League was under control of the Sunnis, the main branch of Muslims, who systematically excluded the members of the Shia sect. Others saw the special electorates working against the best interests of the Muslim masses, since the most conservative groups of Muslims were favored by the property franchise. Among those who in 1910 opposed any further extension of the principle was M. A. Jinnah, who later became the spokesman for the demand for a Muslim state in Pakistan. At the time, he believed that a representative government could be established in India that was not based on religious communities. His change of mind reflected later developments in India's search for nationality, many of them the product of India's involvement in World War I, which had a decisive effect on India's national development.

In contrast to 1939, when there was such vociferous protest from nationalist leaders for India being taken into the war against Germany and other Axis powers without any consultation, there was little protest in 1914 or even discussion, as India's resources in manpower and materials were put at the disposal of the war effort. The change is partly an indication of a difference in evaluation of the international situation by the nationalist leaders. In 1914, most of them had accepted the British reading of the situation that India's international interests were identical with those of Britain, while in 1939 men like Jawaharlal Nehru, Subhas Chandra Bose, and Mahatma Gandhi had come to very different conclusions because of their ideological commitments. But the changes were also due to the fact that in 1939 India had become a far more independent and autonomous nation than it had been in 1914, with many of these changes related to the war itself. Some of these, such as the return of Gandhi to India and the emergence of India on the international scene will be noted in chapters 4 and 5, but it will be useful to mention others here, including the impact of the war on the Indian economy.

The economic effects of the First World War on India are hard to disentangle, since many changes might have taken place even without the cataclysm of the war. The general weakening of the economic and political position of Great Britain in relation to the other great powers would have made it difficult for Britain to have maintained its dominance of India. There were, however, changes that can be directly related to the war itself. An immediate impact was to make India more dependent on the British connection, for the growth of trade with other countries, which had been going on since the early years of the century, was suddenly reversed. There was a drop of 43 percent in exports and 34 percent in imports in the first year over prewar averages. This reflected both the loss of such markets as Germany, which had become India's best customer after the United Kingdom, and the diversion of shipping for war purposes. Added to this change in exports and imports was a new demand for supplies for India's own armies and those of Great Britain. The result was that prices rose very sharply for such necessities as salt, kerosene, and cotton cloth. Inflationary tendencies increased because of speculation and hoarding.

Military demands on the railways intensified the distribution problems for these commodities. And while prices of manufactured and imported goods increased, the prices paid for agricultural products went down because of good harvests, which meant that the peasants were hard hit by the rising costs. The cheap food did not help the townspeople either, because of the dislocation of the transportation system. The discontents and suffering occasioned by these economic problems were felt everywhere in India, leading to the first peasant movements under Indian National Congress sponsorship and a series of strikes in 1917 in the great cities. Perhaps more than any other single factor, the economic dislocation caused by the war explains the new openness of the masses to the political agitation initiated by the Congress under the leadership of Gandhi.

Yet at the same time that the economic conditions of the masses were worsening, there was a marked expansion in industrial productivity occasioned by the new military demands and the decrease in imports. The first important steel manufacturing company was established by the Tata family in 1903. The Tatas raised their capital from Indian sources, although they made use of American and European technicians. The achievement of large-scale production virtually coincided with the outbreak of the war, and the Tatas were able to supply large amounts of the steel formerly imported from Great Britain. Other industries, notably textiles and light engineering works, also expanded in response to military needs. The production of munitions and war materials of all kinds was encouraged by the establishment of the Munitions Board in 1917. All of these new industries were severely hit by the loss of military markets when the war ended, but they gave an impetus to industrial development that was never lost.

The expansion of the Indian army was one of the most remarkable wartime phenomena, and it had important psychological and political repercussions. At the beginning of the war the army had consisted of about 230,000 Indians and 80,000 British officers and men, but before the end of hostilities over a million men had been recruited. This was done without conscription, but local landlords in the great recruiting grounds of Punjab and the United Provinces applied pressure in the villages, while increases in pay made army service attractive to the peasants. Hundreds of thousands of these troops served overseas and throughout the Indian borderlands, breaking or disrupting the old ties that bound them to their villages and regions. The recruitment of Indians as soldiers in such large numbers and their use throughout the major theaters of war also reinforced the demand that had long been made by the Indian nationalists for the granting of officers' commissions to Indians. A tentative beginning was made in 1917 when Indians became eligible for commissions as lieutenants. The nationalist interest in the rights of Indians to receive military promotions was important in fostering a sense of respect for Indian soldiers as defenders of the nation, and not just as the mercenaries of the foreign conqueror.

Revival of Nationalist Activity

The ferment engendered throughout India by the war restored the vigor that nationalist politics had lost after the divisions created at Surat in 1907. Factions often worked at cross-purposes, and the old splits between the moderates and the extremists and between the Hindus and the Muslims were not healed, but out of their interaction came a vitality that gave a new direction to Indian nationalism. For some groups the war offered an opportunity to attack the British while they were distracted in Europe. The revolutionary bodies in Bengal and the Punjab continued their policy of political assassination and sabotage, and Indian revolutionaries in exile, notably those in the Ghadr party in the United States, gave them financial help and smuggled arms to them. The exiles received some help from the Germans, but their organization was inefficient, the British watchful, and the Germans unconcerned with India. Their subversive campaign was never really damaging. The terrorists' major accomplishment was to keep local officials off balance and make them aware of the strength of the opposition to British rule in India. The old argument that only a handful of malcontents were concerned with nationalist aspirations began to disappear from official reports, to be replaced by what is perhaps an exaggerated fear of violence and of the power of public opinion. The revolutionaries also supplied martyrs to Indian nationalism, for some of the terrorists were put to death.

The revival of the Indian National Congress as an active political force during the war years owed much to B. G. Tilak, who had been released from prison in 1914, and to a new personality in Indian nationalist life, Mrs. Annie Besant. Mrs. Besant has often been a subject of ridicule in the West, but her contribution to the Indian nationalist movement was serious and long lasting. She had gone to India in 1893 to work for the Theosophical Society, and as an outstanding orator and a writer with a gift for clear, dramatic expression, she had made theosophy a potent force in Indian intellectual life, especially in south India. Theosophy is a complex mixture of mystical symbols and doctrines, but her emphasis on the superiority of Hindu ethical and theological concepts won her a hearing among the educated classes. Although by temperament and political conviction a moderate believing in constitutional gradualism, she allied herself with Tilak in a political campaign that demanded home rule for India. Her hope was that Tilak might be taken back into the Congress, which, revitalized by his energy, could then pressure the government through popular agitation into further constitutional reforms.

Tilak confined his activities to the Marathi-speaking regions of Bombay, while Mrs. Besant used the network of Theosophical Societies already in existence to organize the most extensive propaganda campaign that had yet been attempted in India. The program of the Home Rule League was "Home Rule for India," but there was no demand for British withdrawal. Tilak was too cautious to make such a public statement, and Mrs. Besant hoped for cooperation and friendship between the British and the Indians. The success of the Home Rule League in stirring up popular opinion forced the moderate leaders of the Indian National Congress to cooperate with Tilak, and by 1916 he once more had an important voice in its decisions. His old liberal opponent Gokhale had died in 1915, leaving Tilak a position of undisputed influence in Bombay. At the same time that the factions within the Congress were reuniting, Mrs. Besant and Tilak were working for a rapprochement with the Muslim League.

Such a rapprochement was possible in 1916 because of the changes that Muslim sentiment had undergone in India since the founding of the Muslim League in 1906. Then the emphasis had been on loyalty to the British regime and a dislike of representative government based on a fear of the Hindu dominance. This fear did not disappear after 1906, but it was put in a new perspective by changes in the Islamic world. First of all the nationalist revival in Turkey under the Young Turks in 1908 caught the imagination of many Muslim intellectuals in India. Then when war broke out between Italy and Turkey in 1911, echoes of the ancient antagonism between Islam and Christendom were awakened. A sentimental attachment developed in India toward Turkey as the chief Islamic state, and toward the Turkish sultan as the caliph of the Muslim world community. The entry of Turkey into the war on the side of Germany made her Britain's enemy, thus confirming the anti-British prejudices which were deeper and stronger in many Muslims than the alliances with the British forged by Syed Ahmad Khan and his successors. The new anti-British sentiment found an outlet in a number of newspapers, many of them in Urdu. The most forceful figure in this new movement was Abul Kalam Azad (1888-1958), who became the spokesman for "nationalist Muslims," that is, those who believed that all Indians should join in a common front in the Indian National Congress against British rule.

The outcome of these activities was one of the landmarks in the development of Indian nationalism: the joint meeting of the Indian National Congress and the Muslim League in Lucknow in 1916. The two parties worked out a scheme of constitutional reform, with the overall aim of raising India to equal status with the other self-governing dominions of the British Empire. The first step was to be the proclamation by the king-emperor that self-government would be conferred on India at an early date. Major compromises were made by both organizations, with the Congress accepting the principle of separate representation for Muslims and the League agreeing to the principle of representative government. The Muslims were promised more than their proportional number of seats, but they would not have a majority in any province, not even in Bengal where they were 52 percent of the population, nor could they ever hope to achieve one, since they specifically agreed not to stand in any of the general constituencies. There was a strong emphasis on provincial autonomy and on the full representation of Indians in the army and the Civil Service.

The home rule agitation and the Congress-League Pact at Lucknow demonstrated that there was now widespread support for nationalist aspirations from all segments of the population and that further delay would only weaken the moderate elements. The result was the announcement in Parliament on August 20, 1917, that the policy of the British government and the government of India was "the increasing association of Indians in every branch of the administration and the gradual development of self-governing institutions with a view to the progressive realization of responsible government in India as an integral part of the British Empire." The secretary of state for India referred to this statement as "the most momentous utterance ever made in India's chequered history,"[11] but as far as Indian opinion was concerned, it was only a formal recognition of what had long been taken for granted.

The 1917 announcement promised "responsible government," not "self-government." The distinction was important, since it made clear that the imperial power would still exercise ultimate control, including deciding when India was ready for further advances. But the rulers would no longer be mere bureaucrats. They would become responsive to an electorate and share power with popularly elected ministers. Edwin Montagu, the secretary of state for India, told the civil servants and officials what this meant: "They must learn to be politicians."[12] The transition was not easy for a class that had prided itself on giving the Indian people what was good for them, not what they wanted, making it a point of honor never to explain or argue. It was not strange, as Montagu pointed out, that the strongest opposition to his proposals came, not from the Conservatives in England, but from the bureaucracy in India.

The implications of the 1917 announcement were spelled out in what is known as the Montagu-Chelmsford Reforms, after Montagu and Lord Chemsford, then governor general. The most striking feature was the introduction at the provincial level of the principle of dyarchy, or divided responsibility. All the branches of the provincial administration were divided, with some under the direct control of the governor, who would continue to be a British appointee, and some under the control of ministers responsible to the elected legislatures. Among the "reserved" subjects were finance, police, and the administration of justice; the "transferred" subjects included education, public health, public works, and agriculture. The legislative councils were greatly enlarged, and although the governors still nominated some members, the majority were to be elected.

This last provision raised the thorniest problem of constitutional reform: the nature of the franchise. The Montagu-Chelmsford Reforms recognized that communal electorates perpetuated and deepened class divisions, teaching people to think in terms of partisan groups rather than of the nation, and that to give a minority representation because it was weak was a positive encouragement for it to stay weak so that it would not lose privileges. Yet no alternative seemed possible that would be satisfactory to the Muslims, especially after the concessions of the Morley-Minto Reforms of 1909 and the Congress-League Pact of 1916. In the end, special representation was given not only to Muslims but also to numerous other groups: Indian Christians, Sikhs, Anglo-Indians, European landlords, universities, chambers of commerce. Hindus did not receive separate electorates, but they voted in the general constituencies, where it was assumed they would be in the majority. The right to vote was based on property qualification as well as race and religion, and it differed from province to province depending upon the strength of minority groups. The qualifications were also different for the central Legislative Council. Approximately 5.5 million persons received the vote and, since women were excluded, this meant about 7 percent of the adult male population.

* * *

The 1919 Constitution was, in many ways, a generous and forward-looking document, yet it did not concede that India was a nation. Instead, it spoke of India as "a sisterhood of states," presided over by a central government dealing with matters of common concern.[13] In 1885 this might have been a promise that would have caught the imagination of the nationalist leaders; by 1919 it was outdated.

NOTES

1. Quoted in S. Gopal, *British Policy in India, 1858-1905* (Cambridge: Cambridge University Press, 1965), 298.

2. Speech by D.F. MacKenzie, August 7, 1899, in Proceedings of the Council of the Lieutenant Governor of Bengal 1899, Vol. 31.

3. Great Britain, *Parliamentary Papers*, 1905, Vol. 71, Cd. 2746, 17

4. R. C. Dutt, *The Economic History of India in the Victorian Age* (London: Kegan Paul, 1950), xviii-xix.

5. Quoted in Wolpert, *Tilak and Gokhale*, 196-197.

6. Qureshi, The Struggle for Pakistan, 29-30,

7. Muslim Resolution at Dacca, December 30, 1906," in C. H. Philips, et al. eds,, *The Evolution of India and Pakistan, 1858-1947* (London: Oxford University Press, 1962), 194.

8. Minto to Morley, November 4, 1906, in ibid., 78.

9. Resolutions of the Twenty-Fourth National Congress, 1908, in *The Indian National Congress.*

10. H. Vishandas, in *Report of the Twenty-Fifth National Congress, 1910* (Allahabad: Indian Press, 1911), 89.

11. Great Britain, *Parliamentary Papers*, 1918, Vol. 8, Cd. 9109, "Report on Indian Constitutional Reforms."

12. Edwin Montagu, *An Indian Diary* (London: Heinemann, 1930), 216.

13. *Great Britain, Parliamentary Papers,* 1918, Vol. 8, "Indian Constitution Reforms," 277.

CHAPTER 4. THE EMERGENCE OF GANDHI

Before the Constitutional Reforms of 1919 were drafted, a preliminary report noted that the granting of voting rights in India was only a partial step toward public participation in government. "We have to bring about," the report noted, "the most radical revolution in the people's traditional ideas of the relation between ruler and ruled, and it will be a difficult and even dangerous business, for it is neither safe nor easy to meddle with traditional ideas in India."[1]

The task of transforming the attitudes of the Indian masses toward their rulers was undertaken, quite self-consciously by Mohandas Karamchand Gandhi (1869-1948). His successes and failures constitute in large measure both his own political biography and that of the Indian nationalist movement.

Gandhi was not the father of the Indian nation, as he has often been called, for the essential groundwork had been laid by the time he made his initial impact on Indian life. His peculiar genius was his understanding that the existing Indian social structure, with the enormous importance of its religions symbols, could be made part of the new political process. His great success was in giving millions of people for the first time a sense of involvement in the nation's destiny. More than any other leader Gandhi helped to create the psychological climate that is a prerequisite of nationalism, in which individual identity is dependent upon national identity. But this extraordinary achievement, which was perhaps unmatched by any other leader in modern times in the magnitude of the numbers involved, carried with it the fulfillment of the demands of the competing Muslim nationalism. The tensions created by Gandhi's leadership, dynamic and necessary though they were for Indian nationalist experience, completed the Muslim nationalist awakening that had begun in the late nineteenth century.

Gandhi's active involvement in the Indian political scene dates only from 1919, but by then he was already one of the best-known Indians of his generation, respected alike by the Indians and the British. He had won his reputation in South Africa, where he had worked for twenty years on behalf of the Indian community in their struggle against the discriminatory laws and practices of the South African government. Although he abandoned a successful law practice to live a life of poverty in the commune that he founded on the basis of Tolstoy's Christian primitivism, he remained attached to the law courts. His skilled mind was able to operate within the framework of British jurisprudence to gain redress from injustices. His devotion to nonviolence in South Africa, as later in India, was directed by the strain in the Indian religious tradition that believes violence leads to the enslavement of the soul. He was also influenced by the emphasis in the radical Christian pacifist tradition of repaying evil with good, of turning the other cheek, and of expressing the divine will through an acceptance of suffering. Such ideas became the rationale for his "experiments with truth," attempts to live what he considered a wholly natural life. Many of these experiments were concerned with areas that seemed to others irrelevant to political life, such as diet and sexual continence. But the one direct political consequence was what he called the technique of *satyagraha*, or nonviolent action. Especially when the weak confronted their oppressors, this was the ideal weapon, with the aim not conquest but a change of heart leading the strong to seek reconciliation with those they had wronged. Such ideas were remote from the political philosophy of the Indian moderate leaders, but men like Gokhale, who introduced Gandhi to the Indian political world, saw that behind those ideas was the same assumption that guided their own activity—that if the possessors of power could be brought to see the justice of the demands made upon them, they would yield.

During the war years, although Gandhi was in India, he held aloof from politics. To Edward Montagu, the secretary of state, he seemed to be, in contrast to some of the other Indian leaders, "a social reformer with a real desire to find grievances and to cure them, not for any reasons of self-advertisement, but to improve the conditions of his fellow man."[2]   But there was another side to Gandhi's noninvolvement in nationalist politics during the war years. He was a leader, not a follower. "You have every right to kick me out, to demand my head, or to punish me whenever and howsoever you choose," he once told his followers, "but as long as you chose to keep me as your leader you must accept my conditions, you must accept my dictatorship."[3]   Such an understanding of leadership would be difficult to enforce in a nationalist movement still dominated by the great figures of the past—Tilak, Gokhale, S. N. Banerjee, Lajpat Rai, C. R. Das, and Mrs. Besant. Neither his methods nor his understanding of the Indian situation matched with theirs, whether they were moderates like Banerjee or radicals like Tilak. His only recourse was to stand on the sidelines of the national movement, but he did not wait idly. As part of the preparation for the deeper involvement that he expected, he turned his attention in a direction that, as commonplace as it may now seem, was then novel: He began an investigation of the grievances of the peasants and workers.

Because of his record of dealing with the problem of indentured laborers in South Africa, Gandhi was urged in 1917 to go to Champaran in Bihar to see what could be done to help the peasants who were in debt to the indigo planters. Since indigo planters, many of whom were European, were notorious for their ill-treatment of the peasants who worked for them, Gandhi's appearance as the champion of the peasants aroused great interest, although the negotiations were inconclusive. The effect of his presence as reported by a British official in the area was a foreshadowing of the next thirty years.

> We may look on Mr. Gandhi as an idealist, a fanatic, or a revolutionary according to our particular opinions, but to the raiyats he is their liberator, and they credit him with extraordinary powers. He moves about their villages asking them to lay their grievances before him, and he is transfiguring the imaginations of masses of ignorant men with visions of an early millennium.[4]

One side of Gandhi's genius was his appeal as a charismatic leader to people in whom the vocabulary of the old nationalist politics had awakened no response. The other was his ability as a negotiator with the planters and government officials to obtain a modest redress of the peasants' grievances. The same techniques were demonstrated later in the year when serious labor troubles developed in the great textile mills in Ahmedabad, near Gandhi's home. The chief British official in the area asked him to make peace between the mill owners and the workers; but when the owners refused to accept arbitration,

Gandhi advised the workers to go on strike. He lacked the funds to support the strikers, and when they began to waver he went on a fast, not to intimidate the mill owners, he insisted, but to purify the workers so they would have the courage to endure suffering and starvation. The result was that the employers agreed to arbitration, and the workers accepted less than they had originally demanded.

Reactions to the Rowlatt Acts

Gandhi's influence at Champaran and Ahmedabad provided him with a base for political operations and opened up new possibilities for channeling the resentment against British rule and the desire for participation in public life into new forms of political action. By 1919 he was ready to use his power in the service of Indian nationhood.

Although the formal center of political concern continued to be the deliberations of the Indian National Congress on the new constitution, three specific issues usurped public interest after 1918: the Rowlatt Acts, the Amritsar massacre, and the Khilafat agitation. It was these issues, not the broader question of constitutional change, that provided Gandhi with his platform for entrance into Indian politics.

The Rowlatt Acts permitted the imprisonment without trial of persons suspected of subversion. Even before the acts were passed they had aroused violent opposition in all sections of the Indian political world. This reaction was a reflection of the curious relationship that still existed between the Indian nationalists and the British, based on the presumption that the governing power was committed to the extension and protection of the political freedoms guaranteed by British law and jurisprudence. Gandhi's own commitment to action within the legal framework was shaken, for, as he put it, the government itself had moved outside this framework by passing laws that were "unjust, subversive of the principles of liberty and justice, and destructive of the elementary rights of individuals on which the safety of the community as a whole and the state itself is based."[5] His remedy was to call for a one-day *hartal*, or general strike, on April 6.

Despite Gandhi's emphasis on the peaceful nature of *hartal*, there were many outbreaks of violence as mobs clashed with the police. The situation was already very tense in the Punjab, and when Gandhi attempted to enter the province, he was arrested and sent back to Bombay. The arrest of other popular leaders led to further violence, and the civil authorities, convinced that they could no longer maintain order, called in the military. All processions and demonstrations were forbidden, especially in the city of Amritsar, where a number of Europeans had been murdered by a mob after the police had fired on a procession. In disregard of the order of General Reginald Dyer, the officer commanding the troops in the area, a meeting was called in protest on April 13. Thousands of people had gathered in Jallianwala Bagh, an enclosed square in a congested part of the city, when Dyer arrived with 150 soldiers—one hundred were Indian. He stationed them at the only exit from the enclosure and gave the order to fire. A British journalist who was present described Dyer's action:

> Without a word of warning, he opened fire at about a hundred yards range upon a dense crowd. . . . The panic stricken multitude broke at once, but for ten consecutive minutes he kept up a merciless fusillade. . . on that seething mass of humanity, caught like rats in a trap, vainly rushing for the few narrow exits or lying flat on the ground to escape the rain of bullets, which he personally directed at the points where the crowd was the thickest. The "targets," to use his own words, were good. . . . He had killed, according to the official figures wrung out of the government months later, 379, and he left about 200 wounded on the ground, for whom, again to use his own words, he did not consider it his "job" to take the slightest thought.[6]

Nothing of this kind had happened in living memory in India, and Indian political leaders of all persuasions denounced the Amritsar massacre as a betrayal of the British promises for constitutional reform. They did not all agree, however, that the time had come to end attempts at cooperation. Rabindranath Tagore, who had received the Nobel Prize for his poetry, showed his disapproval of Amritsar by renouncing the knighthood the British had given him; but he feared that the violence of the mob would be equally destructive of the values and decencies of life. At the very beginning of the twentieth century he had expressed his foreboding: "The naked passion of self-love of Nations, in its drunken delirium of greed, is dancing to the clash of steel and the howling verses of vengeance."[7] It now seemed that India would be caught up in the same demonic force of nationalism that was destroying the West. The Gandhian movement, by appealing to the masses even though it used the language of nonviolence, seemed to Tagore to threaten to let loose in India the same floods of unreason. He warned Gandhi that the violence that had followed the first *hartal* had shown that "power in all its forms is irrational. . . . Passive resistance is a force which is not necessarily moral in itself; it can be used against truth as well as for it."[8]

Gandhi had come to somewhat the same conclusion as he heard of outbreaks of violence that were occurring throughout the country, and he called for an end of the strike. He had made, he said, a "Himalayan miscalculation," in starting a *satyagraha* movement before the people were educated: "Before one can be fit for the practice of civil disobedience one must have rendered a willing and respectful obedience to the slate laws. . . . It is only when a person has thus obeyed the laws of society scrupulously that he is in a position to judge as to which particular rules are good and just and which unjust and iniquitous."[9]

It was a sense of timing, then, not a change of heart about the rightness of his methods, that led Gandhi to urge the end of the first tentative nonviolent protests in the spring of 1919. The decision that the people were not yet ready for a confrontation with the British and that the old methods of cooperation would have to continue was strengthened by the government's appointment of the Hunter Commission to inquire into the Amritsar massacre, which Gandhi expected to condemn the actions of General Dyer and the political authorities. Even if they were not condemned, awaiting the outcome of the commission's deliberations would give him more time to continue the education program for an effective nonviolent movement. When the Indian National Congress held its annual session at Amritsar in December 1919, he led the fight for a decision to cooperate with the government by helping to work out the new constitution. This was a direct challenge to the old extremists and their supporters who favored refusing any further compromises. Tilak, attending his last session of the Congress, argued for denunciation of the constitution as "inadequate, unsatisfactory, and disappointing"; but Gandhi carried the day, and the resolution approving cooperation was passed.

Khilafat Movement

Within a year Gandhi was to make what seemed a complete about-face: He led the Indian National Congress into the non-cooperation movement, rejecting all the forms of participation in the constitutional framework he had persuaded the nationalists to accept in December 1919. The report of the Hunter Commission and the growing unrest among Muslims associated with the Khilafat Movement were the immediate determinants of this new direction in Gandhi's leadership.

Commenting on the report of the Hunter Commission on the Amritsar massacre, Sarojini Naidu, one of the ablest of the many women who became leaders of the nationalist movement, remarked, "Our friends revealed their ignorance; our enemies their insolence."[10] Although the Hunter Commission concluded that the military measures were unduly harsh, the report stressed the provocation of the mob. The report shook Gandhi's remaining faith in British good intentions and released him from his pledge of cooperation.

The Khilafat Movement arose out of the victorious Allies' treatment of Turkey, which had supported the Germans and shared in their defeat. General sympathy for the suffering of a Muslim country was sharpened by the position of the Turkish sultan as caliph (or khalif), the chief dignitary of the Islamic world. The caliph had not been of great importance to Indian Muslims previously, except for the *ulama*, or Islamic theologians, who had always been inclined towards an anti-British position. The Khilafat Movement, which was organized in India to protest the division of the Ottoman Empire and the consequent weakening of the authority of the caliph, did not have any very clearly defined aims. It was essentially an emotional reaction to a humiliation of Islam by the Western—and Christian—nations.

Gandhi saw in the anti-British sentiment engendered by the Khilafat Movement the possibility of a rapprochement with the Islamic community in 1919. Accepting the presidency of the Khilafat committee, formed to protest the dismemberment of Turkey, Gandhi worked closely with the leaders of the movement in India, with the result that the committee agreed to his proposal to initiate a program of non-cooperation. Gandhi's Hindu colleagues had misgivings over this decision, but Gandhi saw it as the great breakthrough in the cause both of Muslim-Hindu unity and of a national acceptance of the method of *satyagraha* as a way of gaining freedom. To those who reminded him of the violence, including the dreadful events at Amritsar, that had followed the first experiments in *satyagraha* on April 1919, Gandhi replied that no country has ever risen without being purified through the fire of suffering and that India could not escape from slavery without paying the costs of self-purification.

Non-Cooperation Movement

Gandhi's task was now to convince the Indian National Congress to adopt a policy of nonviolence and non-cooperation. Excitement mounted as Gandhi's appeals for Hindu-Muslim unity and the acceptance of the program of non-cooperation spread throughout the country. A special session of the Congress convened in September 1920 in Calcutta and accepted Gandhi's proposals. The government's treatment of the Muslims and the condoning of the Amritsar massacre left the people of India no alternative, according to the resolution, but to adopt "the policy of progressive nonviolent non-cooperation, until the said wrongs are righted and *swaraj* is established."[11]

There was no definition of *swaraj*, and the vagueness was deliberate. For the educated classes, who were deeply committed to Western political institutions, it meant democratic, parliamentary government on the British model; for Gandhi it had an almost apolitical meaning. "Abandonment of the fear of death" or "the ability to regard every inhabitant of India as our own brother or sister"[12] were some of the definitions he used in an attempt to give content to the term; but fundamentally it encompassed a style of living and an attitude summed up in his own life. This meant the renunciation of much from the modern Western world —including industrialism and technology—that the older generation of nationalist leaders, moderate or extremist, had regarded as essential for the future well-being of India. That non-cooperation struck at the heart of the old collaboration was made clear in his enumeration of the steps that were to be followed:

1. surrender of titles and all honorary offices under the government
2. withdrawal of children from schools and colleges
3. boycott by lawyers and litigants of law courts
4. refusal of candidates to stand for election in the hew legislative councils and of voters to vote
5. boycott of foreign goods.

The resolution concluded with a strong plea for the revival of hand-spinning and hand-weaving in every home, partly as an economic measure, but more importantly so that "an opportunity should be given in the first stage of non-cooperation to every man, woman and child for . . . discipline and self-sacrifice."[13]

None of the measures that Gandhi proposed were wholly new—the Bengal extremists had organized effective boycotts of British goods in 1905—but taken all together, and including such momentous political steps as the refusal to take part in the elections to the new councils, the Congress was being asked to make fundamental decisions about Indian nationhood. The emphasis was no longer on hurting the British or even on making India strong through home industries; the demand was for a radical reorientation of national life. Rabindranath Tagore, speaking for the intellectual elite, sensed that the anti-intellectual and anti-rational elements might combine with the emphasis on the Indian past to frustrate the growth of community based on reason and mutual understanding. "Our present struggle to alienate our heart and mind from the West," he wrote, "is an attempt at spiritual suicide."[14] He was impatient with the emphasis on spinning in the new program. *Swaraj*, he argued, "cannot be established on cheap clothing; its foundation is in the mind."[15] Tagore, who first called Gandhi "Mahatma," now saw a special danger in the willingness of the people to accept Gandhi's words as truth without any kind of verification.

> Those for whom authority is needed in place of reason will invariably accept despotism in place of freedom. . . . We have had enough magic in this country, magical revelation, magical healing, and all kinds of divine intervention in mundane affairs. . . . Where Mahatma Gandhi has declared war against the tyranny of the machine which is oppressing the whole world, we are all enrolled under his banner. But we must refuse to accept as our ally the illusion-haunted, magic-ridden, slave mentality that is at the root of all the poverty and insult under which our country groans.[16]

The Gandhian message was thus for many in 1920 a call to leave that search for accommodation with the modern world, which had been the hallmark of the nationalist movement, and to replace it with an inward-looking vision of traditional Indian society, purified and cleansed, but nevertheless premodern and preindustrial. This could only end in suffering and loss for the participants, most of whom had careers based on the educational and legal institutions they were being called upon to boycott. And while they were being asked to give up the opportunities of exercising power through participating in new legislative councils, they were being told at the same time that they must renounce the use of violence, the alternative method that had been used with telling effect against the British in the early years of the century.

In personal terms the acceptance of non-cooperation meant that power in the nationalist movement would pass from those who now controlled it—C. R. Das, Motilal Nehru, Annie Besant, M. M. Malaviya, Lala Lajpat Rai, M. A. Jinnah—to Gandhi and his followers. Most of the old leaders, with the exception of Jinnah, were to make some kind of accommodation with Gandhi, but power is never easily given up. This was particularly true when they felt that they stood for the modern world over against Gandhi's traditionalism.

Complicating this division was the seeming contradiction of the very considerable support Gandhi received from the great industrialists of Western India, notably the cotton manufacturers. A cynical explanation is that they saw in Gandhi a power that could free them from the competition of European industries, but another factor may be equally important and not really out of keeping with the first. The industrialists of Western India were drawn, on the whole, from the traditional trading classes and were far less committed to the values of the modern world, less alienated from the Indian tradition, than the educated elite of Calcutta and its environs. Gandhi appealed to this sense of tradition and helped them to fulfill their classic role as men of affairs who recognized saintliness and paid for its upkeep but did not feel compelled to emulate it. But they were modern men, too, in many ways more so than the lawyers, journalists, and teachers who had shaped the early phases of nationalism. The anti-intellectualism of the Gandhian movement of which Tagore complained was not just the obscurantism of the rural past. It was also an expression of the values of business and commercial classes which were becoming a potent force in Indian political life. The old nationalist movement had drawn both its leadership and its support from a relatively small segment of society, and the success of the Gandhian movement in reaching out to new groups inevitably made for tension.

Non-Cooperation Begins

When the Indian National Congress met for its regular session at Nagpur at the end of December 1920, Gandhi was in a position to win assent for his revolutionary program, even from some of those who had opposed him at Calcutta. He won overwhelming approval for the non-cooperation resolution, but he also showed his knowledge of the needs of a modern political party by preparing a new constitution that revolutionized the working of the Congress as a political organization. Village cells were made the basic unit of the Congress, and arrangements were made to set them up throughout the country. These were then grouped into districts and provincial committees, with election to the larger unit coming from below. At the top was the All-India Congress Committee with the executive power in the hands of the small Working Committee. Since anyone who paid four annas a year (about ten cents) could be a member of the Indian National Congress, its membership was drawn from a wide spectrum of society, and the system of committees made for a democratic structure. The whole organization, however, could be tightly controlled by the Working

Committee. The Congress also became a continuously functioning organization, and the executive could make its power felt throughout the country. At Nagpur, Gandhi's critics began to see that, while he might use the vocabulary of religious sentiment, he was also a superb political tactician.

Even in the perspective of history it is hard to say whether the first non-cooperation program was a success or a failure. Elections were held; the legislative councils conducted their business; the schools and colleges were not emptied; foreign goods continued to be bought and sold; and in the end the program was formally revoked. But if, as Gandhi himself would have insisted, results are measured in terms of means, not ends, then the non-cooperation program during 1921 brought about changes both in the quality of Indian nationalism and in the response of the administration to it. The watershed of 1921 ended for many the long dream of collaboration with the British.

Of even greater significance, the 1921 movement awakened a response throughout India. The masses had often been stirred before, for nothing is more false to the realities of Indian society than to picture it as apathetic and unmoved; its susceptibility to passionate involvement is attested by a multitude of religious movements and sectarian groups. But in 1921 this capacity for passion—and, Gandhi argued, for suffering—was harnessed for the first time to the aims of a nationalist organization. A high administrative official summed up the situation late in 1921 by saying that Gandhi "is now regarded not only as a great national hero, but, by the ignorant, as semi-divine."[17] What he missed was of crucial importance: If Gandhi was regarded as semi-divine, it was because he was a great national hero, and not the other way about. Divinities are a commonplace in India, and in themselves are not likely to impress the masses, who may be ignorant but are generally shrewd. The quality that in India defines divinity is power, and Gandhi now possessed power.

The non-cooperation movement that began in January 1921 was not a civil disobedience campaign. That was to come later. The first stage required the education of the masses in the true meaning of *swaraj*, gaining recruits for propaganda and organizational work, inspiring faith in the resolutions passed by the Congress, and, always a matter of the greatest concern for Gandhi, raising money to support the movement. Gandhi and his followers moved about the country making speeches, holding meetings with key provincial leaders, and filling the columns of the movement's newspaper, *Young India*, with discussions of the meaning of non-cooperation. Jawaharlal Nehru has left an account of what the movement meant, especially to the young intellectuals:

> Many of us who worked for the Congress program lived in a kind of intoxication during the year 1921. We were full of excitement and optimism and a buoyant enthusiasm.... We worked hard, harder than we had ever done before, for we knew that the conflict with the Government would come soon.... We had a sense of freedom and a

pride in that freedom. The old feeling of oppression and frustration was completely gone. There was no more whispering, no roundabout legal phraseology to avoid getting into trouble with the authorities. We said what we felt and shouted it from the house tops.[18]

This sense of excitement, of possibilities opening up for India, led many individuals to perform dramatic acts of self-sacrifice in the service of the nationalist cause. Thousands of students left the government colleges and joined the new National Colleges set up by the Congress. A number of distinguished lawyers, including Vallabhbhai Patel, Rajendra Prasad, Rajagopalachari, all of whom were later to hold high positions in the first government of independent India after 1947, gave up their practices. The spinning of thread and the wearing of homespun cloth, *khadi* was an integral part of the program. "Love of foreign cloth," Gandhi preached, "brought foreign domination, pauperism and what is worse, shame to many a home."[19] The simple white "Gandhi cap" became a symbol of support for the national cause. In a country of extraordinary diversity of dress and manners, the adoption of such an easily recognizable symbol was a stroke of genius, the one thing that high caste and low, rich and poor, the Punjabi, the Madrasi, the Bengali, could use without much difficulty. In the same way the spinning of thread might not do much to alter economic conditions, but the experience of working together in great mass meetings gave people an exhilarating sense of participation in the political process, as did another common feature of the movement, the burning of foreign cloth. People would collect the cloth and then gather for a great bonfire. Gandhi's defense of this practice, which seemed to many so wasteful in a land where people went naked because they could not afford clothing, exhibited the blend of passionate religious imagery and practical common sense that was at once appealing and confusing. To wear foreign clothing was sinful, he argued, because it deprived the Indian weaver of the right to work. "I must consign my foreign garments to the flames and thus purify myself. . . . I must refuse to insult the naked by giving them clothes they do not need, instead of giving them work which they sorely need."[20]

The involvement of women in the political struggle, a new element in the nationalist movement, was closely related to the emphasis on spinning and the regeneration of the country's economic life. Telling them that the economic and moral salvation of India rested with them, Gandhi appealed to the women to set an example of self-denial, asking them to give up the use of foreign goods for both themselves and their children. A woman must "refuse to adorn herself for men, including her husband, if she will be an equal partner with man." Traditional Indian society emphasized the necessity of the good woman submitting herself to her husband's wishes, while at the same time it exalted her role as mother and giver of life. Gandhi's message that women could achieve an equality with men, or even in fact a kind of superiority through methods based upon the most time-honored concepts of wifely duty, must have had a profound psychological appeal. Furthermore, the virtues that Gandhi extolled as the basis of *swaraj* were those associated with the classic Indian wife. Meekness and obedience were the other side of strength and courage. Men were fond of speaking of the "weaker sex," but this was because they lacked understanding of the true meaning of strength. The female sex is "the nobler of the two, for it is the embodiment of sacrifice, silent suffering, humility, faith and knowledge. . . . A woman's intuition has often proved superior to man's arrogant assumption of superior knowledge."[21]

Gandhi was appealing to the masses of Indian women, but the ones who responded most strongly, and who were able to play a part in political life perhaps unmatched by that of women anywhere else in the world, were women of the upper and middle classes. Women provided a reservoir of intelligence and skill that had never before been tapped for the national cause, and thousands of women found release from the stultifying boredom of the routines of upper-class Indian life by throwing themselves into the Gandhian movement. They became his most ardent disciples, providing him with unpaid assistants for organizational work and stirring society by their willingness to march in processions and go to jail. Their reward was high office and influence.

As with all aspects of the development of the nationalist movement, the activity of the Indian leaders was only part of the picture; the response of the government was crucial in defining its form and direction. The acquiescent attitude of the government that emerged in the months after the program of non-cooperation was announced in September 1920 was regarded by many British officials—and also by the many Indians who still gave their full support to the British—as a sign of weakness that encouraged disloyalty. When Gandhi said, "Non-cooperators are at war with the Government, they have declared rebellion against it," the case for his arrest seemed clear. But the government held back from arresting him, for despite the Rowlatt Acts, the government moved within a legal framework that required actual proof of criminal action. Gandhi had used a vocabulary that implied rebellion, but he had not in fact broken the law. The government was anxious not to make a martyr of Gandhi and the other leaders.

Civil Disobedience

During the last months of 1921 there was an increase of violence throughout India. How much of this was the product of the non-cooperation program is hard to say, but in many instances it clearly grew out of deep-seated local frustrations and tensions that found an outlet in the nationalist movement. Within the Indian National Congress itself there was growing dissatisfaction over Gandhi's reluctance to initiate full-scale civil disobedience throughout the nation. Gandhi hesitated but finally agreed that each province should make its own plans for starting mass civil disobedience, including the refusal to pay taxes; but he insisted that all those who participated should first pledge themselves to nonviolence, hand-spinning, Muslim-Hindu unity, and the eradication of discrimination against the lowest castes, the "Untouchables." Behind the pledge was his fear of what might happen once the campaign got under way. He wanted its advocates to realize that "Mass civil disobedience is like an earthquake, a sort of general upheaval on the political plane. When the reign of mass civil disobedience begins, there the subsisting Government ceases to function. . . . The police stations, the court offices, etc., all shall cease to be Government property, and shall be taken over by the people."[22]

Finally Gandhi gave the word: Mass civil disobedience would start on January 31, 1922, but it would begin with a trial in the district of Bardoli in Bombay led by Gandhi himself. Even at this point he held off, giving the governor general a chance to prevent civil disobedience by showing his change of heart through releasing political prisoners and restoring the freedom of the press. The country had followed all these steps with mounting tension, and when the governor general's refusal came, Gandhi's followers were ready for decisive action.

But just at this moment word reached Gandhi of an outbreak of violence in the village of Chauri Chaura in the United Provinces. A group of non-cooperators who had been harassed by the police surrounded the police station and set fire to it. Twenty-two of the policemen were either burned alive or were killed by the mob as they tried to escape. Gandhi was horrified by the brutality of the incident and, in his own language, concluded that "God spoke clearly through Chauri Chaura. . . . He has warned me . . . that there is not yet in India that nonviolent and truthful atmosphere which alone can justify mass civil disobedience." He issued an order calling off the whole campaign. His followers, many of whom were in jail, were dumbfounded at this abrupt reversal, especially after Gandhi's ultimatum a few days before to the governor general declaring that civil disobedience would begin unless the government changed its policies. Gandhi admitted that this was "the bitterest cup of humiliation to drink," but it was the voice of Satan, he said, that appealed to his pride by reminding him of his "pompous threats to the Government and promises to the people of Bardoli." Not to call off the movement was to deny the truth.[23]

Jawaharlal Nehru tells how those who, like himself, were in prison reacted with amazement and resentment to the news of Gandhi's action. Thousands of people were ready to go to prison for their political beliefs, and the whole country was responding in excitement and expectation to Gandhi's plans. Suspending civil disobedience just when it seemed to be on the point of making an impact on the nation seemed inexplicable. It was, however, the product of something more than a quixotic intuition. His religious idiom suggested that his main concern was the inviolate purity of the doctrine of nonviolence as a political technique, but behind this was a shrewd assessment of the realities of Indian life. The violent episode at Chauri Chaura had convinced him that he must go slowly, for he knew that the poverty and frustrations of Indian life made violence endemic. He was an anarchist in his view of the perfect society, but he had no expectation that the mere destruction of the existing order could lead to anything but new forms of tyranny. He had meant what he had said, he insisted, when he promised that *swaraj* could come in a year, but only if there was a change of heart on the part of the people. From the standpoint of his ethical theories, the pervasive violence of the past year had shown that the people were not yet ready for the purifying experience of *satyagraha*, of civil disobedience conducted without violence even under the severest provocation.

The success of Gandhi in identifying nonviolence as the peculiar characteristic of Indian life, in the minds of Indians as well as foreigners, has tended to mask an aspect of Indian life that is of the greatest importance to modern Indian political life, namely the frequency of outbreaks of violence. While we do not possess the kind of historical data that would permit us to say with assurance that there was less violence in previous periods of Indian history than there was after 1920, it seems reasonably clear that there has been more of what is referred to as "communal violence," that is, outbreaks where the targets of attack are other religious groups. Many nationalist leaders at the time had the easy explanation that the riots were engineered by the British as part of the strategy of "Divide and Rule" to prevent Muslims and Hindus from uniting in a common front. Aside from the lack of any real proof of this having happened, it is hard to believe that they would have taken the enormous risks of creating an uncontrollable situation. Nor is there any evidence that, as often suggested by foreign observers, that Hindus and Muslims harbor undying hatreds for each other for historic and religious reasons. While such antagonisms were undoubtedly appealed to, the violence of the pre-independence period, as in the post-independence period, seems explainable to a large extent by a number of factors that are part of the reality of modern Indian life that were not present to the same extent in earlier times.

One such factor is a sense of change, carrying with it new possibilities, new ways of doing things, and, conversely, dissatisfaction with the old. Especially young men in a traditional society, with all its conventions and constraints, often responded to these possibilities with the use of violence. Closely related to this was the economic dislocation and unemployment occasioned by the end of the war, and, especially in the Punjab, with the return of thousands of demobilized soldiers. But the most important factor was undoubtedly the new electoral politics, in which politicians in India as elsewhere saw the advantages in appealing for support to groups or communities, and these were usually identifiable through religious designations. Especially in the cities, another factor in the riots were members of the underworld culture, known in India as "goondas," men living on the margins of society who were available to stir up violence and to profit from it. To all of this explosive mix, an appeal to religion gave a potent legitimacy, for whatever the actual motivations or causes of a violent outbreak, actions, however horrendous, could be condoned on the grounds that the righteous cause had to be defended against the onslaughts of evil.

The working out of these factors in a variety of combinations can be seen in a number of incidents in the 1920s. The most serious outbreak of violence since 1857 came on the Malabar coast, where what can be seen in one reading is simply a classic case of peasants rising and killing oppressive landlords. But the rebelling peasants were Muslims and the landlords were Hindu, so the affair had from the beginning a religious coloration of Hindus against Muslims as well as rich against poor. In the Punjab there were tensions, although not a great deal of actual violence, when in events that foreshadowed the 1980s, a group of militant Sikhs denounced the older generation of Sikhs for having made too many concessions to Hindu practices, and demanded a purifying of the leadership of the religious shrines and temples. In Bihar and the United Provinces there were frequent clashes over such matters as the slaughter of cows by Muslims and the playing of music in front of mosques by Hindus on Muslim holy days. This whole volatile situation was in the background, then, when Gandhi called off the first civil disobedience movement.

Gandhi's Arrest

Gandhi was also aware, as many of his followers were not, that behind the façade of political unity the non-cooperation movement was rapidly disintegrating. With most of the ablest leaders in jail, it would be without direction. The Muslim leaders saw little chance of gains for their particular interests from Gandhi's tactics, and as Turkey itself moved to destroy the power of the caliph, the whole Khilafat issue, which had been used so skillfully by Gandhi two years before to forge an alliance, was now of little importance. And on the simple level of organization, always of the greatest concern to Gandhi as a practical politician, the Indian National Congress showed signs of serious weakness that would make a long struggle difficult. Gandhi had emphasized that he would need complete cooperation; what he was demanding was complete obedience. He now knew that the majority of the leaders were no longer with him and that the enormous popularity he enjoyed among the masses was very often based upon a false image of his power and his intention. "I know that the only thing that the Government dreads," he wrote, "is this huge majority I seem to command. They little know that I dread it even more than they." He was a prisoner of the violence and frustration that had found a focus in the nationalist movement, and by this time he was "actually and literally praying for a disastrous defeat."[24] The obvious defeat would be his arrest. In his own religious terminology this would be a purification; in political terms it would give him time to redefine his purposes and regroup his forces for another non-cooperative movement.

Gandhi was not arrested until March 10, 1922, and the governor general's delay was justified, for his action aroused none of the violence that might have followed if Gandhi had been arrested earlier. At his trial Gandhi pleaded guilty to the charge of preaching disaffection to the government. In passing sentence on March 18, 1922, Justice Broomfield acknowledged that Gandhi was:

in a different category from any person I have ever tried or am likely to have to try. . . . In the eyes of millions of your countrymen, you are a great patriot and a great leader. Even those who differ from you in politics look upon you as man of high ideals and of noble and even saintly life.[25]

*   *   *

The first chapter of the Gandhian era of Indian politics ended with the Indian National Congress in disorganized confusion, its leaders in jail, and the non-cooperation movement, which had preempted the loyalties and energies of the nationalists for two years, suspended. Each of the subsequent campaigns was to end similarly. But the movement had opened up Indian society to the nationalist cause, and Gandhi could use the symbols of defeat as well as those of success for his appeal. Jawaharlal Nehru, in trying to explain Gandhi's hold over intellectuals like himself and hard-headed, skeptical politicians like his father, once spoke of those qualities of Gandhi which had a universal appeal: his steely will, the combination of humility and controlled power, his ability to hold an audience. But beyond this was the way the masses reacted to his spell. Many foreigners also reacted to that spell, of course, but there was often a fulsome condescension in their praise that was absent in the reaction of the Indian masses. In his skillful use of the values and symbols of the Indian tradition, he dramatized himself as the embodiment of the nation, even while, undoubtedly with perfect sincerity, he denigrated the personal acclaim. An important element in this ability to appeal to the tradition was his long period of separation from it in England and South Africa. Only someone who was wholly immersed in the tradition, and yet who had looked at it from the outside, could have used it so intuitively. Thus the prison sentence became part of the drama of renunciation and suffering he envisaged as the way India must follow to find true freedom. Prison became the substitute for the banishment to the forest that plays the central role in so many of the great legends of India, where the hero accepts the sentence gracefully and turns the forest into a spiritual retreat from which he returns strengthened and purified.

Gandhi emerged from prison in 1924 confident that the future was with him, not with those who were seeking to redirect the nationalist movement back into the old channels through participation in the legislative assemblies and other institutions set up by the administration. For the next twenty years the tensions between the two interpretations—the Gandhian insistence on social salvation through personal commitment as opposed to the policies of institutional participation—governed the development of Indian nationalism.

NOTES

1. Great Britain, *Parliamentary Papers*, 1918, Vol. 8, "Indian Constitutional Reforms," 113-114.
2. Quoted in B. R. Nanda, *Mahatma Gandhi* (London: Allen & Unwin, 1958), 153,
3. Quoted in Jawaharlal Nehru, *An Autobiography* (Bombay: Allied Publishers, 1962), 46
4. Quoted in Nanda, *Mahatma*, 159.

5. *Satyagraha* of February 24,1919, in D. G. Tendulkar, *Mahatma*, 8 vols. (New Delhi: Publications Division, Government of India, 1960), Vol. I, 241.

6. Quoted in ibid., 258.

7. Rabindranath Tagore, *Nationalism* (New York: Macmillan, 1917), 133.

8. Tagore to Gandhi, April 12, 1919, in Tendulkar, *Mahatma*, Vol. I, 259.

9. Mohandas K. Gandhi, *An Autobiography*, M. Desai (tr.) (Boston: Beacon Press, 1959), 470.

10. Quoted in Nanda, *Mahatma*, 180.

11. Gandhi, in *Young India*, June 16, 1920, quoted in Tendulkar, *Mahatma*, Vol. I, 355.

12. Quoted in Nanda, *Mahatma*, 205.

13. Cf Tendulkar, *Mahatma*, Vol. II, 10-11.

14. Tagore to C. F. Andrews, March 13, 1921, quoted in John Broomfield, *Elite Conflict in a Plural Society* (Berkeley: University of California Press, 1968), 150.

15. Tagore, "The Call to Truth" in de Bary, *Sources of Indian Tradition*, 794.

16. Ibid., 795-796.

17. Sir William Vincent, minutes of October 10, 1921, quoted in Nanda, *Mahatma*, 225.

18. Nehru, *Autobiography*, 69.

19. Quoted in Tendulkar, *Mahatma*, Vol. II, 55.

20. Gandhi, in *Young India*, October 13, 1921.

21. Quoted in Tendulkar, *Mahatma*, Vol. II, 50.

22. Gandhi at Congress meeting, Delhi, November 4, 1921, quoted in ibid.

23. Gandhi in *Young India*, February 16, 1922, quoted in ibid., 111.

24. Gandhi in *Young India,* March 2, 1922, quoted in ibid., 122.

25. Quoted in Philips, *The Evolution of India and Pakistan*, 224.

CHAPTER 5. THE POLITICS OF RIGHT MISTAKES

The excitement generated by the non-cooperation program from 1920 to 1922 was followed by a period of frustration and indecision. The optimistic slogan of "*swaraj* in a year" was mocked by Gandhi's abrupt ending of civil disobedience. And with most of the nationalist leaders in jail, there was little hope of reviving agitation. Yet the government did not really profit from the failure of the first Gandhian assault. The new constitution, which had seemed so radical to many British politicians, had been universally condemned in India for its timidity in moving the country toward responsible government. There was widespread unrest throughout the country leading to numerous violent outbreaks, of which the Hindu-Muslim riots were the most public example. Economic depression added to the general malaise characterized public life in the 1920s. There were, nonetheless, developments during the period that moved India toward *swaraj* in the Gandhian sense of national integration and a growth in respect, although by very different paths from those he envisaged. Despite the hostile reception that the new constitution had received, the legislative assemblies promoted forms of political participation that became the basis for the development of a successful system of party government. At the same time, India also became involved in the international political community in ways that defined her national existence in the eyes of the rest of the world, while giving the nationalist movement itself a new perspective.

India's International Status

India's changed international status was a direct outcome of her contribution to the Allied cause during World War I, for even though her external affairs were wholly under the control of Great Britain, she was one of the signatories of the Treaty of Versailles. This made her automatically a member of the League of Nations under the first clause of the Covenant, which assigned original membership to the signatories of the treaty, despite the fact that she would have been excluded by the second clause, which confined membership to self-governing states.

The anomaly of India's being recognized as an independent state by the international community and yet being denied responsible government in internal affairs became a sore point with Indians of all political persuasions. The members of the new Liberal Foundation, the old Congress moderates, were probably more sensitive to the indignities inherent in the ambiguities of India's international situation than were the more radical nationalists. Being products of an educational system and an intellectual milieu that had made them outward looking and responsive to the political values of the Western world, the liberals attributed great importance to India's identity as an autonomous nation in a world setting. India's failure to secure a permanent seat in the League Council and to be given proportionate representation in the Secretariat was especially galling to them, linking their sympathies with the rest of the Indian nationalist movement, even though they dissented from the direction it had taken since the advent of Gandhi. But despite these slights, membership in the League of

Nations gave her representation in many international bodies, particularly in the influential International Labour Organization. The Indians who attended international meetings were usually men of great ability, such as Srinivasa Sastri, who made India visible in a new and impressive way to the diplomats and civil servants of the West. Within the British Empire itself India was given more or less the same status as the dominions at the various imperial conferences that were called in the 1920s. Participation in the League of Nations and other international bodies meant that in theory and in fact India was not a "new" nation in 1947; it also gave her a nucleus of officials experienced in diplomatic negotiations.

The treatment of Indians abroad was an immediate link between internal political concerns and India's new status as a member of the international community. During the nineteenth century hundreds of thousands of Indians had gone to work in Burma, Ceylon, Malaya, South Africa, the Fiji Islands, and the West Indies. Many of these were indentured laborers, attracted by promises of passage and high wages from the poverty of rural Indian life. The result was that by the 1920s nearly two million Indians were living abroad, almost all in British colonies or dominions. Substandard housing, low wages, lack of educational facilities, high mortality rates, and widespread prostitution, due to the low proportion of women to men, combined with social discrimination to make their condition of special concern to Indian reformers. In South Africa the discrimination was legal, with Indians being prevented by law from acquiring land outside specified locations. But despite the many disabilities imposed upon them, Indians had prospered in South Africa as elsewhere, and it was this prosperity, as well as their very real difficulties, that had made it possible for them to bring their case before the Indian public.

Gandhi had, of course, been the most effective spokesman for the cause of Indians abroad during his career in South Africa. He and his friends had won a sympathetic hearing from the government of India, which recognized that the question of Indians abroad had explosive political consequences. The government of India reported to the secretary of state that the question of the treatment of indentured laborers was the cause of more bitterness than any other issue in Indian politics.

An act to forbid the recruiting of indentured labor in India was passed in 1916, but the system was not finally abolished until 1920, and still indignities lingered. In the history of Indian nationalism, overseas Indians served the same function that minority groups had served elsewhere: a source of irritation for the host country and a focus of indignation for nationalist sentiment at home.

Another aspect of the emigration problem was the right of Indians to enter "white" British dominions, particularly Canada and Australia. The numbers involved were minuscule, but the situation came to be of passionate concern to Indian nationalists in the 1920s as India received recognition in the League of

Nations and in the British Empire on a level of equality with the self-governing dominions. Since as British subjects Indians could claim access to the dominions, special discriminatory regulations were necessary to exclude them. This discrimination against Indians overseas by other countries of the empire was an important factor in the anti-Western sentiment that became obvious after the end of World War I. This was pointed out by a correspondent of the London *Times* in 1922, when he deplored what he called "the most distressing feature of the whole situation," the fact that "behind all immediate grievances and discontents, whether Caliphate, Sikh, or Non-cooperationist, there is a continual growth of racial antagonism."[1]

India's needs and aspirations were also shown in the 1920s by a renewed interest in the economic basis of nationhood. In general this continued the emphasis of the earlier nationalists on the economic disadvantages India suffered by being compelled to be a supplier of raw materials to the industrialized West. But the specific grievance was the tariff structure. The British government had insisted throughout the nineteenth century that tariffs be kept at a minimum, despite the obvious disadvantage this gave to the development of industries in India, and in opposition to the government of India's desire to use import duties as a means of raising needed revenues. For Indian nationalists this was evidence, as one newspaper put it, of "how Englishmen are blinded by selfishness; how in their anxiety to protect the interests of their own countrymen, they do not even hesitate to injure the interests of others—to draw the knife, so to speak, across other people's throats."[2]

The framers of the 1919 constitution had recognized the resentment over tariffs as one of the stumbling blocks to the working of the reforms. The inescapable conclusion, according to a parliamentary committee, was that India should have fiscal autonomy, so that she could make tariff arrangements fitted to her needs. The recommendations of the official commission followed the economic thinking of the nationalist leaders for the previous forty years: There should be a policy of protection for selected industries and the elimination of export duties. The change in India's relation to world markets was indicated by the fact that the competition was no longer with the English cotton manufacturers, but with the Japanese. The long struggle for fiscal autonomy in one sphere was thus won long before political independence was achieved. Such a victory lacked the drama of the political arena, but it was of great importance in the process of defining India as a national unit.

Division in the Nationalist Movement

In more strictly political terms the focus of nationalist interest was the question of participation in the second election for the legislative councils in 1923. The underlying issue was whether Gandhi and his program would still dominate the Indian National Congress, which would mean a refusal to participate in the elections, or whether there would be a return to a more normal pattern of political activity, with Congress leaders running for office. The conflict was solved in one of the compromises typical of Indian nationalist history. When their proposal to contest the elections was voted down by those who remained loyal to Gandhi, C. R. Das and Motilal Nehru resigned and formed the Swaraj party. The Congress then voted to permit those who had no conscientious objections to participating in the elections to do so, while the others should continue the Gandhian program of social work with the masses. The Swarajists, for their part, agreed that if their method failed, they would join a new civil disobedience campaign.

The Swaraj party, representing the Indian National Congress in everything but name, emerged as the largest single political party and the only one with anything approaching an all-Indian organization. Yet it by no means won sweeping victories. Only in the Central Provinces, an area relatively lacking in a history of political activity, did the Swarajists win a clear-cut majority. With about one-third of the 145 seats, they dominated the central Legislative Council; and in Bengal, Bombay, and the United Provinces, three areas of vital political importance, their bloc of votes was often a decisive force. The Liberal Federation had won many seats in 1920, but in 1923 they lost most of them through the opposition of the Swarajists.

In later nationalist versions of Indian history, the Liberals tend at this point to disappear from the story, but in fact, despite their small representation in the legislature, they continued to have a very important part in Indian national development. They were respected by the government, and although sometimes denounced as collaborators by the nationalists, they frequently provided liaison between the nationalists and the officials. They were also the spokesmen for many Indians, especially those in official positions, who by either temperament or status were unlikely to be attracted by the Gandhian ideology with its austerity and its rejection of industrialism and the modern world. Large numbers of this class were never overtly identified with the nationalist movement, but the Liberals gave them at least a semblance of political representation.

Another important result of the elections in 1923, as in 1921, was the victory in Madras of the Justice party, a reminder that the content of Indian nationality must not be equated with the Indian National Congress. The Justice party was distinctive in that it represented the hostility of the non-Brahmans, who made up 95 percent of the population, toward the age-old dominance of the Brahmans in social and political life. The leaders of the movement were not from the most economically and socially oppressed classes, but were those with some economic and political power who resented the Brahman monopoly in such crucial areas as education and the public services. The Justice party also spoke for a kind of nascent subnationalism—the South with its Dravidian languages, especially Tamil, against the North, with its Indo-Aryan languages. The Indian National Congress was suspect because its leaders in the South, as in the North, were mainly from the Brahman caste or other high castes. In this situation the possibility was present for the development of a regional nationalism that would challenge the claim of the Congress as the spokesman for an Indian nationalism that embraced the whole country. That this kind of regionalism, which became such a potent factor in Indian political life after 1947, was not stronger in the South in the 1920s was due to the internal weaknesses of the Justice party itself, as well as to the lack of cultural homogeneity in Madras. The province included not only the Tamil-speaking majority, but also millions of Telegu speakers and substantial numbers of other language groups. The Justice party had no program or ideological position, apart from its anti-Brahmanical stance, on which to base an appeal. Furthermore, the Justice party's opposition to the Congress made it generally pro-British, or at least pro-government, a handicap in a situation where nationalism was increasingly identified with a commitment to ending British rule.

Because the system of dyarchy, with responsibility for government divided between the nominated governor and the elected ministers, applied only to the provincial governments, not to the central Legislative Council, the provinces became the major centers of political activity and interest. Decentralization had been one of the objectives of the 1919 constitution, and as the provincial governments became more important and their decisions became of greater popular concern, provincial politics provided the nationalist leaders with their sphere of influence, rather than the all-India setting of the earlier phases of the nationalist movement. This provincial setting was a significant factor in the weakening of the power and prestige of the Indian National Congress during the mid-twenties. Therefore, to some extent the new constitutional experiment worked against the continued growth of a generalized nationalist sentiment. By having provided the political leaders with provincial, rather than national, forums, dyarchy gave modern institutional form to the cultural and linguistic regionalism that had seemed to many observers to be the distinctive characteristic of India.

This strengthening of regionalism made a vital contribution, however, to Indian nationhood and the sense of nationality by forcing Indian politicians to deal with the realities of administrative power and by forcing the bureaucracy to think and act politically. In the fifteen years in which the new system functioned with varying degrees of success in different provinces, the normal patterns of administration were maintained and new ones initiated, such as the vote for women, compulsory education in some areas, and the encouragement of local self-government on the village level.

The transitional nature of dyarchy made the system peculiarly frustrating to Indian nationalists in the 1920s. There was an air of impermanence about it, with a promise for change explicit in the whole constitutional framework, and the nationalists were anxious to have this pledge redeemed. The problem for them, as for the government, was to find a method. When they entered the provincial councils, their goals had been clear: Through unrelenting opposition to all government measures, they were to bring about a revision of the constitution that would replace dyarchy with genuine responsible government. The government argued that it was precisely this attitude that made the advance to responsible government impossible, since the purpose of the constitutional experiment had been to provide training in ministerial responsibility to the elected representatives of the people.

The search for nationhood had reached the point where fundamental decisions had to be made about the direction which would be taken by the Indian National Congress. The Swarajists were arguing for a political solution based on compromise and negotiation, set within the framework of political realities as defined by the transitional 1919 constitution. Gandhi was insistent upon his vision of an India that had no need for such compromises. For the realization of his vision, however, Gandhi needed the Congress, including the energy and intelligence represented by the Swarajists, and he fought to prevent the Swarajists from pursuing policies that would alienate them from the Congress in the same way the Liberals had been alienated.

Without any positive platform, and weakened by resignations and the lack of support from Gandhi and the Congress organization, the Swaraj party virtually disintegrated in the elections of 1926. Its place was taken by various other groups, most of whom were short-lived as political entities, but whose formation showed the growing divergences within the nationalist movement. Gandhi watched the factional struggles but made little attempt at this point at reconciliation. He regarded the question of elections to the councils as irrelevant to his main concern—the political education of the masses—and he was content to let the parties destroy each other. His own role was clear in his mind: "I must hold myself in reserve, till the storm is over and the work of rebuilding has commenced."[3]

While he waited, Gandhi's own energies and those of his closest disciples went into what he called the "constructive program" in contrast to the work of those who entered the councils and engaged in political activities on the national and provincial level. He asked in 1927: "How many of us can take a direct part in the working of that programme? . . . How many of us are entitled to elect members to these legislative bodies? Are the millions of villagers enfranchised? . . . What then is the programme that can weld together the thirty crores [300 million] of people scattered on a surface 1,900 miles long and 1,500 miles broad in 700,000 villages?"[4] When Strachey and the others pondered this question, they did so rhetorically. They believed that nothing could unite India. For Gandhi there was "one simple and unequivocal answer . . . the spinning wheel and khaddar [homespun]."[5] For this reason he watched, with some satisfaction, as the political parties fought each other in the councils.

One of the groups that helped destroy the Swaraj party as an effective political force was a coalition headed by two of the most famous of the older generation of leaders from the Indian National Congress, M. M. Malaviya and Lala Lajpat Rai. They spoke for a strong faction within the Congress that felt that the interests of the Hindu majority, as opposed to those of Muslims, had not been properly protected by the Swarajists in the legislative councils. They did not represent a new movement within the Congress so much as one that had been quiescent since the Lucknow Pact of 1916 and the Khilafat Movement of the early 1920s. B. G. Tilak's vigorous emphasis on the importance of the Hindu elements of Indian culture had been muted in the years when Gandhi was making common cause with the Muslims, but there had always been segments of the nationalist movement that felt the Hindu heritage had been betrayed by excessive concessions to the Muslims, on the one hand, and to Western secular ideas, on the other.

The Hindu Mahasabha had been formed to safeguard the Hindu way of life in 1906, but it did not come into prominence until the 1920s. It was not a political party and did not run candidates for elections, but it included many members from the Congress, with Mulaviya and Lajpat Rai among its leaders. The revival and strengthening of the Hindu Mahasabha in the mid-twenties and its very considerable accession of power within the Indian National Congress were related to the worsening of Hindu-Muslim relations, perhaps the most significant feature of Indian political and social life in the period.

By the mid-twenties Hindu-Muslim riots had become commonplace. Charges that the riots were caused by British *agents provocateurs* were often made but have never been proved, and in any case the British could not have created the violence had there not been deeply rooted antagonisms. As suggested in an earlier chapter, these antagonisms became visible in the late nineteenth century as a nationalist ideology was articulated, with its inevitable appeals to religion, language, culture, and history, all of which were divisive, not cohesive, forces. The emergence of Gandhi sharpened these distinctions, despite the fact that he was an adamant spokesman for Hindu-Muslim solidarity. On the one hand, by making the Khilafat Movement central to the nationalist cause in 1920, he had, despite all his disclaimers to the contrary, emphasized the importance of being a Muslim, rather than an Indian, nationalist. For both Hindus and Muslims it indicated the primacy of religious identifications in Indian social life. Even more important, and again despite Gandhi's denial that this was the increasing use of an essentially Hindu vocabulary of politics, Gandhi's extraordinary empathy with the Hindu masses depended upon the formulation of a nationalist ideology in terms that were comprehensible to them. The corollary was that this nationalism became less appealing to Muslims, especially to the Muslim intellectuals who did not have the instinctive response to the Gandhian ideology that the Hindu intelligentsia had.

The direct result of the worsening of Hindu-Muslim relations was the attempt by M. A. Jinnah to revitalize the Muslim League and make it an active political force. It had been moribund since the start of the Khilafat Movement, which had absorbed the energies of the Muslim political leaders. But after he had left the Indian National Congress over the non-cooperation and civil disobedience issues, Jinnah saw the possibility of using the League as a pressure group to gain constitutional protection for the Muslim minority. He succeeded in drawing the League together again as a functioning political organisation, but it had no popular support from the masses or from the religious leaders, many of whom regarded Jinnah and his followers as heretical modernists. In addition, the League itself was divided by internal quarrels. The opportunity to make the League a more powerful force in Indian politics came at the end of the 1920s in connection with the appointment by the British government of the Simon Commission to examine the need for further constitutional changes in India.

First Demand for Independence

It is ironical that the announcement of the Simon Commission in 1927 brought new life to the Indian nationalist movement on all levels, breaking the spirit of malaise and frustration brought on by the divisions within the Congress and the viciousness of the Hindu-Muslim rioting. The 1919 constitution had made provision for reviewing its effectiveness after ten years. But the British Conservatives appointed the commission, headed by Sir John Simon, two years early because they feared that the nationalist cause would gain too much sympathy if the Labour party took power. Indian leaders of all political views had been demanding a commission for some time, but when Indians were not included as members, the Simon Commission was denounced as a new insult to Indian national life. Political India had found a common cause once more, and India's search for nationhood took on a new sense of urgency.

The older generation of nationalists, including Gandhi, who found it difficult to visualize an India that was not in some way related to Great Britain, argued that dominion status for India was the limit of realistic possibilities. By 1928, however, there was a group of young men within the Indian National Congress demanding that full independence should be the stated aim of the Congress. The leaders in this revolt were Jawalarlal Nehru, the son of Motilal, and Subhas Chandra Bose, a young Bengali who aspired to the position of leadership once held by C. R. Das. They brought fresh ideas and new vitality into the Congress, for both had been influenced by contemporary European socialist and Marxist thought, and, more than any other of the Congress leaders, they saw Indian politics in terms of ideology. But despite Nehru's socialism and his distaste for religious symbols, he was always drawn emotionally toward Gandhi in a way that Bose never was. And from the very beginning Gandhi recognized that Nehru's ideological positions were far more flexible than those of Bose, whose allegiances and sympathies with the revolutionary tradition of Bengali politics were a barrier to wholehearted acceptance of the Gandhian program, with its ethic of nonviolence.

The divergence between the political understanding of Nehru and Bose and that of Gandhi came to a head over the Congress' position on India's future constitutional relationship with Great Britain. Nehru and Bose, with strong support from within the Congress, demanded that India's goal should be complete independence, not dominion status. By the end of 1928 it seemed that a split in the Congress was inevitable, so sharply had the issue divided the party. But Gandhi once more devised a formula for compromise: They would ask for dominion status, but if it were not granted by the end of 1929, then the Congress would begin a new civil disobedience movement. This not only prevented a division within the Congress, but it also brought Gandhi back into full participation in political life, for when the British did not agree to grant dominion status, Gandhi began a new civil disobedience campaign.

The second civil disobedience campaign began in March 1930, eight years after the collapse of the first one. Gandhi proceeded cautiously, despite the impatience and enthusiasm of the supporters, as he was still uncertain that the masses were ready for the kind of movement he envisaged. The educated classes had independence as their slogan, but at one time Gandhi had defied anyone to give him a translation of the word "independence" in any Indian language that would be intelligible to the masses. What they needed was some symbol that touched their daily lives. He found it in the salt laws, which made the manufacture of salt a government monopoly. Gandhi's argument was that the laws were unjust, since they increased the price of a commodity that is a necessity of life. Gandhi's method for breaking the salt laws was dramatic and appealing. It began with a march from his headquarters near Ahmedabad in Gujarat to the seacoast at Dandi, 240 miles away, where salt was manufactured from sea water.

The breaking of the salt laws at Dandi was the signal for the beginning of civil disobedience throughout the country, and the government soon took action. Numerous outbreaks of violence took place. The Indian National Congress accused the police of provocation, but the government placed the blame on the attacks of mobs on government and private property. Many people were killed, and thousands arrested, including all the leaders of the Congress. Most of those jailed were ordinary members of the party or people involved in the riots, but they also included men of wealth and power such as the Nehrus. Gandhi himself was not arrested until May 1930, since the government was afraid his imprisonment would evoke a new round of disorders.

The civil disobedience campaign continued for six months more, but with the leaders in jail there was little hope for an organized movement. Gandhi began conversations with the governor general through the mediation of the Liberal leaders. Gandhi's announcement that, in return for concessions from the government, the second civil disobedience campaign had been suspended came as a blow to his followers; after refusing to negotiate the previous year, he seemed to have given in now for very minor concessions. There was no mention of dominion status, much less independence, but only a concern with what seemed to many of them minor items: the release of prisoners, the calling of a round-table conference, the permission for peaceful picketing of liquor shops, and the right of those who lived near the sea to make their own salt. 1930 had been, as Nehru put it, "a wonder year," when the whole country seemed willing to follow Gandhi's bidding in resisting the British. Now once more, as in 1922, Gandhi seemed to have let his followers down, just when they might have shaken British power.

At this point of low morale, the nationalist movement found a martyr in Bhagat Singh, a young Sikh revolutionary, who was found guilty of a political murder. The extraordinary popularity he achieved was embarrassing to the Congress leaders, who were committed to the position that Indians had accepted the ideal of nonviolence. But the emotional response that Bhagat Singh's cause engendered was a useful antidote to the pessimism and frustration that followed the ending of the civil disobedience campaign. When Bhagat Singh and his accomplices were hanged, riots broke out in which hundreds of people were killed and wounded. And although Gandhi deplored the violence, he extolled Bhagat Singh's bravery and sacrifice. His attitude at such times often confused his admirers in the West, many of whom were Christian pacifists, but for Gandhi the willing sacrifice of blood by the innocent was a necessary foundation for a strong nation. "I would not flinch," he once declared, "from sacrificing even a million lives for India's liberty."[6] But though he was fascinated by the metaphors of martyrdom, with their undertones of purification by blood, this aspect of his thought, as with so much of his ideology, was marked by ambiguity. For example, the actual physical death of martyrdom, Gandhi transmuted into the symbolic death of the self through fasting and other austerities.

Hindu-Muslim Relations

The abandonment of the civil disobedience campaign in 1931 marked the end, or at least the postponement, of the debate over dominion status versus independence, one of the two great issues that had arisen out of the Simon Commission. The other issue was the question of Hindu-Muslim relations, which, in terms of the constitutional discussion, was concerned with the guaranteed representation of Muslims in the central and provincial legislative assemblies. Muslim leaders, including Jinnah, had taken an active part in negotiations, but they were convinced that the Congress leadership did not take the issue of Muslim representation seriously. By the end of 1928 Jinnah was beginning to abandon his long attempt to foster cooperation between the Muslim League and the Indian National Congress. Although he was still uncertain of the direction in which he should move, the events of 1929 and 1930, with Gandhi's dramatic exploitation of his following among the Hindu masses, had been decisive for Jinnah. He was convinced that the Muslim League, which so far had failed to elicit either interest among the Muslim masses or unified support from even its own leadership, would have to speak for the Muslims.

At this time Jinnah found a powerful ally in Muhammad Iqbal (1877-1938), the greatest literary figure produced by Indian Muslims in the twentieth century. Jinnah and Iqbal are makers of Pakistan, but they are also makers of Modern India in the sense that its political development after 1930 is not intelligible without considering their work. Jinnah has been assigned the role in Indian nationalist history of the fanatical enemy of Indian unity, building a new nation on hates and fears which he either brought into being or fanned into flames. There is very little to justify this reading of his activities in the 1930s.

Jinnah's insistence that the Muslim community, making up one-quarter of the population of India, constituted a special problem that needed careful constitutional definition was rejected by the Congress leadership for a variety of reasons. Gandhi sought a nation animated by a specific spiritual response, and he was genuinely convinced that this could come from all of India's people, irrespective of their religious identifications, since, as he never wearied of arguing, all religions expressed the same truth. He was probably unaware that this involved a peculiarly Hindu definition of truth. From a different standpoint Nehru and his group rejected religion as a significant factor in modern nationalism, arguing that the tensions leading to Hindu-Muslim riots were rooted in poverty and in the ignorance it produced. Another attitude was represented by men such as M. M. Malaviya, who, deeply Hindu in their outlook and allegiances, saw the Muslim demands not just as a threat to national unity, but also to Hindu culture itself. All of the groups were united in arguing that the Congress was demonstrably neither exclusively Hindu nor anti-Muslim since many Muslims were active in it, and a number of Muslims had become presidents of the Congress. Maulana Azad was the most notable of these "nationalist Muslims," as they became known. This Muslim support seemed to confirm the Congress' insistence that it was not a Hindu organization, but the fundamental reality remained that, however apathetic the Muslim masses might be and however divided their leadership, the Islamic community in India possessed all the potentialities to which a nationalist appeal could be made. This ran counter to the definition of nationalism with which the Congress had identified itself, but once this alternative nationalism became an option for Indian Muslims, they were likely to seize upon it as an escape from the political frustrations they shared with other Indians. More than anyone else, it was Iqbal who articulated the alternative to the Congress' brand of nationalism.

In his early writings Iqbal had decried nationalism as a disease of the West that was antithetical to the spirit of Islam, and he had argued that the Muslims of India would find their salvation through membership in the whole Islamic community. The failure of the Khilafat Movement and the rise of strong nationalist parties in many of the Muslim countries turned him inward, and the course of Indian politics after 1928 convinced him that Indian Muslims would have to find their true community in some form of a Muslim state within India. He enunciated this idea for the first time in 1930 when he was president of the

Muslim League. To the Congress' arguments that religion was not a decisive component in nationality and that Hindus and Muslims could find solidarity through a common devotion to India, Iqbal answered that religion and society were organically related in Islam, with one nourishing the other. "Therefore the construction of a polity on national lines, if it means a displacement of Islamic principles of solidarity, is simply unthinkable to a Muslim." Given his premises, the logic of Iqbal's conclusion was irrefutable. "The formation of a consolidated North-West Indian Muslim state appears to me to be the final destiny of the Muslims of at least North-West India."[7]

Iqbal's arguments were never met in a meaningful way by the Congress politicians. Gandhi's answer that all religions could find fulfillment in the new India since they were guardians of the same truth, and Nehru's argument that religion was a man's private concern, having nothing to do with the polity of the state, only strengthened Iqbal's case. While it was true, as Indian nationalists pointed out, that in Western countries different religions and sects lived side by side, united in allegiance to a common nationality, India was different. Hinduism and Islam were not "religions" in the sense that the Western world used the term, Jinnah insisted, but rather were social orders. In the West religious affiliation was one among many aspects of life; in India at this time it denoted the deepest patterns of life and thought. Because of this, as Jinnah put it in a later period, the attempt to meld two basically different social orders into a common nationality "must lead to a growing discontent and final destruction of any fabric that may be so built up for the government of such a state."[8] Jinnah's point was best understood by the Hindu communal groups; from the opposite end of the political spectrum, they too insisted that in India religion was not, as in the West, one preference among many. Hinduism was the heart of Indian civilization and could not be treated as if it were irrelevant to politics.

Renewal of Nationalist Activity

The problems concerning the nature of Indian nationhood and nationality raised by Iqbal and Jinnah received little attention in 1931. The center of nationalist concern shifted to London, where Gandhi had gone to attend the round-table conference called as the result of his pact with the government for ending civil disobedience. Gandhi was the sole official representative of the Indian National Congress, and the drama of one man speaking for the most powerful political force in India caught the imagination of the world. For the moment Indian nationality was concentrated in Gandhi. The talks, however, accomplished almost nothing. The British government and the non-Congress delegates wanted to discuss constitutional details, while Gandhi insisted that the only issue was Indian independence.

Gandhi made no attempt to negotiate the details of a constitutional settlement. By this time it was clear that such negotiations were not part of his style of politics. O. K. Gokhale had once remarked on his extraordinary ability to "enchain the attention of the poor man" and to establish "an affinity with the lowly and the distressed." But he had gone on to say: "Be careful that India not trust him on occasions where delicate negotiations have to be carried on with care and caution . . .acting on the principle that a loaf is better than no bread."[9] This was a notable insight, but it was only a half-truth, since Gandhi had of course negotiated successfully on numerous occasions. But now Gandhi probably felt the stakes were too high to endanger the country by diverting them from the main issues: the unity and freedom of India.

When Gandhi returned to India at the end of 1931 another confrontation between the Indian National Congress and the government became inevitable. There had been incidents of terror in Bengal, and widespread agitation and rioting elsewhere had been brought on by the worsening economic depression. The government insisted that it had to take strong measures to preserve law and order, including the arrest of Congress leaders who participated in the agitations. Gandhi charged that these measures were in violation of the pact he had made with the governor general before halting the civil disobedience campaign, and he announced plans for its resumption. This time the government acted swiftly, imprisoning Gandhi and the rest of the leaders early in 1932 and declaring the Congress illegal. Civil disobedience continued, however, and the police responded by charging on the crowds that gathered in towns and cities throughout the country. Many people were killed and wounded, and more than 100,000 people were arrested. None of the previous campaigns had elicited such widespread support, and there were many acts of individual defiance that thrilled the country, as when Nehru's mother was beaten by the police after she had placed herself at the head of a procession.

The behavior of the police at such times caused special bitterness. The government argued that the police had to use force to protect themselves in the face of the mobs, which was probably true. But the reality of the situation was summed up by an Indian observer in a letter to Ramsay MacDonald, the British Labour prime minister.

> The police in India, ill-educated, ill-paid, and drawn from the lowest strata of society and accustomed to rough modes, when actually authorised and encouraged to strike persons in the streets, irrespective of station, age or sex, cannot be expected to restrain themselves. Stories of inhuman and barbarous chastisement go about, creating bitterness and racial and communal rancour. Believe me, there will be the very devil to pay for another generation.[10]

Yet despite the enthusiasm and self-sacrifice, the civil disobedience campaign was not self-sustaining, and by the summer of 1933 most of its vitality was gone. The Indian nationalist movement never had the spirit of a civil war, with its complete commitment occasioned by the knowledge that one was engaged in a fight to the death in which no quarter would be asked or given. The processions, the speeches, the newspaper reports, the public gatherings were made in defiance of government orders, but always with the assertion that no violence or destruction was intended and that it was the government which was acting illegally and undemocratically in provoking the riots through the violence of the police.

The Indian nationalists in 1932 and 1933 were still appealing, as their predecessors had in the early days of the movement, to British notions of freedom and legality. The result was that the repressive legislation and the attacks by the police weakened their will to resist because they still acknowledged the legitimacy of British rule.

The government's policy was probably the major reason for this exhaustion, but there were other controlling factors. One was that very important segments of the Indian population actively opposed the civil disobedience campaign. These included business and commercial interests and landlords, as well as many intellectuals of moderate political views, such as the leaders of the Liberals, who were convinced that the time had come for careful negotiation for a new constitution. The Muslim League was inactive during these years, but the spirit of malaise that characterized its leadership helped the government, not the Indian National Congress. Jinnah himself left India for London, feeling that there was no hope in a united India for the Muslims, who "were like dwellers in No Man's land; they were either led by flunkeys of the British Government or the camp followers of the Congress."[11] A more complex factor in the weakening of the civil disobedience movement was Gandhi's activity in prison.

Gandhi's return to the forefront of India's political consciousness came with his initiation of a series of fasts while he was still in jail. The first one in September 1932 was a protest against the British decision to give the Untouchables a total of seventy-one seats in the various provincial legislative councils. The grant was made in response to the demand at the round-table conference of Dr. Bhimrao Ramji Ambedkar, the leader of the Untouchables, for the protection of this minority. Gandhi's announcement that he would fast to death unless the award was withdrawn created a dilemma for the British, who feared that Gandhi's death might trigger an outburst of violence the government of India could not contain.

For Gandhi the award of seats to the Untouchables, or, as he preferred to call them, the Harijans, God's People, would be a further division of Indian society, perpetuating their inferiority by giving them a vested interest in their low status. Ambedkar denounced this as a thinly veiled argument for using the 70 million Untouchables as weightage for the Hindus against the Muslims; but as the attention of the nation focused once more on Gandhi, an intricate agreement was worked out. In essence it assured Harijan representatives twice as many places in the legislative councils but did not give them separate constituencies.

By directing his own attention and that of many of his followers into the campaign against untouchability, Gandhi no doubt drew off some of the energy that might have gone into more directly political purposes, but his concern for what he regarded as an intolerable blot on Hindu society stirred the imagination and the conscience of the Indian people. His ceaseless travel from village to village throughout the country was a paradigm in modern form of the wanderings of the traditional Hindu saint, in quest of salvation both for himself and for those who thronged to see him. Even his insistence that everyone, including the poorest people, should give him some contribution for the national cause was rooted in the elemental feeling that both the giving and receiving of alms are marks of spiritual grace.

Another factor that weighed heavily in Gandhi's decisions at this time was the increasing violence of the crowds, especially in the great northern cities, as they confronted the police. Gandhi did not fear bloodshed and suffering when, according to his beliefs, they could be used creatively, but he feared uncontrolled violence. He was especially troubled by a growing challenge to his conception of the Congress as an organization representing all the interests and classes of the nation. The communists and other leftwing groups were active as participants, if not as leaders, in much of the violent agitation of 1932 and 1933, and they denounced Gandhi and the other Congress leaders as the tools of the British imperialists and the Indian capitalists. Gandhi came to the conclusion that he should retire from the Congress because of his estrangement from many of the other leaders. His emphasis on the spinning program and the eradication of untouchability seemed increasingly irrelevant to those who thought the time had come to engage in the administration of the country and to fight in the legislatures for changes in the new constitution the British government had prepared.

1935 India Act

After the second round-table conference had broken up in 1931 without the Indian representatives coming to any agreement on constitutional safeguards for the minority groups, the British officials and the government of India proceeded to draft a new constitution. This was the Government of India Act of 1935, the last in the long series of British parliamentary acts that since 1773 had defined the nature and power of British rule in India. Despite the criticism made of it at the time, the act provided the framework around which the constitution of independent India was built. It once more asserted the primacy of British rule, but although there was no specific mention of either dominion status or independence as future goals, the implicit assumption was that the promise of 1917, the advance toward responsible government, could be fulfilled within the new framework. It was not a transitional document, as the 1919 constitution had been; provisions for change and growth were made, but the act was a definitive solution to what the British regarded as the major political problems of India.

In general terms the new constitution preserved the ultimate authority of the governor general as the representative of the British crown and created a federation in which the princely states had a considerable degree of autonomy and responsibility. The system of dyarchy, which had worked in the provinces, was to be introduced at the center, with responsibility for certain aspects of the administration being turned over to ministers representing the electors, and others being retained by the governor general. But since the princes did not accept the proposals made for their participation, this federal part of the constitution never came into operation. The real changes took place on the provincial level.

The authority of the British government was maintained in the provinces by the governor appointed by the Crown, but the dyarchy of 1919 was abolished. The chief minister would be chosen from the party that commanded the largest majority; the chief minister could then select his own ministers, as in British parliamentary practice. The franchise was given to about 27 percent of the total adult population, including women, making the electorate of thirty-five million one of the largest in the world. The desire to write in safeguards for the rights of minorities led, however, to the fragmentation of this electorate into an extraordinarily complex pattern. There were two kinds of constituencies, general ones and those in which only special classes had a right to vote. Bombay can serve as an example. There were 175 seats in Bombay's Legislative Assembly, with 114 of them for the general population, in effect for the Hindus. Out of this number fifteen seats were reserved for representatives of the Harijans and other culturally and economically backward Hindu groups. The Muslims were given twenty-nine seats, with the rest divided among tribal peoples, Anglo-Indians, Europeans, Indian Christians, representatives of industry, landowners, universities, labor, and women.

To the British the India Act of 1935 was a generous gesture, meeting all the reasonable demands of the nationalists while safeguarding the rights of the minorities, particularly the Muslims, and ensuring the continued guiding hand of British power. Politically conscious Indians regarded it with disappointment and scorn. It cut across what seemed to be the mainstream of national integration, the process that the British themselves had done so much to further through their centralized administration and modern communications. A federal structure was being created out of an existing unitary government, not as elsewhere from a union of states. The complex franchise, with its constituencies for a multitude of racial, religious, and cultural groups, was subversive of Indian nationality. To men like Nehru the communal franchise was a denial of modernity to India, an attempt to relegate it to the status of Lebanon or the millets of the Ottoman Empire. The conviction, long held by the nationalists, that the British accentuated old divisions and created new ones in order to perpetuate their rule was thus strengthened.

The Indian National Congress response was ambiguous. The new constitution was denounced but Congressmen were to contest the elections. They were not to cooperate with the government by taking office, however, if they won a majority of the seats. Instead they were to wreck the new structure from within. When the elections were over, and it was found that the Congress had won majorities in most of the provinces, this decision was changed. On being assured by the governor general that the governor would in normal circumstances exercise his authority only on the advice of the elected ministers, Congress ministers took office in 1937 in seven provinces, including three of the largest and most important, Madras, Bombay, and the United Provinces.

New Strength of the Muslim League

With political power no longer a distant goal to be sought, but a possession to be managed, the stresses that had been apparent for some years became greater. Within the Indian National Congress party itself there was increasing resistance from various groups. One group, led by Subhas Chandra Bose, objected to the dominance of Gandhi and his ideology and the failure, in their view, of the Congress to pursue a socially progressive and anti-imperialist policy. The break came when Bose, having been elected president of the Congress, was forced by Gandhi to resign. Bose then formed a new party, the Forward Bloc. Its manifesto was virtually a rejection of the Congress' commitment to nonviolence and a broadly based consensus. "Only the Left," it declared, "can preserve the revolutionary character of the Congress and bring about an early resumption of the fight for national freedom."[12] Although Bose used the vocabulary of contemporary European socialism, his intellectual and spiritual roots were in the Bengali revolutionary movement. His wartime collaboration with the Nazis was therefore not so much a renunciation of his earlier Marxism as a willingness to use any method to defeat the British. His ardent patriotism, with its atavistic links to religious passion, made an appeal to many Hindus, especially his fellow Bengalis, even if they had no sympathy for his political ideology. The old relationship between religion and nationalism was also seen in the increased activity of the Hindu Mahasabha and allied groups seeking to make Hinduism relevant to the changing political conditions. The reinvigoration of the Muslim League at this time was to a considerable extent a response to this revivalism.

One of the many paradoxes of the history of nationalism in India is that Muslim nationalism, with its explicit grounding in an appeal to a specific religious community, appears to be far less "religious" in its orientation than the nationalism of the Indian National Congress, which very genuinely sought to include Indians of all religious persuasions. Jinnah himself was a rationalist to whom the religious idiom expressed by Gandhi was distasteful, partly because it introduced an irrational element into political discussion, but more importantly because Gandhi had turned the Congress "into an instrument for the revival of Hinduism and for the establishment of Hindu Raj in India."[13]

Jinnah did not strengthen the Muslim League through an appeal to religious emotion. He built his case substantially on the formal recognition by the British in 1909, 1919, and 1935, through the creation of Muslim constituencies that any political settlement would have to take the Muslims as a subnationality into account. This meant that all decisions on India's future always involved negotiations between the British, the Indian National Congress, and the Muslim League. The Congress had unmistakable claims to be the major beneficiary of the devolution of power, but the League insisted that it was the spokesman for the political rights of Muslims that the British as the possessors of power had already acknowledged. Jinnah had a twofold task: to validate the League's claim and to define Muslim political rights in constitutional terms through negotiations between the British and the League.

Although the idea that the Hindus and the Muslims constituted two separate nations that might have to find distinct national destinies was suggested at a meeting of the League in 1930, Jinnah did not concentrate on this theoretical argument after the Congress ministries took office in 1937. He took up instead a practical and explosive political issue. This was the charge, made especially in the rural areas, that the Congress ministries were discriminating against Muslims. Although British observers thought that in general the alleged cases of discrimination were rather trivial, truth or falsity in such matters is hard to distinguish. The important fact was that the Muslims felt they were being discriminated against by the Congress. This belief became one of the realities of Indian politics, the focus for fears and frustrations that had their origin in social and economic conditions that had little to do with actual religious status. But just as the leaders of the general nationalist drive for political freedom and national self-identity had often found it necessary to use symbols and vocabulary that were drawn from Hindu culture, so the leaders of the Muslim League had to use the rubric of Islam in order to make its appeal. With a well-articulated social and cultural inheritance to draw upon, the League was able by the 1940s to identify itself with a subnationalism that had to be taken seriously as a possible expression of the aspirations of the Indian Muslims.

*   *   *

The failure of the Indian National Congress to take the Muslim League seriously in the crucial years from 1937 to 1939 has seemed, to many observers, the final political error made by Nehru and Gandhi. The list that critics draw up is long: the refusal to enter the councils in 1920; then, having decided on civil disobedience, the abandonment of it in 1922 and 1934, instead of moving forward to a final confrontation; the unwillingness of the Congress in the 1930s to negotiate details of a constitutional settlement; and the rejection in 1937 of coalition ministries with the League. Other decisions at these climactic moments, it is argued, would have saved India from the turmoil of the 1940s that ended with partition. But what the critics ignore is that the complexity of Indian political and social life would not have permitted any easy transition to responsible government and independence. The decisions made at the time, especially those in which Gandhi had the major influence, do indeed often seem to have been quixotic and mistaken in their understanding of the possibilities of political action. Yet in the total context of India's long effort to define herself as a nation, they were probably the right mistakes. The frustrations and tensions they engendered were related to the fundamental problem in the devolution of power, the answer in explicit political terms to the question Curzon had asked in 1905: "Who and what are the real Indian people?"[14] Probably, as the events of the 1940s showed, only a complicated and unsatisfactory answer could be given.

NOTES

1. *Times* (London), March 16, 1922.

2. Quoted in Bipin Chandra, *The Rise and Growth of Economic Nationalism in India* (New Delhi: People's Publishing House, 1966) 239.

3. Quoted in Tendulkar, *Mahatma*, Vol. II, 166.

4. Ibid., 234.

5. Ibid., 244.

6. Ibid, Vol. Ill, 52.

7. Muhammad Iqbal, *Speeches and Statements of Iqbal*, "Shamloo" (ed.) (Lahore: Al-Manar Academy, 1948), 9.

8. Speech at Lahore, March 23, 1940, quoted in Kahlid B, Sayeed, *The Political System of Pakistan* (Boston: Houghtan Mifflin, 1967), 40.

9. Quoted in M. R. Jayakar, *Story of My Life* (Bombay: Asia Publishing House 1958), Vol. I, 317.

10. Srinivasa Sastri to Ramsay MacDonald, April 15, 1932, quoted in Kanji Dwarkadas, *India's Fight for Freedom* (Bombay: Popular Prakashan, 1966), 416.

11. Quoted in S. K. Majumdar, *Jinnah and Gandhi* (Calcutta: Firma K.L. Mukhopadhyay, 1966), 155.

12. Subhas Chandra Bose, *Crossroads* (London: Asia Publishing House, 1962). 180.

13. Quoted in Majumdar, *Jinah and Gandhi*, 171.

14. Ralelgh, *Lord Curzon in India*, 584-585.

CHAPTER 6. END AND BEGINNING

By 1939, despite the frustrations and mistakes of the previous twenty years, a sense of nationality, fused from the disparate elements of India's cultural and political traditions, had become an actuality. Regional differences of language, custom, and historical experience were still as great as they had been in 1880 when Strachey declared it was impossible that men of the Punjab, Bengal and Madras should ever feel they belonged to one great nation. But a change had taken place that even those most committed to the value and necessity of British rule found hard to deny. For large numbers of people throughout the country, and by no means for only those who had been directly influenced by Western education, there was an awareness that being an Indian was part of their essential heritage. They had come to share in what, as was suggested in the first chapter, is one of the fundamental aspects of nationality: the sense that "individual identity hinges on the existence of a national identity," with all the attendant psychological involvement that such an identification entails. The announcement in September 1939 that the governor general had declared India at war on the side of Great Britain and her allies, without prior consultation with Indian political leadership, was thus felt as a personal, as well as a national, slight, requiring a new confrontation with the imperial power.

The pattern of events that followed was a duplication of the earlier confrontations: mutual charges of bad faith, the call for civil disobedience, imprisonments, and finally, agreement on issues that might, it seems, have been reached without the years of frustration and delay. The difference between the new phase, lasting from 1939 to 1947, and the previous ones was that this time there was no real doubt that the final settlement would be Indian independence. The issues had narrowed to questions of timing and methods of devolution of power, even though the language of all the protagonists sometimes concealed this. But the fact that the issues were more precisely defined than they had been in the past did not mean that there was less bitterness or more clarity in regard to solutions that would be acceptable to the three negotiating groups—the British, the Indian National Congress, and the Muslim League. It was true, as the governor general was reminded by a delegation in 1939 representing the Liberal Federation, the Scheduled Castes, and the Hindu Mahasabha, that there were interests in India whom neither the Congress nor the League represented. But these interests carried little weight in the final struggle.

Bargaining for Independence

The Indian National Congress at first offered to support the war effort if the British would make an unequivocal statement that India would get freedom after the war, with an immediate grant of a large measure of responsible government at the central level. When the British replied that such a transfer of power could not take place during the war, the ministries in the eight Congress provinces resigned. This decision has often been criticized, but the Congress leadership recognized that if they continued in office, they would be forced to cooperate with the British, and powerful factions within the Congress itself would use this cooperation to undermine their authority. The threat to the leadership came from two main sources: the communists, who in the early stages of the war had denounced it as imperialist aggression, and Subhas Chandra Bose and his followers, who were willing to cooperate with the Germans in return for help in overthrowing the British. Bose and his followers thought the time had come when the nationalist movement would finally move to a direct and, if necessary, violent confrontation with the British. The German triumphs in Europe in the spring and summer of 1940 had set the stage. Bose wrote:

> As every day passes one feels like biting his fingers in helpless agony. Can nothing be done to save India even at this late hour? Will not the enslaved people of India cast off their lethargy and stand up as one man to demand liberty. . . . If Europe is in the melting pot, who can withstand the demand of three hundred and fifty millions of Indians?[1]

When the British refused the Congress' demand for an immediate establishment of an independent government, they argued that this was impossible not only because of the war, but also because they "could not contemplate transfer of their present responsibilities for the peace and welfare of India to any system of government whose authority is directly denied by large and powerful elements in India's national life."[2] What they had in mind, of course, was the Muslim League, and they were thus in effect giving a veto over constitutional change to Jinnah and the Muslim League.

Two-Nation Concept

Jinnah, who up to this time had been struggling to make the Muslim League politically significant, became the spokesman for the Muslims. In future negotiations he did not have to state his aims nor did he have to prove that he spoke for all, or even a majority, of Indian Muslims. His strength was the British insistence that the rights of all minorities be safeguarded.

Although Jinnah did not offer any concrete proposals for constitutional change at this time, he further refined the concept of Muslim nationalism. The only hope for a reasonable life for Muslims was the recognition that Hindus and Muslims constituted two nations. This view found formal expression in a resolution of the Muslim League at Lahore in March 1940:

> No constitutional plan would be workable in this country or acceptable to the Muslims unless it is designated on the following basic principles, viz., that geographically contiguous units are demarcated into regions that should be so constituted . . . that the areas in which the Muslims are numerically in a majority as in the North-Western and Eastern zones should be grouped to constitute "Independent States" in which the constituent units shall be autonomous and sovereign.[3]

This was a more precise definition of Iqbal's idea of Muslim provinces, to which the name of "Pakistan," from the initial letters of the various Muslim majority areas, had been given by an Indian Muslim student at Cambridge in 1933. There was still much ambiguity about what Jinnah really meant, whether he was thinking of two separate Muslim states—one in what is now West Pakistan, the other East Bengal—or if he meant by "states" merely provinces with a large measure of autonomy. But he had given at least a minimal statement of his goal. The idea that Hindus and Muslims could ever evolve a common nationality was, he said at this time, a dream that failed to see that Hindus and Muslims drew their inspiration for nationhood from different sources of history.

The Muslim League's vitality came simply from opposing the Indian National Congress, but the Congress had to have a program to maintain its popular support. In Bengal, Bose's Forward Bloc was winning adherents through its undeviating opposition to the British. In northern India, many Hindus, including Congressmen, dismayed at the growing power of the Muslim League, were convinced that the Congress, by refusing to cooperate with the British, had played into Jinnah's hands. They were also disenchanted with nonviolence, especially as there were renewed outbreaks of Hindu-Muslim rioting in which, the Hindus believed, the Muslims had been the aggressors. K. M. Munshi, one of the most prominent Congressmen and a close friend of Gandhi, expressed a widespread view when he spoke of the "planned Communal frenzy" directed by the Muslim League against Hindu women and children and of how he "boiled with rage at our impotence" in not fighting back.[4]

Allied Pressure

Tension increased after the entrance of Japan into the war at the end of 1941. The rapid advance of the Japanese through Southeast Asia forced all groups to face the prospect of an imminent Japanese invasion. A new factor in the situation was the pressure put on Britain at this time by her allies, China and the United States, to gain India's full support for the war effort by meeting some of the nationalist demands for an immediate move toward granting independence. This was the first time that the Indian nationalists had received any substantial backing from foreign governments. Unlike earlier national movements in Europe and later ones in Asia and Africa, Indian nationalism had few debts to outside political forces.

The Chinese nationalist leader, Chiang Kai-shek, who had been in touch with Nehru at the outbreak of the war, visited India in February 1942 and became convinced that unless the British made some move, Indians would not resist the Japanese. The United States government had already raised the question of Indian independence with Churchill, reflecting pressure from groups in the United States that had long been sympathetic with the Indian cause. And the fall of Singapore made the matter more urgent. Setting up a temporary dominion government of India, Roosevelt urged Churchill, "might cause the people there to forget hard feelings"[5] and to join wholeheartedly in the war against Japan. Some interpreters have suggested that the American intervention was the prime influence in persuading Churchill to open negotiations with the Indian political leaders by sending Sir Stafford Cripps to India. This suggestion is doubtful since there was strong support for such action from the Labour members of the British government, but it may well have been one of the deciding factors.

Cripps Mission

Cripps arrived in India in March 1942, bringing with him the British government's proposal that as soon as the war was over steps would be taken to set up in India an elected body to frame a constitution for a new Indian union. This would "constitute a Dominion associated with the United Kingdom and other Dominions by common allegiance to the Crown but equal to them in every respect." Any province that wished to remain outside this Indian union would have the right to do so and would be given the same status as the Indian union. Meanwhile the government would invite the immediate participation of the leaders of the Indian people in the running of the country. The task of "organizing to the full the military, moral and material resources of India must be the responsibility of the Government of India," with the British government retaining "control, and direction, of the defense of India as part of their world war effort."[6]

The promise of the Cripps mission that Britain would give India her freedom when the war ended was, in words attributed to Gandhi, "a blank cheque on a failing bank." The Indian National Congress leaders were interested only in what Britain had to offer immediately, and when the proposals were examined, this was found to be very little. All the essential powers were to be left with the governor general and the commander in chief of the army; the Indians would find their role through an effective prosecution of the war. There was little reason why the Congress leaders should have been willing to consider this proposal.

One aspect of the proposal made it particularly unacceptable: the statement that a province could, in effect, secede from the Indian union. As a concession to the Muslim League, this meant that the Congress would agree in advance to the partition of the country. Jinnah and the Muslim League did not have to press their position; as in the past and as it was to be later on, all that was necessary was to wait, leaving the action to the Congress. Jinnah knew, as responsible British opinion might have known, that such a proposition was unthinkable to the Congress in 1942. Events finally forced its acceptance in 1947, but in 1942 among the Congress leaders only Rajagopalachari urged that the Muslim League's demands should even be recognized as negotiable. The nation they envisaged was coterminous with the Indian Empire the British had created.

The British insistence on their responsibility to protect minorities had now become a dogma with them, the full implications of which were in fundamental conflict with the Congress' commitment to a united India under a parliamentary democracy. The Muslims were not, of course, the only minority. The Depressed Classes under Dr. Ambedkar's leadership had denounced Cripps' proposals, believing they threatened to return the Untouchables to "the black days of the ancient past" by placing them "under an unmitigated system of Hindu rule."[7] In addition, religious minorities, such as the Sikhs and Christians, were also concerned for their future. But in 1942 only the Muslims were in a position to profit from British concern, and it was Churchill's concentration on the Muslims that made genuine negotiations impossible. When Churchill heard that Cripps had failed, he is said literally to have danced with joy. The failure justified his view that the divisions within Indian life made the continuance of British rule inevitable.

"Quit India" Resolution

After the failure of the Cripps mission the Congress leaders had to show that Churchill's interpretation of Indian nationalism was wrong. This could only be done by an unmistakable response from the Indian people, and for this they turned once more to Gandhi. His answer was a new civil disobedience campaign. Because of the war, with its threat of invasion, the implications of such a course of action were far different from what they had been before. Gandhi's age—he was now 73—and his long experience with nonviolent movements might have made him cautious, but in fact he moved to more extreme positions. Before, he had always counseled careful preparation before starting a campaign, but now he believed that neither he nor the nation had much time. He realized that the result might be anarchy, for he no longer had any illusions about the ability of ordinary people to follow the way of nonviolence. But he was willing to take the risk. Nor did he fear a Japanese invasion. All that mattered was that the Indian people, without help from anyone, British or Japanese, should seize their own future. "That is why," he said, "I have made up my mind that it would be a good thing if a million people were shot in a brave and nonviolent rebellion against the British rule." His friends and opponents were equally shocked by this argument, but he brushed them aside, saying, "they do not know the fire that is raging in my breast."[8]

The result of Gandhi's resumption of leadership was the "Quit India" resolution passed by the Indian National Congress at Bombay on August 8, 1942. As in 1920 there were very few of the leaders who accepted his course wholeheartedly, but they had no alternative to propose to either his passion or his logic. The long resolution demanded the immediate withdrawal of British power from India since "the continuation of that rule is degrading and enfeebling India, and making her progressively less capable of defending herself." Gandhi gave India a mantra, a sacred formula.

The mantra is: Do or Die. We shall either free India or die in the attempt; we shall not live to see the perpetuation of our slavery . . . Take a pledge with God and your own conscience as witness, that you will no longer rest till freedom is achieved and will be prepared to lay down your lives in the attempt to achieve it.[9]

Once more Gandhi had become the apotheosis of the nation. His old opponent, Subhas Chandra Bose, who had by this time joined the Japanese, rejoiced that Gandhi had at last seen what he himself had long preached, that "the destruction of British power in India was the *sine qua non* for the solution of all India's problems." The Congress' resolution, he was convinced, expressed "the wish of the vast majority of the Indian people."[10]

The government was in no mood in the summer of 1942 to wait as it had in 1922 and 1930. Within a few hours of the passing of the resolution, all the leaders were arrested and imprisoned; the Congress was declared an illegal organization; its newspapers were closed; and its funds were confiscated.

After the arrests of the Congress leaders, North India was swept during August and September by a wave of violence unmatched since 1857. Students took the initiative in the early stages, leading processions through the streets, overturning cars and buses, and forcing the shopkeepers to close their stores. Then a second phase began with attacks on government property throughout the country, but especially in the United Provinces and Bihar, the strongholds of the Congress. Hundreds of railway stations, post offices, and other government offices were attacked and damaged. Next came a wave of sabotage, in which telegraph wires were cut and railway bridges and tracks were blown up. This was so successful in Bihar that for some time Bengal was cut off from all communication with the rest of India. Large areas in rural Bihar and Bengal ceased to be controlled the government as the peasants destroyed records and chased out officials.

The Indian historian R. C. Majumdar was hardly overstating the situation when he wrote that "as soon as Gandhi and his followers were removed to prison, the cult of nonviolence, as understood and preached by them, came to an end, nevermore to figure as a potent force in India's struggle for freedom."[11] There was, however, no master strategy for all of India, or at least none that could be put into operation, and even in a single region there might be a number of groups working independently. Perhaps the most effective leadership came from the socialists, whose leader, Jayprakash Narayan, escaped from jail to organize underground resistance. Followers of the old revolutionary parties in Bengal and elsewhere, who had never accepted the Gandhian ideology, also took part in acts of sabotage.

The uprisings of August 1942 had another important result: the further polarization of the Muslim League's position. For Jinnah the "Quit India" resolution was one more example of Gandhi's method of nonviolence leading to a breakdown of law and order, but he was unwilling to take a very strong public stand lest this might antagonize the Hindus, who might then turn on the Muslims. A cautious neutrality was therefore observed by the Muslim League, but even so, in areas of Bihar and Bengal the riots of 1942 often had an anti-Muslim tinge. The Hindu Mahasabha, while opposing Gandhi, made much of the League's failure to support the nationalist cause and called the agitation for a separate Muslim state "outrageous and treacherous."[12]

The dilemma of Indian nationalism was dramatized by Gandhi in 1944, when, after his release from prison because of ill health, he met for a long series of discussions with Jinnah. The basis for the talks was the League's demand for a separate state, and Gandhi seemed willing to go a long way toward making concessions. But what he could not concede was the heart of Jinnah's position: the acknowledgement that India contained two nations, one Muslim, one Hindu. In denying this proposition Gandhi rather surprisingly argued that since foreign rule had united India politically, the only lawful test of Indian nationhood was the fact that all the racial and religious groups had been brought under a common political subjection. "If you and I throw off this subjection by our combined effort," he pleaded with Jinnah, "we shall become a politically free nation." Gandhiji's appeal to a concept of nationhood grounded on the historical fact of a political unity created by a foreign power and looking to a future based in a common struggle for freedom from that power was ingenious. But essentially it was a solution that ignored the existence of a Muslim nationality created by the very success of the Indian National Congress. Jinnah had already crystallized the inchoate fears and aspirations of India's Muslims into another nationalist expression.

Negotiations for Independence

The long-drawn-out negotiations for a settlement began in June 1945 with the governor general, Lord Wavell, bringing together the leaders of the Indian National Congress and the Muslim League to discuss the formation of a new Executive Council. Jinnah's insistence that all the Muslims who were nominated should be members of the League was irreconcilable with the Congress' position that religion was not a factor in political representation. But the real difficulty was that neither the League nor the Congress was much interested in interim proposals. Then with the victory of the Labour party in the British elections in July and the end of the war in August came a change in the political climate. The Labour party was anxious to settle the Indian question, partly because of its old commitments to Indian freedom, but more urgently because its priorities demanded the expenditure of its energies on social change at home, not in holding on to India.

As a preliminary step toward forming a constitutional assembly, elections were held in India in September 1945, for the first time since 1937. The results confirmed the changes that had been apparent in the interval. The Indian

National Congress maintained its unchallenged control of all the general seats, and the Muslim League, which had done poorly in 1937, won 446 out of the 495 seats reserved for Muslims. After the election Congress governments took power in eight provinces; the League took control in two; and a coalition, including Muslim groups that opposed the League, took control of the Punjab.

With popularly elected ministries in office once more in the provinces, the British government sent a Cabinet mission to India in March 1946 to negotiate the transfer of power. The plan that the Cabinet mission brought with them envisaged the creation of an Indian union, in which the central government would have control of foreign affairs, defense, and communications, and the provinces would be left the other powers. The provinces would be formed into three groups, each of which would have separate executive and legislative bodies. This grouping of provinces was intended to satisfy the Muslim League without conceding the establishment of a separate state. There would be one group, made up of the Punjab, the North-West Frontier Province, and Sind, which would have a Muslim majority.

The plan was the subject of intense negotiation during the summer of 1946. There were two basic constitutional issues at stake: first, whether there should be a strong central government or a relatively weak one, with most of the power developing to the provinces, including the right of secession; second, whether the constitution would provide for the continued special electoral representation for religious and other minority groups. On these two issues the Congress and the League had fundamentally different views that were the product of the roles that each had played in the development of nationalism in India. The irreconcilability of these views was marked by the acceptance, with many reservations, of the general scheme of the Cabinet mission plan by both the League and the Congress.

At this point, when agreement seemed to be in sight, Jawaharlal Nehru, as president of the Indian National Congress, declared that although the Congress members were entering the constituent assembly under the rules laid down by the Cabinet mission, once the assembly met they would not be bound any longer by British rules. "What we do there we are entirely and absolutely free to determine."[13] Jinnah immediately denounced Nehru's position as a "complete repudiation of the basic form upon which the long-term scheme rests."[14] A few days later the Muslim League withdrew its previous acceptance of the Cabinet mission plan and reasserted the League's adherence to a separate state of Pakistan as the only possible solution of the problem of Muslim survival.

The most influential Muslim in the Congress, Maulana Azad, has called Nehru's statement "one of those unfortunate events that change the course of history."[15] It completed the process of alienating Jinnah that Nehru had begun with his refusal to include the representatives of the League in the provincial governments in 1937. But speeches do not often change the course of history, and whatever Nehru had done was to express a political reality. An Indian nation had been brought into being, and it would have been impossible to circumscribe the freedom of the members of the constituent assembly by the commitments of the Cabinet plan. As for the League, Nehru's speech freed them from a position to which they had never really given wholehearted assent. From this time on the partition of India became the central fact of political life, although the Congress leaders continued during the next few months to express their unyielding objection to it.

Meanwhile, there were signs that the disorders that many feared would follow the end of British rule had already begun. Hindu-Muslim riots raged in Calcutta during August 1946, leaving at least three thousand dead and many thousands more injured and homeless. The Muslim League has been blamed for the Calcutta killings, since they began on August 16, the day the League had called for "Direct Action" in the form of strikes and rallies against the Congress, but in the end, as a minority in the great city, it was the Muslim community that suffered the most. Reprisals against Muslims also followed in Bihar and East Bengal.

Even more ominous for the government was the mutiny that had broken out in the navy earlier in the year. There were also indications that the tensions between Hindus and Muslims in the civilian population were being transferred to the police and army. It was doubtful if the government could control the situation much longer, even if it had the will to use force. Both the Labour government in Great Britain and the British officials in India wanted to move quickly toward a solution, and Prime Minister Attlee's statement in the House of Commons on February 20, 1947, signaled the end of British rule.

> The present state of uncertainty is fraught with danger and cannot be indefinitely prolonged. His Majesty's Government wish to make it clear that it is their definite intention to effect the transference of power to responsible Indian hands by a date not later than June, 1948,[16]

Lord Louis Mountbatten was appointed governor general to carry out this program.

Partition

In referring to "responsible Indian hands," Attlee was using the language common to British constitutional statements on India since 1909, but now a time limit had been set and the alternatives were stated. There were three possibilities for a transfer of power: It could be given to a government of a united India, as agreed by the political parties; to existing provincial governments; or "in some other way as may seem most reasonable and in the best interests of the Indian people."[17] As Jinnah had long recognized, the choice was up to Indian National Congress. The Muslim League had a veto over transferring power to a united

Defining a Nation: India on the Eve of Independence, 1945

government, for they could demand a price the Congress would be unwilling to pay: a weak central government. The second possibility, the transfer of power to the provinces, meant the creation of perhaps a dozen autonomous states, not counting the hundreds of princely states that would also become independent. Such a choice went against the whole development of Indian nationhood which the Congress had fostered. The third possibility, concealed in the phrase "some other way as may seem most reasonable," meant, in effect, agreeing to the creation of Pakistan, an idea the Congress leaders had always refused to take seriously. It had now become the most realistic of the choices.

The acceptance of partition by the Indian National Congress leaders was a wrenching decision. It was a denial of the Congress' creed that Indian nationalism was not determined by religious affiliation, but by a common culture that transcended religious differences. Partition was an admission of failure, a tacit acknowledgment of the old argument that India was not a nation. The success of the nationalist movement in creating a self-conscious awareness of Indian nationhood made the trauma of partition all the deeper. This was as true for those with a secular vision of India as for those whose perception was deeply colored by religious imagery and passion, who instinctively equated political India as it was when it had came into existence in the nineteenth century with *Bharat Mata*, or Mother India, the holy land of Hindu myth and legend. More than any other religion in the world, Hinduism is bound up with a holy geography, for there is hardly a river or mountain not associated with some event in the sacred literature. And this motherland was being divided.

In the whole complex of issues involved in partition and the actual transfer of power from British to Indian hands, the dominant figure was Sardar Patel, not Nehru or Gandhi. Patel had been important in nationalist politics since the early 1920s but his concern with party organization had not given him the public fame of the other leaders. Now his skills brought him to the forefront, and when he became convinced that partition was the best solution for the impasse, he carried his colleagues with him. His knowledge of Indian regional politics convinced him that throughout the country there were forces at work that would lead to disruption, so that India would be faced with the prospect of not one partition, but many, unless a strong central government took over. Partition was a blow to the dreams of Indian nationalists, but Patel's acceptance of it exacted a heavy price from Jinnah and the League: the partition of Bengal and Punjab. The League had claimed the whole of both provinces as the very heartland of the Pakistan idea. Jinnah would get Pakistan, but it would be, as he said, a "moth-eaten" one. Thirty million Muslims remained in India. There was thus no great triumph in his victory. He was also conscious that many Hindus accepted Pakistan as a way of getting rid of a large number of Muslims, thus making India more truly a Hindu state.

In the end Patel carried even Gandhi to an unwilling recognition that partition was the only practical course, given the attitude of both the Indian National

Congress and the Muslim League. This did not mean that Gandhi gave his approval to the Congress' decision in June 1947 to accept partition; he only acknowledged that he had become "a back number" and that the leaders of the Congress were not with him. According to his biographer, Pyarelal, henceforth "the impossible old man was put on the pedestal, admired for his genius. . . listened to with respectful attention and bypassed."[18] Yet Gandhi did not cease to be what he had been for nearly thirty years, the one acknowledged symbol of the potential of Indian nationality, which was as complex and ambiguous as his words and actions. Nothing proved this ambiguity more clearly than his death seven months later at the hands of Hindus who regarded him as the betrayer of India.

The British government had set June 1948 as the deadline for the transfer of power, but after his arrival in India in the spring of 1947, Lord Mountbatten became convinced that the existing administration, the uneasy alliance of Indian leaders with the British government, should not attempt to hold power for more than a few months. He therefore announced early in June that the transfer of power would take place on August 15, 1947, a year earlier than had been planned. British power in India had been legitimized by its ability to maintain law and order and by the tacit acceptance of the people; now both these sources of authority were rapidly being eroded. As violence spread throughout north India the soldiers and police, the ultimate guarantee of British power in India for nearly two hundred years, became increasingly unreliable instruments of the administration. There was uneasiness among all the classes whose fortunes had been linked with the British: the commercial and professional groups, the industrialists, the landlords, the princes. The British themselves, the administrators and soldiers, were anxious to end their part in the long drama and go home. The basic decision was that power would devolve to two central governments: the existing provinces of Bengal and Punjab would be partitioned so that the areas where Muslims were in a majority would go to Pakistan and those with a majority of non-Muslims would go to India.

*   *   *

When the formal transfer of power to the two governments, India and Pakistan, took place on August 15, 1947, it was acknowledged that the new dominion of India was the successor state to the old government of India, continuing, as the secretary of state put it, "the international personality of existing India." As for Pakistan, the United Nations decided it was "part of an existing state breaking off to form a new State."[19] The legal phraseology neatly summarized the search for nationhood and nationality that defined the modern political history of the subcontinent of India. Just before the separation of the states became final, Nehru had told the constituent assembly in Delhi, "Long years ago we made a tryst with destiny, and now the time comes when we shall redeem our pledge." He had in mind the coming of India's independence, but the tryst with destiny had included the creation of not one nationality, but two. And among the pledges that had to be redeemed after August 15 were the prophecies that had long been made that the withdrawal of British power would be followed by violence and chaos. There were two months of bloodshed as the two nations that had been created out of a common past pulled themselves apart. Gandhi, who had been so central to the whole process as a symbol and a catalyst, now turned away in despair, praying for an end to his life so that he would not have to be a "helpless witness of the butchery by man become savage."[20] But by the end of 1947 the worst of the violence was over, and the two nations recovered their stability, fulfilling the final test of nationhood, the capacity to survive.

There are, however, four general principles that can be identified as part of India's nationalist ideology. First of all is the consensus, rooted in the history of the nationalist movement, that the preservation of the unity of India takes precedence over all other commitments. An emphasis on the importance of national unity runs through the speeches and writings of India's leaders in a way that would be hard to match in any other country. The sources of this concern for unity have been frequently mentioned in this essay. One was the reiteration by the British that Indian unity was an artifact of imperial power and would not survive their departure, coupled with a recognition on the part of some thoughtful leaders that India is indeed, in some fashion, what she was called in the Montagu-Chelmsford Report, "a sisterhood of states," something in fact new under the political sun. This means that nationality is understood primarily in territorial terms, and not, as in the case of Pakistan, in an ideology that is in a curious sense not related to territory. India's national identity has instead as a fundamental referent a territorial base, that is, areas over which India assumed sovereignty in 1957, or which had accrued to her since, by legal or historical right, as in the case of Goa and Kashmir. The stress on nationality as a function of territorial sovereignty of a people deriving their identity from a defined territory is the basis of most nationalism, at least in the West, and it surely constitutes a source of political and social stability. Another item of the national consensus is the conviction that the Government had a primary responsibility for ameliorating the poverty of the masses. The former rulers of India had frequently enough proclaimed—and probably quite genuinely—their concern for the Indian masses, but in post-independence India there was a conviction, unlike under the imperial regime, that there must be radical and widespread social change. This belief in the necessity of social change, and in the duty of government to promote it, is probably one of the crucial differences between imperial and post-imperial rule. There is a wide divergence between the rhetoric of rulers and their actual intentions, not to speak of their achievements, but in India, as in most of the countries that have achieved political independence from colonial rule since 1947, a sense of national identity carries with it a longing for economic betterment. The preservation of national unity and the movement towards economic justice are set in the context of a third element in the national consensus in India. That is the apparently widespread acceptance that a multi-party democracy is peculiarly relevant to the traditions and ethos of the Indian people. The survival of political democracy is surely a reflection of the sense of national identity that was forged in the pre-independence period, as well as one of the factors that continues to maintain it.

A fourth component of the nationalism of modern India is the conviction that India must be given her rightful place in the comity of nations. This demand for a place in the sun did not play as central a role in Indian nationalism as it did in the history of European nationalism, but it has surely been of great importance since 1947. India's sense of nationhood carries with it a demand for recognition that is commensurate with its history, its human resources, and its potential for leadership.

In the last decades of the twentieth century, the environment for the development of nationalism in the subcontinent has altered drastically from the decades before Independence. In the nineteenth century and on through the first half of the twentieth, India was of very great importance in the world balance of power—far more so than her dependent political status would suggest. But it was a role masked and distorted by the imperial connection as well as by the political and economic conditions of the whole of Asia and the Middle East. European expansion from the seventeenth century onwards had given the sub-continent linkages with the world economic and political order that had developed with a European centre.

Power alignments since 1947 have given India an entirely different set of economic and political linkages from those that had existed previously. Linkages with Britain are far less important, for example, than those that many former French colonies have with France. This partly reflects the great resources of India in relation to Britain as well, of course, as the fact that Britain's departure from India coincided with a diminution of her role as a world power. Along with this must be mentioned a fact that often seems odd to foreign observers, namely, the friendly attitude towards Great Britain that existed after 1947. Thus when Mountbatten, the last of the imperial rulers, was assassinated, India observed a period of mourning that one might have thought would have been reserved for a great national figure.

Almost immediately after 1947, India's foreign relations shifted their focus from Europe to the two great non-European powers, the United States and the Soviet Union. Neither had played a role in the independence movement, except for somewhat peripheral roles —the United States through pressures exerted on the British in relation to the war effort, and the Soviet Union through the ideological model it supplied to some of the nationalist leaders. India's relations with the great superpowers have probably obscured the importance of other new linkages that developed after independence. One set of these was with China, with which India had had remarkably little contact since ancient times, when Buddhism had been a medium of transposing Indian intellectual concepts to China. One of the important by-products of European imperialism was that it distorted relations between the Asian countries so that India had little contact in the nineteenth century with any of the other areas of East and South East Asia. India's intellectual life, as well as its economic patterns, were oriented towards Western culture in many ways during the nineteenth century, and renewed contacts with the great civilizations of Asia will surely lead towards changes in India's cultural and intellectual life. But the truly new linkages in India's national life after 1947 came, paradoxically, with the other countries of the South Asian region—Pakistan, Nepal, Bangladesh, and Sri Lanka. The areas that are now Pakistan and Bangladesh had both been integral parts of previous Indian empires, and the cultures of Nepal and Sri Lanka have been deeply influenced by Indian sources. As independent sovereign nations, they posed new issues for India, for during the formative phase of Indian nationalism there had been no genuinely independent nations on the borders of India. Thus in 1947 India found itself as the successor state of the old Government of India in terms of all its internal political and administrative structures but also as the legatee of its foreign policy in the area. This meant having to do what the British government had not had to do in India—come to terms with a ring of sovereign states. All of these relationships with the outside world built upon the national identity forged out of the richness and complexity of India's historical experience.

NOTES

1. *Crossroads*, 292-293.

2. Great Britain, *Parliamentary Papers*, 1939-1940, Vol. 10, Cmd. 6219, in Philips, *The Evolution of India and Pakistan*, 371.

3. Quoted in Sayeed, *The Political System of Pakistan*, 40.

4. K. M. Munshi, *Indian Constitutional Documents* (Bombay; Bharatiya Vidya Bhavan, 1967), Vol. I, 86.

5. R. C. Majumdar, *History of the Freedom Movement* (Calcutta: Firma K.L. Mukhopadhyay, 1963), Vol. Ill, 619.

6. "Draft Proposals," quoted in V.P. Menon, *The Transfer of Power in India* (New Delhi: Orient Longmans, 1968), 124.

7. Quoted in R. Coupland, *Indian Politics 1936-1942* (London: Oxford University Press, 1944), 280.

8. Quoted in Tendulkar, *Mahatma*, Vol. VI, 137.

9. Ibid., 161

10. Subhas Chandra Bose, *The Indian Struggle* (Bombay: Asia Publishing House, 1964), 350.

11. Majumdar, *History of the Freedom Movement*, Vol. Ill, 646.

12. Quoted in Tendulkar, *Mahatma*, Vol. VI, 277.

13. Quoted in Menon, *Transfer of Power*, 283.

14. Ibid., 284.

15. A.K. Azad, *India Wins Freedom* (Bombay: Orient Longmans, 1959) 154.

16. Statement by Prime Minister Attlee, February 20, 1920, quoted in Menon, *Transfer of Power*, Appendix IX.

17. Ibid.

18. Pyarelal, *Mahatma Gandhi, the Last Phase* (Ahmedabad : Navajivan Publishing House, 1958), Vol. II, 153.

19. Quoted in Menon, *Transfer of Power*, 412-413.

20 Quoted in Tendulkar, *Mahatma*, Vol. VIII, 145.

Appendix C: Recommended[DJ4] Reading

GENERAL STUDIES

These books place "the endgame of British rule and the coming of independence" in the wider context of Indian social and political history:

Sugata Bose and Ayesha Jalal, *Modern South Asia: History, Culture and Political Economy* (London and New York: Routledge, 1999). Chapters 13-17 assess current interpretations of the period.

Barbara D. Metcalf and Thomas R. Metcalf, *A Concise History of India* (Cambridge: Cambridge UP, 2002). Chapters 6 and 7 emphasize the consequences of social and political divisions for the partition of India.

Nicholas Mansergh, et al., editors, *India, the Transfer of Power, 1942-1947*, 12 volumes (London: H. M. Stationery Office, 1970-1983). Detailed correspondence that covers the whole process.

R. J. Moore, *Endgames of Empire* (Delhi: Oxford UP, 1988). A narrative account of the period from 1942 to 1947.

SPECIALIZED STUDIES

Ian Copland, *The Princes of India and the Endgame of Empire, 1917-1947* (Cambridge: Cambridge UP, 1988). Important for understanding the role of "Princely India" in the negotiations.

Geraldine Forbes, *Women in Modern India* (Cambridge: Cambridge UP, 1988). Women had a special role in the freedom struggle.

Sumit Ganguly and Neil DeVotta, editors. *Understanding Contemporary India* (Boulder: Lynne Rienner, 2003). A collection of useful essays on such subjects as politics, religion, caste.

J. S. Grewal, *The Sikhs of the Punjab* (Cambridge: Cambridge UP, 1990). Chapter 8 is an evaluation of the Sikhs' participation in the independence movement, especially in the period after 1930.

Mushirul Hasan, *Legacy of a Divided Nation: India's Muslims since Independence* (London: Hurst, 1997). Valuable background for understanding the period from 1942 to1947.

Christophe Jaffrelot, The Hindu Nationalist Movement and Indian Politics, 1925 to the 1990s (London: Hurst, 1993).

Lisa McKean, *Divine Enterprise: Gurus and the Hindu Nationalist Movement* (Chicago: University of Chicago Press, 1996). Good material on the Hindu Mahasabha and other Hindu movements.

V. P. Menon, *The Transfer of Power* (Princeton: Princeton University Press, 1957). Detailed study of the political process from 1945 to the coming of independence.

B. B. Misra, *The Bureaucracy in India* (Delhi: Oxford University Press, 1977). Detailed study of how the British ruled India and how they transferred that rule in 1947.

G. D. Overstreet and M. Windmiller, *Communism in India* (Bombay: Perennial Press, 1960). Material on the attitude of Indian Communists to the national struggle.

B. R. Tomlinson, *The Economy of Modern India, 1860-1970* (Cambridge: Cambridge University Press, 1993). Evaluation of the impact of foreign rule on the Indian economy is an essential element in the discussion of decolonization.

Peter van der Veer, *Religious Nationalism: Hindus and Muslims in India* (New Delhi: Oxford UP, 2000). A background study that emphasizes religion, not politics.

Eleanor Zelliott, *From Untouchable to Dalit: Essays on the Ambedkar Movement* (New Delhi: Manohar, 1992). The search for social justice by the groups once called "Untouchables" but who prefer "Dalit," the oppressed.

BIOGRAPHICAL STUDIES

In the period between 1942 and 1947, a number of remarkable people dominated Indian public life, including:

Ambedkar

Gail Omvedt, *Ambedkar: Towards an Enlightened India* (New Delhi: Penguin, 2004).

Azad

A. K. Azad, *India Wins Freedom*, new edition (London: Sangam Books, 1988).

Gandhi (His writings have been published in many volumes, and there are hundreds of biographies and studies, many of which are listed in these two volumes.

M. K. Gandhi, *My Experiments with Truth* (Boston: Beacon Press, 1957). While this autobiography does not cover the period of the transfer of power, it illuminates his actions.

Judith Brown, *Gandhi: Prisoner of Hope* (New Haven: Yale University Press, 1989).

Dennis Dalton, *Mahatma Gandhi: Nonviolent Power in Action* (New York: Columbia UP, 1993). Relates Gandhi's religious beliefs to his political actions.

Hari Singh, Maharajah of Kashmir

See Copland and Menon, above.

Alastair Lamb. *Kashmir, A Disputed Legacy* (Karachi: Oxford University Press, 1993). A controversial account of the ruler's role.

Jinnah

Stanley Wolpert, *Jinnah of Pakistan: His Life and Times* (New York: Oxford University Press, 1984). Chapter 18 is a sympathetic account of Jinnah's role.

Akbar S. Ahmed. *Jinnah, Pakistan and Islamic Identity: The Search for Saladin* (London and New York: Routledge, 1997).

Copland and Menon (above) have different evaluations.

Nehru

S. Gopal, *Jawaharlal Nehru: A Biography,* vol. 2 (Cambridge: Harvard University Press, 1976). Chapter 6 examines Nehru's role in negotiations.

Judith M. Brown, *Nehru: A Political Life* (New Haven: Yale University Press, 2001). Good explanation of Nehru's political ideas and his vision of India's future.

Nizam of Hyderabad

Zahir Ahmed, *Life's Yesterdays: Glimpses of Sir Nizamat Jung and his Times* (Bombay: Thacker, 1945). An uncritical biography.

V. P. Menon, *The Story of the Integration of the Indian States* (Madras: Orient Longmans, 1985). There are many references to the ruler of Hyderabad here and in Copland (above).

Master Tara Singh

J. S. Grewal has material on Master Tara Singh and the independence movement.